Fundamentalism

Prophecy and Protest in an Age of Globalization

This book investigates the origins of fundamentalism, outlining its characteristics and the history of key fundamentalist movements around the world, with examples from Christianity, Islam, Buddhism, and Hinduism. The book argues that fundamentalism develops when modern lay religious leaders challenge the authority of secular states and traditional religious establishments. These new leaders and their followers seek to infuse religious values and practices into all spheres, especially law, politics, education, and science. The patterns of religious authority and leadership that characterize fundamentalism have their roots in a Christian context but were globalized through intense intercultural contacts after the mid-nineteenth century. Fundamentalism is a thoroughly modern and global phenomenon because it presupposes the globalization of ideas and practices concerning religious leadership and organization, as well as universal changes in the relationship of religion to modern societies and states.

Torkel Brekke is a Professor of the History of Religions and South Asian Studies at the University of Oslo. Before being appointed to his current university position, he completed his DPhil at Oxford and served as advisor in the Norwegian Ministry of Defence. He also works for the think tank Civita. Professor Brekke has written and edited several books, including *Makers of Modern Indian Religion* and *The Ethics of War in Asian Civilizations*, and his articles have appeared in numerous journals.

Fundamentalism

Prophecy and Protest in an Age of Globalization

TORKEL BREKKE
University of Oslo

CAMBRIDGE
UNIVERSITY PRESS

32 Avenue of the Americas, New York NY 10013-2473, USA

Cambridge University Press is part of the University of Cambridge.

It furthers the University's mission by disseminating knowledge in the pursuit of education, learning, and research at the highest international levels of excellence.

www.cambridge.org
Information on this title: www.cambridge.org/9780521149792

First published 2012
Reprinted 2013

A catalog record for this publication is available from the British Library.

Library of Congress Cataloging in Publication data
Brekke, Torkel.
Fundamentalism : prophecy and protest in an age of globalization / Torkel Brekke.
p. cm.
Includes bibliographical references and index.
ISBN 978-0-521-76625-8 (hardback) – ISBN 978-0-521-14979-2 (paperback)
1. Religious fundamentalism. I. Title.
BL238.B74 2012
209–dc23 2011023536

ISBN 978-0-521-76625-8 Hardback
ISBN 978-0-521-14979-2 Paperback

For Kristian, Iris, and Marius

Contents

Acknowledgments

The idea for this book came up in a conversation with Beatrice Rehl of Cambridge University Press at a conference in Oslo in 2008, and most of it was written during autumn 2010 and spring 2011 while I was on sabbatical leave from the Institute for Cultural Studies and Oriental Languages at the University of Oslo. I thank colleagues and students at my department in Oslo for years of discussion and encouragement, and I am grateful to the University of Oslo for a grant that made it possible to spend my sabbatical in Oxford. In spring and summer 2011, I was a visiting scholar at the Oxford Centre for Buddhist Studies, and I am grateful for its hospitality. Friends and colleagues in several departments of Oxford University and at Wolfson College made the stay very rewarding.

I am particularly grateful to Peter B. Clarke for reading a draft of the first part of the book and making useful comments. Peter was a generous scholar and will be missed. I thank Mahinda Deegalle for his advice and for sharing unpublished material about Buddhism and politics in Sri Lanka, and Suwanna Satha-Anand for advice regarding Buddhism in Thailand. Hilal Ahmed offered valuable advice about Islam in contemporary India, and Dale F. Eickelman did likewise about questions related to recent developments in religious authority in Islam in the Middle East. I thank Werner Menski and Surendra Subramanian for advice on how to approach the question of Hindu law and fundamentalism. I am also grateful to Martin Riexinger for sharing unpublished material about Islam and creationism.

On matters of South Asian religion, I am indebted, as always, to Richard Gombrich and Sanjukta Gupta. I also thank Lars Tore Flåthen for letting me read some of his research on modern Hinduism and education. Through the years, I have received a lot of good advice about Sikhism from Gurinder Singh Mann, and some of this has been relevant to this book, although I did not have space to treat Sikhism in depth here.

I have over the past few years been invited to give an introductory lecture, followed by a seminar, as part of a course about fundamentalism at the Centre for Theology and the History of Religions at the University of Lund in Sweden. The discussions with staff and students in Lund have been valuable in the development of some of the arguments in this book.

Finally, I would like to thank colleagues at the think tank Civita for years of intellectual debate, some of which has been relevant to the subject of this book.

Introduction

"How did it feel to be named a cause of the invasion of Iraq?" I ask. The overweight mullah on the sofa looks at me. Then he breaks into laughter. His wife appears in the doorway with some tea and biscuits. She is just back from work. It is 2004, and this is my second interview with mullah Krekar. It takes place in the living room of his small apartment in Oslo, Norway. On the wall above the sofa is a picture of the Kaba in Mecca. On another wall is a bookshelf with books in Arabic. In the corner is a desk with a computer and a phone.

On February 5, 2003, U.S. secretary of state General Colin Powell presented the United Nations with data that would be the basis for the American justification of the war against Iraq. He said: "But what I want to bring to your attention today is the potentially much more sinister nexus between Iraq and the al Qaeda terrorist network, a nexus that combines classic terrorist organizations and modern methods of murder." Powell described a situation where Ansar al-Islam, headed by mullah Krekar, was harboring al Qaeda fighters from Afghanistan and at the same time collaborating with Saddam Hussein. According to Powell, mullah Krekar's group was *the sinister nexus*, the link between Saddam Hussein and international terrorism, which was a central argument for invading Iraq and making sure its potential weapons of mass destruction did not find their way to al Qaeda groups operating in Iraqi Kurdistan or other regions.[1]

It is hard to know exactly what was correct and what was not in Secretary Powell's assessment of the situation, and that is not really important here. It seems very likely that Mullah Krekar had links to al Qaeda, but he insists he did not have any contact with Saddam Hussein's regime.[2] After all, the Iraqi leader had used massive violence to crush Kurdish calls for autonomy. Being a Kurd, the mullah strongly disliked Hussein's policies. Mullah Krekar was the leader of the militant fundamentalist organization Ansar al-Islam, and in this capacity he was engaged in a civil war against secular Kurdish organizations competing for political control in Iraqi Kurdistan. He was a military leader fighting for the establishment of an Islamic state in the region. In the mind of a fundamentalist like mullah Krekar, however, the establishment of one small Islamic political entity must be seen as a step on the way to a larger goal: the (re)establishment of the Islamic caliphate.

Mullah Krekar is an example of how some fundamentalists use violent means to achieve their religious and political goals. In a later chapter of this book, I will return to this issue. I will look more closely at Muslim fundamentalist ideas about the caliphate, and I will discuss how fundamentalists in other world religions want to establish states, or change existing ones, to make politics conform closely to their conceptions of a religious ordering of society. Some Christian fundamentalists feel that the state should base its politics on biblical norms. Quite a few Buddhist and Hindu fundamentalists want a *Dharmarajya* (politics in accordance with religion), and some Sikhs want a Sikh state or *Khalistan.* Some Jews have religious visions of the state of Israel or reject the state as such on religious grounds.

[1] The case is treated in detail in Torkel Brekke, "Sinister Nexus: USA, Norge og Krekar-saken," *Internasjonal Politikk* 63, no. 2 (2005): 279–96.

[2] Brynjar Lia, Irak og terrortrusslen: Eit oversyn over terrorgrupper med tilknyting til det irakiske regimet. FFI/Rapport/2003/00940 (Kjeller: Forsvarets forskningsinstitutt, 2003).

In the worldviews of fundamentalists within these traditions, politics is a sphere of human activity and ideology that was originally tied to religion in an organic way. In their eyes, the separation of politics and religion is a tragedy. Many of them would add that the separation of religion from other spheres, such as law, science, or education, is a negative effect of the same process of modernization and secularization. However, before we look in detail at how fundamentalists in the world religions believe that each of these societal spheres should be reconquered by religion, which is the subject of Chapters 5 to 9, we need to establish a framework for our discussion. We can start by taking a brief look at the word "fundamentalism" and the debates that have taken place concerning its meaning, application, and relevance.

SHOULD WE USE THE WORD "FUNDAMENTALISM"?

The word "fundamentalism" is used to describe many different things in everyday speech. After the financial crisis of 2009, several economists criticized what they saw as *market fundamentalism*; that is, the conviction that markets correct themselves and that governments should stay out of the economy. In other words, the language of religion was brought into a different sphere to denote views and attitudes that were perceived as rigid and irrational. This use of the term "fundamentalism" probably tells us more about the views of the person using the term than about the nature of the thing that receives the negative label. In public debates and everyday conversation, the term "fundamentalism" is used widely simply to name persons or attitudes that we do not like.

There is also the opposite trend: the word "fundamentalism" is sometimes used in a very narrow sense. Some academics are of the opinion that fundamentalism is really an exclusively Christian phenomenon, and they believe that the term should not be used to describe people, organizations, and communities outside the

Christian world. They claim that it is meaningless to speak of fundamentalism in Islam or Buddhism, for instance. In a relatively recent work on the creation of an Islamic state in Iran, one author writes that she rejects the term "fundamentalism" in the case of Iran "as it reflects a different, Christian religio-political environment, and finds no corresponding term in Islamist vocabulary."[3] This way of discarding the term "fundamentalism" altogether simply by pointing out that it originated in a Christian context has become common among academics. One expert on Buddhism has argued that "fundamentalism" is a term that is not suited to describing Sinhalese Buddhists, even militants among them, because they do not want to return to the fundamental textual sources of their tradition and they are not concerned with the literal truth of those texts, unlike Christian fundamentalists.[4]

It is true that the word "fundamentalism" comes from a Christian context. It was first used in the early twentieth century by American Protestants who saw themselves as defenders of the fundamentals of the Christian religion against the onslaught of modern, liberal theology and critical textual scholarship that seemed to undermine the special status of the Bible. Fundamentalist is a good description of these Christians: they even used the word themselves. They saw their own activities as fundamentalist and were proud of that. To borrow a useful concept from the anthropologist Clifford Geertz, "fundamentalism" was an experience-near word to them.

In Geertz's thinking, experience-near words are the words we use in our daily life to describe our own activities and the world we see around us. Experience-distant words are words

[3] Vanessa Martin, *Creating an Islamic State: Khomeini and the Making of a New Iran* (London: I. B. Tauris, 2000), p. xxi.

[4] Richard Gombrich, "Is the Sri Lanka War a Buddhist Fundamentalism?" in *Buddhism, Conflict and Violence in Modern Sri Lanka*, ed. Mahinda Deegalle (London: Routledge, 2006), pp. 22–37.

that are applied as analytical categories from outside.[5] Scholars who insist on saving the term "fundamentalism" exclusively for groups in the Christian tradition because it is a Christian word assume that we must describe social phenomena, such as religion, in experience-near terms. But this is an assumption that, if taken to its logical conclusion, makes all academic study of other cultures impossible. We can illustrate this by looking at the word "religion."

The word "religion" comes from a Christian context. It is a word in the Latin language. Cicero, one of the greatest writers to use the Latin language in the ancient Roman world, wrote extensively on the nature and origins of different conceptions of gods, and he used the word "religion" at least partly in the same sense as people use it today.[6] Modern European languages – such as English – have all inherited this word from the ancient Romans. No other culture or society used the word "religion" for the simple reason that their languages were not derived from Latin. Moreover, it is in Europe that people started seeing religion as a special sphere of social life that could be analyzed apart from other spheres, such as politics, science, or law.

In Arabic, one has the word "*din*," and this word refers to some, but not all, of the same things in the Arab world as the word "religion" in the Christian world. Likewise, in Indian languages, such as Hindi, we find the word "dharma," and there is some degree of overlap between dharma and religion. However, it is certainly not the case that the words "religion," "*din*," and "dharma" refer to exactly the same things. In fact, it is often impossible to find a word in a different language that means

[5] Clifford Geertz, *Local Knowledge: Further Essays in Interpretive Anthropology* (New York: Basic Books, 1983), p. 57.

[6] Of special interest is Cicero's attempt to define religion by offering an etymology of the word. In fact, he gave two different etymologies. See Cicero, *De natura deorum. Academica*, with an English translation by H. Rackham (Cambridge, Mass.: Harvard University Press, 1994), pp. 192–93.

exactly the same as the words we use in English. This is one of the good things about studying a different language: one discovers that the world can be categorized in radically different ways from what one is used to.

If the word "fundamentalism" cannot be used to describe social phenomena in Islam or Hinduism merely because it is taken out of its Christian context, we can make the same argument for the word "religion." However, if we want to study and describe other societies and cultures, we cannot accept the claim that we must only use experience-near terms. If we insist on using only words derived from a culture and its language when describing social life in that culture, we effectively give up research altogether.

So, on the one hand, we should avoid using the word "fundamentalism" about all those views that we happen to find zealous or narrow-minded. On the other hand, we cannot restrict the word to developments in the Christian world. In my view, fundamentalism is a special kind of reaction to certain developments in the modern world that have taken place in many, perhaps in most, religious traditions. We find fundamentalism a notable religious response to global developments reaching different societies and cultures at different times between 1800, at the earliest, and today. In other words, fundamentalism is a reaction to processes that take place at a particular stage in world history.

THE FUNDAMENTALISM PROJECT

Since the 1990s, there has been a growing awareness about the renewed importance of religion in public and private life in many parts of the world. Most sociologists of the 1960s and 1970s insisted that modernity produced secularization more or less by necessity. Secularization means that religion is losing status and significance in society, and we will return to this idea shortly. However, since the late 1970s, things have happened in the world that made it clear that religion was not about to disappear in spite of the predictions of the social sciences. One clear indication of the importance of religion in American culture was the reemergence of fundamentalism in the shape of a movement called the Moral Majority in the late 1970s. On the global scene, the Islamic revolution in Iran in 1979 was a clear indication that religion could still play a significant political role. During the same period, labor migration to Europe from countries such as Turkey, Pakistan, and Morocco resulted in the creation of new religious communities of Muslims in many European countries and, at least since the 1980s, this has led to a new awareness of the religious identity of both immigrants and host populations.

It would be misplaced to offer reviews of a number of books about fundamentalism here, but there is one work that must be mentioned because it has set a standard for later studies of fundamentalism. This is the Fundamentalism Project commissioned by the American Academy of Arts and Sciences. Between 1988 and 1995, the Fundamentalism Project produced five volumes that approached fundamentalism from different angles. The Fundamentalism Project brought a lot of new data and new theoretical insights, but it has also received criticism from those who disagree with the basic premise of the project, that there exist religious movements across the globe that share enough traits to lump them together under one heading.

In order to study fundamentalism across cultures, the editors of the Fundamentalism Project had to take what we might call an *ideal type* as their point of departure, and the construction of this ideal type was a main goal in the first of the five volumes. Some scholars would reject such a research strategy and insist that we restrict the use of the term "fundamentalism" to its original context, Christian movements that are self-consciously fundamentalist, but this is a misconceived criticism, as I just explained.

The Fundamentalism Project is one important point of departure for this book, and to disregard its many important contributions would be ridiculous. However, the volumes were published in the early 1990s, and much has happened in the world since then. There are now enough books treating Muslim fundamentalism exclusively to fill a small library. There are several reasons why Muslim fundamentalism has received more attention than other forms of fundamentalism. With the revolution in Iran, it became clear that Islam had potential for motivating and justifying strong social and political movements, although, as I will explain later, the Islamic revolution in Iran might not be a very good example of fundamentalism. As the modern jihadist network created in Afghanistan and Pakistan during the Soviet invasion started looking at the West as its enemy in the early 1990s, radical Islamic movements came to be perceived as a formidable security threat. Then came 9/11 and several other terrorist attacks, and interest in al Qaeda and related networks exploded.

There are now many books treating fundamentalism with different perspectives, but most of them have little to say about fundamentalism outside the Abrahamic traditions: Judaism, Christianity, and Islam. This is partly because fundamentalism is most obviously present in the Abrahamic traditions, but it is also because people who are interested in fundamentalism often have their primary training in these traditions, whereas people who specialize in other religions, such as Buddhism, Hinduism, or Sikhism, have been reluctant to enter into a comparative debate to see whether "their" traditions fit the theories and concepts used to study fundamentalism in the Abrahamic religions. One aim of this book is to find a way to bring other religions into the debate about the nature and causes of fundamentalism. This is of particular interest to me because much of my background as a scholar is in the study of the religious traditions in South Asia.

FUNDAMENTALISM: WHERE AND WHEN?

Let me say a few words about the choices I am going to make in this book. I am going to look at a number of organizations, movements, and individuals belonging to what we have come to know as "world religions." In the discipline called history of religions, or religious studies, it has for some time been fashionable to discuss how our idea of world religions arose and developed, but I will not go into this debate here. A basic assumption I am making is that there are movements, people, ideas, and practices in the world religions that are so similar that we can use the same word to refer to them. This is necessarily an assumption shared by any book dealing with fundamentalism as a cross-cultural phenomenon.

However, I work with an additional and stronger assumption that is not shared by many other books on the subject. I believe that the right way to study fundamentalism in the world religions is to look at movements within different traditions as sharing basic historical origins. The Fundamentalism Project and several other studies say that we can compare movements in different religions and put the label "fundamentalism" on them because they are similar. They share some characteristics. There is a family resemblance. I claim that there are movements in the world religions that we can call by a common name not only because there is a family resemblance but because they are in fact results of the same global historical processes. They have the same form *and* the same origins. It is the aim of the early chapters of this book to explain these common origins.

To do this, I will look at fundamentalism in Protestant Christianity in the United States; this is, after all, the "original case" of fundamentalism. I will also look at Muslim fundamentalists in the Middle East and South Asia. One important focus will be on Maulana Maududi and the fundamentalist party he established, the Jamaat-e-Islami, which has branches in several South Asian countries.[7] Maududi was the person who more than anybody formulated a modern Muslim fundamentalist ideology,

[7] It is not unusual to confuse South Asia with Southeast Asia. Whenever I use the term "South Asia," I refer to the region comprising India, Pakistan, Bangladesh, Sri Lanka, Nepal, and Bhutan.

and he had a great impact in many Muslim societies. I will also look at relevant movements in other parts of the Muslim world, such as Egypt, and the Muslim Brotherhood will be an important example of Muslim fundamentalism in the Middle East.

Hindu fundamentalism is less well known than Christian or Muslim fundamentalism, but it could be argued that Hindu fundamentalists have had more political success than most others because they were able to put their leaders into government in the period 1999 to 2004. My focus will be on certain organizations, the Rashtriya Swayamsevak Sangh (RSS), the Bharatiya Janata Party (BJP), and the Vishva Hindu Parishad (VHP), and certain key individuals, especially ideologues like M. S. Golwalkar (1906–1973) and Deendayal Upadhyay (1916–1968).

Buddhist fundamentalism will be discussed, too, and here I intend to focus on two societies in particular: Sri Lanka and Thailand. They both have majority populations belonging to the branch of Buddhism we call Theravada, and they have both experienced very dramatic changes in their meeting with the modern West since the nineteenth century, although the political contexts were very different. In the Buddhist case, I intend to focus on key leaders, religious and political, who have defined new religious roles since the late nineteenth century, such as the Sri Lankan activist Anagarika Dharmapala. I will also look at more recent movements, such as the Thai Buddhist movement called Santi Asoka, but for reasons of space I must skip the many interesting modern Buddhist movements of Japan, such as the Soka Gakkai, that have been favorite subjects for many sociologists of religion.

There are several important religious traditions that will not be dealt with in any detail. I will not look at Jewish fundamentalism partly because this is a tradition I know much less about than the ones mentioned so far and partly because it has been well documented and explained by others. Within Catholicism, the groups that are often called fundamentalists are the ones that rejected the changes in the Mass and other reforms after the Second Vatican Council, which opened in 1962 under

Pope John XXIII. Some Catholic protest groups repudiate the authority of the church and call for a return to the true rituals. However, I will not bring Catholicism into my discussion of fundamentalism.

When I started writing this book, I intended to include fundamentalism in Sikhism because I have over the past few years done interviews with fundamentalist Sikh leaders in India and studies of Sikh fundamentalist literature. Sikhism is an interesting and underexplored tradition. Sikhs themselves have a word – *mulvad* – connoting a polity and society organized according to scriptural religious authority, and in their approach to the holy text, the Guru Granth Sahib, conservative Sikhs share the same abhorrence of modern textual interpretation and exegesis as Protestant Christian fundamentalists.[8] Unfortunately, space did not allow the inclusion of Sikhism here.

Let me say a few words about the historical limitations, too. I see fundamentalism as religious reactions against great changes happening in the modern world, and I believe we should restrict the use of the term to movements that arose well after 1800, or probably even later, say 1850. I disagree with the view that fundamentalism has existed for centuries in some world religions, such as Christianity or Islam. It is not difficult to understand what somebody means when they say that certain premodern currents in Islam were instances of fundamentalism because these movements strongly defended the position that the Qur'an is the eternal, uncreated word of God and should be accepted unconditionally. For instance, Hanbalism, one of the four schools of law in Sunni Islam, arose in strong opposition against rationalism and against heterodox currents in ninth-century Baghdad that seemed to relativize the status of scripture and tradition.[9]

[8] Harjot Oberoi, "Sikh Fundamentalism: Translating History into Theory," in *Fundamentalisms and the State*, ed. Martin E. Marty and R. Scott Appleby (Chicago: University of Chicago Press, 1993), p. 256ff.

[9] See a useful discussion of this problem in Said Amir Arjomand, "Unity and Diversity in Islamic Fundamentalism," in *Fundamentalisms Comprehended*, ed. Martin E. Marty and R. Scott Appleby (Chicago: University of Chicago Press, 2004), pp. 179–98.

However, I believe that the changes that have taken place in the world since the nineteenth century are so different from previous periods, and I think the threat that modern fundamentalists are reacting against is so special, that we need a name for modern movements that clearly distinguishes them from the conservative and puritan movements of the past. The scripturalism and conservatism of the fourteenth-century Muslim theologian Ibn Taymiyya, or of the original Wahhabi movement of the eighteenth century, arose from internal processes in the Muslim world and not as the result of the enormous changes brought about by Western political and cultural dominance, modernization, and globalization, which really started making an impact only in the nineteenth century. So, although Ibn Taymiyya or the Wahhabis were sources of inspiration for fundamentalists in the twentieth century, they were not fundamentalists themselves.

RADICAL CONSERVATIVES

But is it not the case that all fundamentalists are conservative? Isn't fundamentalism just another name for conservative religion? And if that is the case, why do we need the label "fundamentalism"? These questions about the relationship between fundamentalism and conservative religion are common, and their answer may serve as a first step toward a sound concept of fundamentalism.

Political philosophers would tell us that conservatism is not an ideology but rather a general approach to political and social life. Libertarianism and socialism are real ideologies with certain doctrines and views, whereas conservatism is rather an approach to politics that emphasizes slow change rather than revolution, and praises the values and wisdom of tradition regardless of the content of that tradition. Thus, conservative religion would refer to organizations or communities that cherish and hold onto established truths and traditions. Conservative religion would resist change on many levels: in doctrine, in ritual, and in religious values and norms guiding social life.

Many fundamentalists are conservative in their theological outlook. As we will see, American Protestant fundamentalism started as a reaction against new ways of reading the Bible and new ways of interpreting the contents of scripture. The groups that we describe as fundamentalist in Judaism are mostly conservative in their interpretation of Jewish tradition, although theology has a very different position in Judaism than in Christianity. Fundamentalists in the Sunni Muslim world are also less concerned with theology than most Christian fundamentalists. In the Sikh religion, it seems reasonable to say that fundamentalists are conservative in their interpretation of both scripture and ritual, whereas in both Hinduism and in many parts of the Buddhist world it would seem that theology is not really that relevant to the debate or the struggle between fundamentalists and others. So if we ask whether fundamentalists are theologically conservative, the answer is certainly yes for Protestant Christian fundamentalists, but the question may be less relevant for fundamentalists in many other religious traditions.

On the other hand, if we look at views about social philosophy, most fundamentalist groups seem to be decidedly conservative. Conservatives are often critical of the developments in family patterns and sexual norms that they believe characterize the modern, secularized world. They would hold that it is a religious duty to build a family and have children (unless you devote your life to religious studies inside monastic walls). They would reject homosexual partnerships as immoral, and they would see extra- or premarital sex as sinful. Similar conservative attitudes on matters of social life, family life, and sexuality would be found among all fundamentalists in all the major religions that we will look at in this book.

However, in matters of religious authority, fundamentalists are *not* conservative. On the contrary, one of the key characteristics of fundamentalism in most religious traditions is its rejection of the religious authority associated with traditional religious hierarchies and organizations. Fundamentalists reject the priestly authority that is backed up by hierarchy and traditional education. Instead, they espouse prophetic authority earned by charisma and gifts in preaching. Although it may seem like a contradiction in terms, fundamentalists are radical and conservative. They are *radical* because they reject traditional authority, and they are *conservative* in the sense that they often want to retain traditional understanding of doctrine and rituals and in the sense that they want traditional religious values to guide social life.

I would like to stress this point already in the introduction because we will return to it several times throughout this book and it is important that the reader understand why religious authority is such a crucial issue if we want to understand fundamentalists. On this subject, much of what I have to say is inspired by the work of the great German economist and sociologist Max Weber.

PART I

THE HISTORICAL AND IDEOLOGICAL CONTEXT OF FUNDAMENTALISM

1

Religion and Modernity in the West

A standard account of history, found in different versions in many books, sees modernity as a powerful force that undermines tradition and religion, and fundamentalism is commonly explained as a reaction against this force. In this type of account, fundamentalism is the struggle of religious groups and individuals to halt and reverse what is seen as the negative side of modernity. This account of fundamentalism is not incorrect, but because both modernity and religion are so many different things, we have to specify exactly what aspects of modernity and religion we are talking about if this explanation is to have any relevance and precision. That will be the aim of this chapter.

Fundamentalism is a relatively recent thing, as I insisted in the introductory chapter. It is probably meaningless to talk about fundamentalism until about 1850. What is so special about modern times? Let us for a minute think of the difference between *cyclical* changes and *linear* changes. By *cyclical changes* I mean transformations in religious organizations and ideologies that may occur again and again over centuries and even millennia. They are changes that take place *within* a structure so that the structure itself is not basically changed. Cyclical religious reform movements have always been around. We can identify any number of such reform movements in the history of Islam, Christianity, and Buddhism. Typically, when the legitimacy of an established organization and its elites crumbles, new leaders, sometimes called *prophets*, come along and lead a religious reform that results in a reshuffling of power and authority.

Many of the earlier reformers in the world religions called for a return to the fundamentals, to what they see as the *real* words of the Buddha, to the *real* code of religious discipline, or to the *real* Bible or Qur'an, and they have attacked what they see as later innovations. When reform has been carried out (or crushed), a new process of establishment and routinization may set in.

Such historical movements calling for a return to the fundamentals are not instances of fundamentalism. What is important about modernity is that it initiates change in all world religions that is not cyclical but linear. The changes brought about by the transformation in the economy, politics, science, and education over the past two centuries have shattered the very societal structures within which previous cyclical changes could take place. Instead, we are looking at changes that have set all world religions on a course that has no precedent in history. Fundamentalism is a reaction within this completely new context: the modern world.

MODERNITY AND RELIGION

The word *modernus* is Latin and was used at least as early as the fifth century CE, long before what we think of as modern times. In academic discourse, however, modernity is one of those very big and unwieldy concepts that social scientists and historians use to refer to certain key aspects of European societies after the Renaissance and Reformation, the two great processes that transformed the culture of the continent beginning in the fifteenth century. During the Renaissance, Europeans rediscovered the classical thought of Greek and Roman literature, and the Reformation set in motion far-reaching changes in the way many Europeans thought of themselves in relation to God, the church, and other Christians. These changes led to a transformation in religious authority, first in Europe and then, over time, globally, that will be crucial to my argument about fundamentalism.

In much historical research, modernity stands in an ambivalent relationship to religion. Modernity makes life difficult for organized religion, but at the same time religion may be an important element in the development of key aspects of modernity, such as capitalism. Max Weber made a famous argument about the links between the religious ideology of the Reformation and the development of modern capitalism in his classic essay *The Protestant Ethic and the Spirit of Capitalism.* In the medieval Christian world, religious zeal was confined to monasteries, and although he started out as a monk himself, Martin Luther turned so against the otherworldliness of the monastic tradition that he organized kidnappings of nuns. Reformers like Luther demanded that zeal and devotion should be transported out into the world, and that Protestants should bring religious zeal into their jobs. This created a completely new attitude toward work, captured in the German word *Beruf*, which means *calling.* At the same time, the religious attitude of the reformers was such that they frowned on personal consumption and luxuries. Thus, economic gains made from hard work could not be spent on useless pleasures but had to be invested in new and rational production, which created an expanding search for new avenues of investment. This new Protestant ethic would, in Weber's account, produce the spirit of modern capitalism.

Changes brought about by the transformation of the economy affect the everyday world of people in a profound sense. As an example, we may consider the important sectoral transformation that has accompanied industrialization in modern times. In preindustrial societies, 90 percent of the population was typically involved in agriculture. During the 1800s and 1900s, almost all of these jobs disappeared as a result of mechanization. Machines make modern agricultural work efficient and far less reliant on manpower than before. The consequence is that a tiny percentage of the population are employed in agricultural work in modern industrialized societies. In the developed countries of North America and Western Europe, almost the entire population is employed in manufacturing goods or in services. Very few people today herd cattle and till the soil. Instead, we make products or sell our skills and knowledge in a market. This has produced huge cultural, social, and psychological changes. One influential book about fundamentalism has called these changes *the Great Western Transmutation.*[1]

If we want to understand the challenges that the shift from agriculture to industry poses for a society, we may look at what is happening in the rapidly developing economies of the world today. In countries such as India and China, governments are eager to promote sectoral change because they know that economic growth requires that more people leave agriculture and enter manufacturing and services. In many parts of the countryside in these societies, people find the transition challenging. It requires new and advanced skills and breaks up old and established social structures, and although it can offer great opportunities for some, it results in deep feelings of insecurity for others.

The sectoral transformation has also led to a complete change in where people live their lives. Take a look at Great Britain. In 1801, about one-fifth of Britons lived in towns and cities of 10,000 inhabitants or more. In 1851, two-fifths lived in towns and cities, and in 1901 the share was three-quarters of the population. In other words, during the industrialization of Great Britain, which took place between 1800 and 1900, people stopped living in the countryside and moved to the cities. In

[1] Bruce Lawrence, *Defenders of God: The Fundamentalist Revolt against the Modern Age* (Columbia: University of South Carolina Press, 1989), pp. 47–52.

the second half of the 1800s, the number of big cities grew rapidly. The cities of Europe and America became more densely populated, and this created new service industries for feeding and transporting city-dwellers, and for building and maintaining their homes. These new demands produced a number of new employment opportunities. The manufacture of goods and trade in them require centralized sites of production and new systems of communication and distribution. Factories need workers who organize and coordinate their lives according to daily and weekly rhythms of production, so industrialization creates new conceptions of time.

Industrialization created economic growth of an order that was unprecedented in world history, but it also resulted in new social problems and an increasing awareness of social and economic inequality. Many Christian leaders of the late nineteenth century looked at the consequences of industrialization as the greatest challenge of their time. American industry makes profit the goal and man the means to produce it, lamented the German Baptist intellectual Walter Rauschenbusch (1861–1918) of New York. In 1907, Rauschenbusch wrote a book entitled *Christianity and the Social Crisis.* He insisted: "The spiritual force of Christianity should be turned against the materialism and mammonism of our industrial and social order."[2] It was in this rapidly changing world that fundamentalism first appeared.

MODERNITY, MODERNISM, AND THE ORIGINAL FUNDAMENTALISTS

Whereas one may discuss *modernization* as a great historical process involving many aspects of culture, science, politics, and economy, *modernism* is something narrower and easier to

[2] Extract from Walter Rauschenbusch, *Christianity and the Social Crisis,* in *A Documentary History of Religion in America,* ed. Edwin S. Gaustad, with revisions by Mark A. Noll (Grand Rapids, MI: Eerdmans, 2003), p. 110.

handle.[3] Modernization is a historical process, whereas modernism is an ideology.

Fundamentalism in American Protestantism started in the early 1900s as a defensive reaction against liberalism and modernism. The standard way to relate the story is to place the roots of the threatening forces of modernism and liberalism in the Enlightenment era. This was when the modern scientific worldview was born and when the urge to question or relativize the basic doctrines of Christianity became fashionable. However, the history of the eighteenth century is also the history of the greatest revival movements in Christianity. In fact, the period we often call the Enlightenment era might as well be thought of as a time of intense religious revival in the Protestant Christian world. How should we think about the relationship between, on the one hand, the culture of secularizing modernism and, on the other hand, the culture of religious revivalism born in the same period, the middle of the eighteenth century?

There was not always conflict between these currents of thought, and it is not at all clear that there was a gulf separating the mentalities guiding the Enlightenment thinkers and the champions of Christian revivalism from the mid-eighteenth century. For instance, John Wesley was a religious entrepreneur and a great evangelist, but at the same time he was highly educated and fascinated by developments in the sciences. He studied and commented on works by Descartes, Locke, Newton, and others, and he recommended many of the important works published in the natural sciences to the thousands of Methodist preachers he recruited to spread his religious message. Wesley even wrote a number of shorter works on science to make the latest discoveries accessible to ordinary people. In short, the key figure in the evangelical awakening in the English-speaking world was firmly rooted in the Enlightenment.[4]

[3] See, for instance, Lawrence, *Defenders of God*, p. 27.

[4] J. W. Haas, "John Wesley's Views on Science and Christianity: An Examination of the Charge of Antiscience," *Church History* 63, no. 3 (September 1994): 378–92.

Two great cultural currents were born in the eighteenth century: secularist modernism and Christian evangelical religiosity developed in Europe and America. Fundamentalism in America and Europe inherits and employs the religious styles of one of these currents to fight the other. There was an intense cultural and religious struggle between fundamentalists and modernists in the first decades of the twentieth century, and it is from this struggle that we get the concept of fundamentalism.

So what was the nature of this cultural current and the ideology called *modernism* that the early American fundamentalists, the "original" fundamentalists, struggled against? "What then is Modernism?" asked Shailer Mathews (1863–1941), professor of theology and dean of Chicago Divinity School, in a book called *The Faith of Modernism*, published in 1924. Mathews was a modernist and a liberal, and he was at the forefront in the cultural struggle against fundamentalists in America in the 1920s. His answer was that modernism was simply the application of the modern scientific method to religious tradition in order to find those core values that were relevant to contemporary life.[5]

To somebody like Mathews, modernism was a positive philosophy that should be combined with Christian doctrine to make a modern version of Christianity. There were really two main components of the culture of modernism: Darwinism and higher biblical criticism. Darwinism involved a completely new perception of time and the origins of life, including humankind. Higher biblical criticism was the name given to the new methods and attitudes applied to the academic study of the Bible in European and American universities. We will return to both of these elements of modernism in later chapters.

The struggle between fundamentalists and modernists was not a struggle between Christians and atheists. Fundamentalists both in Christianity and in other religions seldom bother with nonbelievers. Their struggle is mostly against co-religionists who do not

[5] Quoted in Gaustad, *A Documentary History of Religion in America*, p. 404.

take religion seriously enough. Shailer Mathews was a churchgoing Baptist and taught courses on New Testament theology at Chicago. In his book *The Faith of Modernism*, he touched on the historical and theological issues that were so crucial to the fundamentalists, such as the virgin birth and the bodily resurrection of Christ. Mathews was a believing Christian, but on issues like these he wrote with a sense of ambiguity and evasion that vexed more traditionally minded believers. The important thing about Christ, according to Mathews, was not the historical factuality of virgin birth and the resurrection but rather the hope for a better social order where institutions would embody the goodwill of Jesus. In fact, Mathews wrote, Jesus "did not demand belief in the inerrant Bible, his virgin birth, his atoning death, his physical resurrection, or his physical return."[6] The modernists undermined and relativized the fundamentals of Christian doctrine, in the eyes of the fundamentalists.

"We suggest that those who still cling to the great fundamentals and who mean to do battle royal for the fundamentals shall be called 'Fundamentalists,'" wrote Curtis Lee Laws, the editor of the Baptist magazine *Watchman-Examiner*, in 1920.[7] The natural defense against the modernism espoused by people like Mathews was to insist even more strongly on fundamental doctrines. The struggle between fundamentalists and modernists raged within and between Baptist conventions held during the late 1920s. Important defenders of the fundamentals of Christianity against the onslaught of modernism and liberalism were people like the aggressive Fort Worth pastor J. Frank Norris and the vocal Baptist preacher William Bell Riley, the latter of whom established the World's Christian Fundamentals Association in 1919.

It would be a bad idea to spend too much space here on the details of the rise of American fundamentalism in the early

[6] Martin E. Marty, *Modern American Religion*. Volume 2: *The Noise of Conflict, 1919–1941* (Chicago: University of Chicago Press, 1991), p. 202.

[7] Ibid., p. 160.

twentieth century. This issue has been treated extensively by others. We are concerned with fundamentalism as a global phenomenon, and the details of the classic American case are interesting mainly to the extent that they can be brought to bear on our larger questions. The main contention of this book is that fundamentalism is a specific type of reaction against the erosion of religious authority in public and private life in the modern world. I am concerned with the form that this reaction has taken in different cultures, and I want to pay particular attention to the types of religious and political actors that define fundamentalism.

Fundamentalism as a global phenomenon is more about religious authority and styles of religious leadership than the specific doctrines that fundamentalists attack or defend. In fact, fundamentalism as a global phenomenon is at least as much about form as about content. The doctrines and values that are important to Christian fundamentalists are not the same as those addressed by, say, Hindu fundamentalists, simply because the norms, theologies, and rituals of the two world religions have always been, and continue to be, very different. However, there has been a global convergence of the *uses* of those elements, and with increasing interreligious communication and influence, the styles of religious leadership and organization and the attitudes toward religious authority, implicit and explicit, have much in common across these cultural divides. This is what makes it possible to identify fundamentalism as a global phenomenon.

Therefore, what are important in the case of early American fundamentalism to our discussion of fundamentalism in the world religions are ideas of religious authority and leadership. The most striking fact about fundamentalism and other important modern strands of Christianity, such as Pentecostalism and charismatic groups, is that they all have taken Protestant values and attitudes concerning religious authority to their extremes. They generally start out as antiestablishment movements where the skills and the charisma of the individual pastor are more important than formal training and positions in a church hierarchy. The modern Protestant groups in America and Europe have taken the Reformation idea of the priesthood of all believers seriously.

The religious styles of fundamentalists, charismatics, and Pentecostals have common sources in Methodism and, more generally, in the religious awakenings of America and Britain since the mid-1700s. Many observers of modern Christianity are eager to demonstrate that fundamentalists are different from Pentecostals and Evangelicals. For instance, it is common to note that Pentecostals are different from fundamentalists because they emphasize empowerment through spiritual gifts and because Pentecostals seem to have fewer problems than fundamentalists with key aspects of modernity.[8] The beliefs of Pentecostals are embedded in testimonies, ecstatic speech, and bodily movements, whereas fundamentalists have formal theological systems and are much more concerned with the status of Scripture.[9] We could add that fundamentalists are more explicitly and self-consciously engaged in a struggle against cultural currents they observe around them, whereas Pentecostals and Evangelicals in general tend to build lower fences between their own communities and society at large.

So fundamentalists struggle against an ideology and a mentality we may call *modernism* and against aspects of the historical process of modernization. The aspect of modernization that bothers them the most is *secularization*. Secularization is the process whereby religion loses its authority and relevance in public and private life, and we cannot engage in a serious discussion of fundamentalism without understanding this process and the

[8] David Martin, *Pentecostalism: The World Their Parish* (Oxford: Blackwell, 2002), p. 1.

[9] Harvey Cox, *Fire from Heaven: The Rise of Pentecostal Spirituality and the Reshaping of Religion in the Twenty-First Century* (Cambridge, Mass.: Da Capo Press, 2001), p. 15.

challenge it has posed, and continues to pose, to people who see religion as crucial to a healthy and moral society.

There are three distinct ways in which secularization has taken place. First, the societal spheres have been differentiated from each other, and religion in particular has been differentiated from other societal systems, such as law, education, and politics. Second, there has taken place a privatization of religion in the sense that religion has been pushed out of the public sphere and relegated to the private. Third, some argue that a decline in religion has taken place, meaning that religious beliefs and worldviews have become less relevant to people in general. Let us look briefly at the three components of secularization before we move on.

SECULARIZATION AS DIFFERENTIATION

In order to understand the concept of differentiation, we should take a brief look at the ideas of Talcott Parsons, an eminent American sociologist who wrote extensively on the nature of modern societies. He was particularly interested in America, the country where modernity was most complete in the postwar period, but he also did research on Europe and Asia.[10] Parsons analyzed society as a system consisting of different units, each with its own function to perform for the system as a whole. Differentiation is the division of a unit in society into two or more units, each having new functions for the system.[11]

For instance, in premodern societies, economic activity went on in the household. In modern societies, however, most economic activity takes place in factories, offices, and shops – outside the household. This change is the result of differentiation. The unit of the traditional household was differentiated into

[10] Roland Robertson and Bryan S. Turner, eds. *Talcott Parsons: Theorist of Modernity* (London: Sage Publications, 1991), pp. 254–55.

[11] See, for instance, Talcott Parsons, *The System of Modern Societies* (Englewood Cliffs, N.J.: Prentice-Hall, 1971), p. 26.

the modern household and the modern workplace. This change involved transformations in roles and norms. The result was what Parsons called "a more evolved" system, where the two new structures perform their functions better than the one undifferentiated structure. Another example, which is more important for an understanding of today's fundamentalism, is that in premodern societies there is no sharp distinction between religion and law. A hallmark of modern societies, however, is the differentiation of secular law from religious law. Such changes are crucial stages in the development of societies from premodern to modern forms. Parsons used the term "evolution" when he wrote about such development, and he often pointed out that he took biological evolution as the model for social change. Even if we are skeptical about such parallels between biology and society, and there are good reasons for such skepticism, there are important insights in the way Parsons describes differentiation, and many later social scientists have taken his work as their point of departure.

In his books and articles, Talcott Parsons often refers to the academic predecessors who influenced his own perspectives on the development of modern societies, and among the most important are two social scientists who took great interest in the role of religion in society: Max Weber and Emile Durkheim. In several books, Parsons relies on Durkheim's famous study of aboriginal Australian religion as a typical example of a "primitive" society.[12] (I put the adjective "primitive" in quotation marks because this is not an acceptable description of any society in modern anthropology.) Durkheim's goal was to find the most primitive society and its elementary forms of religion. In Parsons's view, it was not a bad idea to compare primitive societies with modern ones in order to understand the evolution

[12] See, for instance, Talcott Parsons, *Societies – Evolutionary and Comparative Perspectives* (Englewood Cliffs, N.J.: Prentice-Hall, 1966), chap. 3; Talcott Parsons, *Social Systems and the Evolution of Action Theory* (New York: The Free Press, 1977), p. 284ff.

of institutions and culture, but he also said that if we want to understand the difference between undifferentiated and differentiated societies we must not make the mistake of looking for simplicity versus complexity.

An undifferentiated society, such as the aboriginal society of Australia, has extremely complex kinship relations, but its kinship is not much delimited from economy, politics, and religion. On the other hand, in modern societies, kinship is rather simple compared with "primitive" societies, but kinship is clearly differentiated from these other structures. Internal complexity, then, is not the key to understanding the relative differentiation of one component of society. The key is the autonomy of the component relative to other components of the same social system. "One major point," Parsons writes, "is that differentiation is not only internal complicatedness, but differentiation *from*."[13] Thus, kinship is differentiated *from* economic structure. Politics is differentiated *from* law. For our purpose, it is the religious structure that is most important. Religion is differentiated *from* kinship, economy, law, science, politics, and other components of society. Fundamentalism is a reaction against this process. Let us see why.

In the thinking of Parsons, the evolution of societies from undifferentiated to differentiated forms has a number of important implications. First of all, such evolution entailed great changes in the values of society. All societies have value systems that are internalized by their members and are crucial to the legitimation of social order. Traditional societies have institutionalized values that are very particular and tied to the culture of that one society. A society undergoing a process of differentiation encounters a problem. It has to formulate a new value system that is appropriate to the new and more complex system that emerges through the process of differentiation. When a society becomes secularized and makes room for a plurality of

[13] Parsons, *Social Systems and the Evolution of Action Theory*, p. 285.

worldviews, when one dominant religion loses its grip on other spheres of society, values must necessarily become more general in order to accommodate and integrate everybody. In the words of Parsons, the new value pattern must be couched at a higher level of generality in order to legitimize the wider variety of goals and functions appearing through differentiation.[14] This is the process that Parsons called *value-generalization*, and he believed that this process was an important source of turmoil because some people and groups would react negatively to such changes. They feel commitment to the older values and resist the introduction of new and more general norms. "Such resistance may be called 'fundamentalism,'" Parsons suggested.[15]

In most premodern societies, some set of practices and worldviews that we may call *religion* has a crucial role in expressing values for society as a whole. When religion is differentiated from other components of society, and when its mores become irrelevant to other components because the values of society have been generalized, one may expect reactions from people and groups who believe that such value-generalization is a harmful thing. This reaction is seen among Christian, Muslim, Hindu, Buddhist, and Sikh fundamentalists, who react against liberal individualism, humanism, egalitarianism, and the other values that characterize modern societies. Thus, in the sociological thinking of Parsons, fundamentalism is the negative reaction against the generalization of values in a society that undergoes development through differentiation.

Modernity undermined religion by compartmentalizing society and throwing out religion as the ultimate source of authority in the emerging spheres of social life. The long process of differentiation can be traced back to the transformations in European society caused by the Renaissance and the Reformation of the late fifteenth and early sixteenth centuries. The Enlightenment,

[14] Parsons, *Societies*, p. 23.

[15] Ibid.

starting in the late seventeenth century, was also a process of change that advanced differentiation. In a classic book about Enlightenment thought, the German philosopher and historian Ernst Cassirer devoted a chapter to the changing role of religion in the thought of Enlightenment thinkers and observed how the various fields of knowledge – natural science, history, law, politics, art – gradually withdrew from the domination and tutelage of theology.[16]

There are powerful forces in the process of modernity that undermine the position of religion in public life, and perhaps in private life, too. The aim of fundamentalists everywhere is to reverse some of these processes by fostering a process of de-differentiation through which religion would regain some of its lost authority over other spheres of society. What such a de-differentiation might look like would depend on the cultural context. In the chapters of Part II, I will present some examples of how fundamentalist movements approach important spheres such as science, education, law, and politics with a view to de-differentiate religion with these secular social realms.

PRIVATIZATION OF RELIGION – AND DE-PRIVATIZATION?

The second element in the process of secularization is the privatization of religion. This means that religion in modern societies has lost its accepted role in public life, and religious symbols and behaviors have been relegated to the private sphere. Perhaps the individualization and privatization of religion follows from

[16] Ernst Cassirer, *The Philosophy of the Enlightenment*, trans. Fritz A. Koelln and James P. Pettegrove (Princeton, N.J.: Princeton University Press, 1951), p. 159 (first published in German in 1932). See also a short summary of the links between differentiation and fundamentalism in Anson Shupe, "Religious Fundamentalism," in *The Oxford Handbook in the Sociology of Religion*, ed. Peter B. Clarke (Oxford: Oxford University Press, 2011). Oxford Handbooks Online, March 8, 2011, http://dx.doi.org/10.1093/oxfordhb/9780199279791.001.0001.

differentiation because it forces people to live according to different types of rationality in different spheres of life. If somebody in a modern society wishes to see a doctor or a lawyer about an issue, he or she normally does not bring religious beliefs to the table. They are irrelevant in the sphere of scientific medicine. Modern life confines religion to one limited compartment of life for most people. Religion becomes a matter of private choice.

Does the process of privatization make religion weaker? Or is it conceivable that religions in their privatized forms may continue to be an essential part of the lives of individuals and groups? Whereas some social scientists have insisted that privatization does not necessarily lead to loss of belief, others have asserted that privatization is a serious challenge to religion because it removes the social support from religion that is vital to maintaining and reinforcing shared beliefs and worldviews. Moreover, privatized religion makes evangelizing less relevant and produces a sort of relativism that is fatal to shared beliefs.[17]

In places where the privatization of religion has been elevated into national ideology, many people are inclined to interpret the appearance of religious symbols in public as a process of de-privatization. France is the best example of such a society, where many people see the peculiar French version of secularism called *läicite* as vital to the political and cultural life of the republic. This has caused the French debate about Muslim symbols, such as women's headscarves, to become very emotional.[18]

In many European countries, some of the greatest struggles concerning the political management of religion are about questions of private and public religion. Some European states

17 Steve Bruce, *God Is Dead: Secularization in the West* (Oxford: Blackwell, 2003), p. 20.

18 For a short summary of the debate, see Olivier Roy, *Secularism Confronts Islam*, trans. George Holoch (New York: Columbia University Press, 2007).

say to their citizens that it is okay to wear religious symbols in your home but insist that they must be left behind when you go to work or when you enter a lecture hall at a university, and in several countries there are now debates about how to manage ostentatious public manifestations of religion. Religious groups' self-conscious entry into the public sphere seems to be one of the hallmarks of our time, and although this is perceived as a threat by sections of the public and by several secular-minded politicians, it is far from clear that this development constitutes a challenge to the differentiation of the societal spheres.[19]

A significant number of people in the modern world refuse to keep their religious beliefs, symbols, and behaviors limited to the private sphere. They believe that religion should be taken into the public sphere again because they feel that leaving their beliefs, behaviors, and symbols behind when they enter the public sphere amounts to a lack of commitment or a compartmentalization of life that does not make sense to them.

Does the idea of privatization and de-privatization of religion make sense if we apply it in a comparative and global perspective? The distinction between a public and a private sphere arises in European and Western societies through a long historical process. The idea that something is public may be found in texts from Greek and Roman times. In the early period of the common era, the Romans instituted laws that built on the assumption that certain things and places – such as roads, aqueducts, and theaters – belonged to the public in general rather than to private individuals. There was an important distinction between such public works and the things that went on inside the household of a Roman family.

With the expansion of Western political practices and ideologies, the concept of distinct public and private spheres has been introduced into many other societies. However, there is naturally

[19] An influential analysis of this and related questions is Jose Casanova, *Public Religions in the Modern World* (Chicago: University of Chicago Press, 1995).

a wide variety of ways in which the relationship between such spheres is conceptualized in other parts of the world. Some of the tension arising from immigrant religious practices in Europe probably has something to do with different conceptualizations of such spheres.

It seems that many societies in the world are witnessing a process of de-privatization, where people refuse to restrict their religious identities to the private sphere, and if we want to talk about a process of de-secularization in our time, we should probably specify this to mean de-privatization and not de-differentiation. However, in many places we could also ask whether people in general ever accepted the privatization of religion. If they did not, the concept of de-privatization does not make sense.

As we will see later in this book, many fundamentalists would like to take their symbols and rituals into the public realm, but it is often just as important to understand the opposite process. Fundamentalists believe that the modern state has wrongly appropriated a number of fields and emptied them of religious and moral content. Look at the education of children and issues concerning family matters and child-rearing. Fundamentalists want to take these fields out of the hands of the state and put them back into the private sphere. They want to assert the sanctity of the private sphere and resist what they see as a colonization of their lives by public authorities. If we see the public and private spheres in opposition to each other, then fundamentalists often want to defend the boundaries of the private sphere, and this sometimes leads to conflicts between fundamentalists and state authorities.

SECULARIZATION AS DECLINE IN RELIGIOUS AUTHORITY

The third element of secularization is the decline of religion in the everyday lives of people. For some time, it was believed by most sociologists that religion would decline because it was made redundant by modernization. Europe has often been presented as the standard case of secularization because so many Europeans have lost their attachments to the historically dominant religions of their countries. If we look at statistics of religious behavior and belonging in European societies, it is obvious that many Europeans do not feel at home in the established churches. People go to church less and find new alternatives to the traditional rituals at the important occasions in life, such as weddings and burials. Perhaps it is possible to see the decline in belonging to traditional religious organizations as a symptom of the decline in religious belief.

Those who hold the belief that modernization will lead to the decline in religion more or less by necessity often trace the start of the process to the Enlightenment. A long tradition of historical research has located the core of the Enlightenment in the thought of the great French thinkers of the mid-eighteenth century, such as Diderot, Montesquieu, and Voltaire, whereas other research has focused on slightly earlier developments in science and philosophy in Britain, spearheaded by John Locke and Isaac Newton. By any account, the Enlightenment marks the most dramatic step toward secularization and rationalization in Europe's history.

Whereas moderate Enlightenment thinkers sought to forge a synthesis of the new philosophy and the valuable elements of the old order, there were a number of more radical men who completely rejected Christianity and the ecclesiastical order. The Enlightenment produced ideas and values that spread to ever larger sections of societies and institutions in Europe and America during the nineteenth century, and some see this as one of the most important shifts in the history of man, as ideas and values extended across the globe through Europe's interaction with other continents and civilizations.[20]

[20] See, for instance, Benjamin Israel, *Radical Enlightenment: Philosophy and the Making of Modernity, 1650–1750* (Oxford: Oxford University Press, 2001), p. vi.

In the early eighteenth century, skepticism and outright atheism were confined to limited communities of intellectuals, particularly in France. Nevertheless, it was easier to hold and proclaim atheist views during this period than, say, one or two centuries earlier. It was easier not because the church or the state had become tolerant all of a sudden – in many parts of Europe, the control of religious behavior was very strict – but rather because new ideas had become possible. The historian Lucien Febvre argued that atheism in the sense we use it today, as disbelief in God, was unthinkable in sixteenth-century Europe. Many people were accused of atheism, and it was seen as a despicable and dangerous condition, but in reality it was not much more than a label that somebody would stick on a person who did not think about or practice religion in the correct manner.[21] Real atheism was only possible later, after the Enlightenment. It is difficult to know exactly what people believed, and what was possible to believe, in earlier times, and perhaps Christian theologians themselves created the potential and the conditions for disbelief by spending so much intellectual resources on proofs of God's existence.[22]

Atheism is a position that is gaining adherents in many parts of the Western world, but if we take a look at the state of religious beliefs and participation in the world today, it does not seem very plausible to hold that religion is in a state of general decline. Some scholars even insist that we are witnessing a religious revival, and they typically point to the global awakenings taking place in Christianity and Islam as evidence of this. Even in the case of the most secularized continent, Europe, the relationship between religious belonging and religious belief is a

[21] Lucien Febvre, *The Problem of Unbelief in the Sixteenth Century: The Religion of Rabelais*, trans. Beatrice Gottlieb (Cambridge, Mass.: Harvard University Press, 1982).

[22] See the discussion in the Preface to Alan Charles Kors, *Atheism in France, 1650–1729*. Volume 1: *The Orthodox Sources of Disbelief* (Princeton, N.J.: Princeton University Press, 1990).

contested issue for sociologists. The decline of the state churches in Europe does not necessarily mean that Europeans entertain fewer or weaker religious beliefs. A more plausible interpretation is that people feel that the old churches with monopolistic positions in national religious markets do not supply the kinds of religion they want.[23] If we look at how Europeans describe their values and beliefs in the European Values Surveys, it seems that there is a disconnect between institutional belonging and private belief. Many Europeans do believe in God and in life after death, for instance.[24]

Fortunately, for an understanding of the most important characteristics of fundamentalist movements, we do not need to make up our minds about the question of whether religious belief necessarily will decline as a consequence of modernization. *Religious authority* is the important aspect of religion for our exploration of fundamentalism in world religions, and I think that a scrutiny of historical data must lead to the conclusion that all world religions have experienced secularization in the sense of decline in religious authority. The great changes taking place in religious authority structures, particularly in the relative positions of religious elites and laypeople, and a change in the possible roles of these groups, were a necessary condition for the development of religious fundamentalism in all religious traditions. I will look more closely at this process in Chapter 3.

Secularization is many different things. On the one hand, it refers to the large processes whereby the key sectors of society, politics, economics, law, science, and other areas become independent from religion. On the other hand, secularization

[23] Jonathan Fox and Ephraim Tabory, "Contemporary Evidence Regarding the Impact of State Regulation of Religion on Religious Participation and Belief," *Sociology of Religion* 69, no. 3 (2008): 245–71.

[24] See the discussion of the surveys in Grace Davie, *Religion in Modern Europe: A Memory Mutates* (Oxford: Oxford University Press, 2000), pp. 5–23.

is also the process whereby religion loses its power over the lives of families and individuals. For now, we can make the summary statement that to understand fundamentalism we need to understand both *secularization as differentiation* and *secularization as the decline of religious authority.*[25]

[25] Mark Chavez, "Secularization as Declining Religious Authority," *Social Forces* 72, no. 3 (March 1994): 749–74.

2

Religion and Globalization

If we limited our exploration of fundamentalism to the Christian tradition, or to the Abrahamic religions, we might be content with a presentation of modernity that restricted itself to the transformations linked to industrialization, with all its consequences for culture and society in the Western world. However, we want to understand *global* historical trends that have led to the emergence of fundamentalist movements in several of the world religions. In this chapter, I will look at how colonialism and the piecemeal building of European empires were part of the process of modernity and how the colonial expansion of Europe laid the foundation for the diffusion of new styles of religious leadership and religious organizations in other cultures. Between 1800 and 1950, the European empires, the British in particular, provided the institutions through which modern Christian concepts and ideals of religious leadership and organization were communicated to Muslims, Hindus, Buddhists, and Sikhs. This global exchange of concepts and values is a side of modernity that is somewhat underexplored but nevertheless of vital importance for an understanding of fundamentalism outside the Christian world.

The modern historical development of Europe is not a model or standard that other societies necessarily will emulate. However, it is obvious that the West has exerted great influence on other cultures and societies over the past two centuries, and nobody seriously doubts that intensive interaction across cultures is a defining feature of the modern period in world history. The modern age stands out as distinct from earlier epochs because of the intensity and systematic nature of the cross-cultural interactions that have driven it.[1] In the most general sense, the interactions between Western and non-Western societies in the modern period, and particularly since the nineteenth century, make up the context for the development of fundamentalism in the world religions.

THE GLOBALIZATION OF DIFFERENTIATION

The role of the European colonial empires, the British in particular, was crucial for the development of fundamentalism in non-Western religious traditions. I am not primarily thinking of negative reactions against colonial rule. In fact, reactions were not always negative, as certain groups in several societies benefited from the new opportunities brought by colonialism. It is far more important to understand the long-term changes brought about by the colonial expansion of Europe. Colonized peoples came, at least partly, to analyze their own social reality, including their own religious traditions, using the categories of the colonizers and the missionaries who came in their wake. In the words of an anthropologist of southern Africa, "we have grossly underestimated the pervasive significance of Christ's foot soldiers, at home and abroad."[2] Africans increasingly came

[1] See, for instance, Jerry H. Bentley, "Cross-Cultural Interaction and Periodization in World History," *The American Historical Review* 101, no. 3 (June 1996): 749–70, especially p. 769.

[2] Jean Comaroff, "Missionaries and Mechanical Clocks: An Essay on Religion and History in South Africa," *The Journal of Religion* 71, no. 1 (January 1991): 1–17 at p. 3.

to argue with whites in their own master languages, the same historian continues, using its political and poetic possibilities.[3] A similar point can be made with regard to other parts of the world, and this process laid the foundation for religious opposition to modernity in many places in Asia and Africa.

One of the most important aspects of modernity as a global condition is the fact that it has universalized a set of reference points, a set of concepts, a *language* one might say, that everyone has to use if they wish to take part in debates about matters concerning politics and society. This language of modernity includes concepts such as equality, justice, freedom, autonomy, rights, democracy, citizenship, nationhood, development, and public and private spheres. These concepts are originally carried by words in European languages and then translated when used by people in other societies. With translation, meanings may change in subtle but significant ways.

Still, since the end of the nineteenth century, debates about the place of religion in society or the political management of spheres such as religion, law, education, and economy increasingly have been held in this new and global language. Whether somebody applauded or opposed secularization, or whether they welcomed or lamented the general undermining of the authority of religious elites, they had to formulate their debates in the new language. This is one more reason why we must see fundamentalisms globally as movements with a common history. Fundamentalists in Islam, Christianity, Buddhism, Hinduism, and Sikhism do belong to the same category, not only because they share diffuse family resemblances, as The Fundamentalism Project argued, but also because they share the same historically conditioned way of reasoning and arguing about important matters.

The expansion of Spain and Portugal in the Americas and in Asia beginning in the early 1500s was the beginning of European colonialism. Contact with unknown peoples on the

[3] Ibid., p. 16.

other side of the Atlantic produced new and disturbing political and moral questions in Europe. Were the Indians natural slaves because they seemed, in the eyes of some Spanish observers, to lack the ability to build advanced societies? Or were they human beings with the same rationality as Europeans and therefore to be treated as equals?

Early colonialism had great consequences for the peoples of the Americas, but in most parts of Asia there was no real impact from Spain and Portugal's expansion in the 1500s. The Indian subcontinent at this time had empires that were bigger and mightier than Portugal, and the Asian empires that experienced the earliest European expansion were not vulnerable like the Indians of the Caribbean. During the 1500s, the Spanish and Portuguese carried on with their trading and their missionary activity, the Dutch soon joined in, and in the early 1600s traders and sailors in England and France, too, saw the opportunities. In the early 1600s, British colonialism started with the first steps of the British East India Company to establish a presence in Bengal. The eighteenth century certainly saw great political transformations in some parts of Asia, but from local sources it seems that a real impact on culture and religion was not felt until the early nineteenth century. Colonialism shaped the world between 1800 and the middle of the twentieth century to such a degree that we cannot even begin to understand fundamentalism as a global phenomenon without appreciating colonialism's impact on society and religion on different continents. The colonial expansion of Europe led to the global diffusion of secularization, especially in the sense of differentiation, and thus laid the foundation for fundamentalist reactions against this process.

Talcott Parsons noted that England had become by the end of the seventeenth century the most highly differentiated society in Europe – more highly differentiated than any previous society in history.[4] The main units of society – religion, politics, law,

4 Parsons, *The System of Modern Societies*, pp. 50–70.

and economy – had crystallized as distinct subsystems. This is another way of saying that England was the most modern society at that time. England would become the greatest colonial power beginning in the early nineteenth century, and millions of people in Asia and Africa would meet modernity in its English version. Through the bureaucracies and governments of the British Empire, differentiation and its values would be spread to other societies and implemented with varying degrees of success.

Let us take a couple of examples that will become important later in this book. Science was among the important societal spheres to be differentiated from religion in many societies as a result of contacts with the West. Science became a new and dominant sphere through the new systems of education, the new colleges, the new curricula, the new professions, and the new scientific outlook on nature and society. Technological innovation, exchange, and diffusion were important aspects of the period of intense globalization of the nineteenth century. One notable book on the subject has argued that new machines, railways for instance, became the measure of human achievement during the nineteenth century, and that Western politicians defended colonialism with the need to civilize other societies by spreading technology and science.[5] *Rationality* was one of the great catchwords of British culture in the late nineteenth century, and the Western-educated elites in the colonies adopted the word (or translations of it) as the label of a modern, progressive worldview.

The globalization of differentiation was also clearly visible in the sphere of law. During the colonial era, many legal traditions were marginalized through the introduction of secular courts. Law was differentiated from religion and from other societal spheres. The legal customs of European countries have had an enormous impact on law in the rest of the world. Throughout

5 Michael Adas, *Machines as the Measure of Men: Science, Technology, and Ideologies of Western Dominance* (Ithaca, N.Y.: Cornell University Press, 1990).

history, intense contacts between societies have resulted in one society borrowing from another to modify its own legal system. Often a foreign legal system has replaced a local one more or less completely; scholars of comparative law call these imported legal systems "legal transplants."[6] In many colonized societies of the nineteenth century, elements of local legal traditions were replaced by European law. The process of legal transplantation often led to reactions, as when *sharia* (i.e., Islamic law) was gradually replaced by British or French legal customs in Asian and African societies, or when Hindu law was reformed in India, or when the Thai king reformed both monastic and lay Buddhist law in the nineteenth century without being colonized at all but as a natural response to the globalization of modernity. We will return to this in Chapter 6, which is about fundamentalism and law.

Saying that societies in Asia and Africa were introduced to modernity through contacts with Western societies is not the same as saying that all these non-Western societies integrated the institutions, concepts, and values of modernity to the same degree, in the same manner, or at the same time. Modernity necessarily took different shapes in different parts of the world because existing cultures and institutions provided varying contexts in which modernity could take root and develop. The modernizing process turned out to be less homogenizing than some expected. Multiple modernities developed.[7] Nevertheless, there were general trends shared by all societies that experienced modernity. Structural differentiation of the spheres of society was one such basic and universal trend, although the organization and internal relations between such spheres developed in different ways.

6 Alan Watson, *Legal Transplants – An Approach to Comparative Law* (Charlottesville: University of Virginia Press, 1974).

7 A good place to start an exploration of modernity in different parts of the world and an explicit criticism of earlier modernization theories is the issue of the journal *Daedalus* 129, no. 1 (Winter 2000), which has the title *Multiple Modernities.*

COLONIALISM AND MISSIONARIES

Styles and modes of religious behavior, models of religious leadership, and religious organizational forms diffused from Protestant Christian Britain and America to many corners of the globe beginning in the early nineteenth century. This diffusion was a precondition for the development of religious movements that we call fundamentalist in Muslim, Hindu, Buddhist, and Sikh societies. What were the institutions and mechanisms by which this diffusion took place?

By the end of the nineteenth century, many societies in the Middle East, throughout Africa, and in South Asia and Southeast Asia were directly or indirectly ruled by European states, first of all Britain and France. The British Empire covered about a quarter of the globe and a quarter of its people. The promotion of British institutions, culture, language, and ideas amounted to the most important spurt of globalization the world has ever seen. It is what one historian has called *Anglobalization*, observing that it is almost impossible to imagine what the world would be like without the British Empire.[8]

Societies that were not directly ruled by European powers – such as Turkey, Thailand, and Japan – were often heavily influenced by Western institutions, technology, and culture. Their leaders realized they needed to adopt modernity more or less wholesale in order to strengthen their power and defend themselves against other modern states and their gunboats. This was the essence of the Meiji restoration of the late 1800s, which was a program of self-imposed modernization that shook the foundations of traditional Japanese culture and society and set Japan on a course of westernization that would also carry the seeds of militarization and nationalism.[9]

[8] Niall Ferguson, *Empire – How Britain Made the Modern World* (London: Penguin, 2004), pp. xxii–xxiv.

[9] See, for instance, Morris Low, *Building a Modern Japan: Science, Technology and Medicine in the Meiji Era and Beyond* (New York: Palgrave Macmillan, 2005).

Important elements of modernity were exported to societies in Asia and Africa through the colonial expansion of European powers starting in the early 1800s. Globalization involved the exchange of ideas, including religious ones. People from Egypt to Malaysia were exposed to a style of religious leadership developed in the Protestant cultures of Anglo-America, and this amounted to the diffusion of what we may call a new religious style. The British and American Protestant missionaries who worked in the Middle East, South Asia, and Southeast Asia had a peculiarly Protestant Christian way of doing religion. This Protestant style of doing religion and of being religious was often adopted, completely or in part, by people in many societies with traditionally Muslim, Hindu, or Buddhist cultures, but this did not necessarily imply conversion.

I am certainly not claiming that modern Christian concepts, values, and patterns of organization and behavior were adopted or localized without modifications. On the contrary, there were great differences in the way people interpreted and domesticated the impulses coming from the Christian world, which dominated the globe beginning in the nineteenth century. Communities that converted to Christianity would necessarily adapt new concepts to an existing worldview, and this meant that the understanding of even the most basic Christian concepts – such as God, the death and resurrection of Christ, or sin and redemption – varied a great deal between different cultures.[10] The point is that in most parts of the world, even among the majority who did not accept Christianity, the religious and cultural impulses coming from the political centers of the West were so strong that they did have a significant impact on religious concepts and patterns of organization and behavior

[10] Elsewhere, I have explored the misunderstandings and disagreements about the interpretation and translation of the word "baptism" in India. See Torkel Brekke, "Mission Impossible? Baptism and the Politics of Bible Translation in the Early Baptist Mission in Bengal," *History of Religions* 45, no. 3 (February 2006): 213–33.

among Muslims, Hindus, Buddhists, and Sikhs. In Chapter 3, I will discuss modern styles of preaching as an example of how a certain religious practice was adopted and localized by new religious leaders in other cultures.

Religion was not the reason or main motivation for the piecemeal development of the colonial empires. In the beginning, during the seventeenth and eighteenth centuries, empires were built by people eager to get rich through trade, and the traders often felt that missionaries were a nuisance. The East India Company, the business enterprise that in fact created the British Empire in South Asia in the seventeenth century, was very skeptical about missionary activity in its domains. With the revision of the company's charter in 1813, this changed, and the working conditions for Protestant missionaries in the British Empire in Asia improved throughout the later nineteenth century.

Toward the end of the eighteenth century, Christian evangelists started to have a real impact on the debate about the larger purposes of governing other peoples. During the late eighteenth and early nineteenth centuries, the Christian world witnessed the establishment of a number of voluntary societies for the propagation of Christianity in remote corners of the world. The new zeal demonstrated in this work was a result of the Christian revivals and awakenings in Anglo-America, which carried with them a new sense of responsibility both in regard to personal religiousness and holiness and on matters of civic and social life.

Different non-Western societies responded in different ways to the efforts of Christian missionaries during the period of intense globalization in the nineteenth century. The pattern seems to be that societies that were attached to old and self-conscious religions with holy scriptures were more difficult to change. In societies where, for instance, Islam, Hinduism, or Buddhism had been established for some time, and where people had a clear idea of belonging to these traditions, the Christian missionaries often had a hard time. Some Protestant missionaries were of the opinion that hunter-gatherer societies, such as Australian Aborigines and Native Americans, were incapable of understanding and adopting revealed religion.[11] However, in societies where scriptural religious traditions were absent and where there was no literate and self-conscious religious elite, missionaries often met with less resistance. The huge African country of Sudan provides an example of this contrast. In the northern part of the country, where people were Muslims, the missionaries of the Church Missionary Society (CMS) experienced deep skepticism and converted virtually nobody after their arrival in 1899. In the south, however, during the same period the CMS experienced mass conversions to Christianity by people who were not Muslims but belonged to nonscriptural African traditions.[12] What such conversion actually *meant* to individuals in different parts of Africa or Asia is a different matter.

Similar patterns can be seen in South Asia. From the early years of Protestant missionary activity in the early 1800s, the missionaries had little success among Muslims, Hindus, and Buddhists. They met resistance, and sometimes aggression or ridicule, from the elites of these religions. The people who were easily converted were typically tribal peoples at the fringes of Hindu culture either because they belonged to the low and underprivileged strata of society known as Untouchables, or Dalits, or because they belonged to tribes who were not part of Hindu civilization. For instance, the tribes of Northeast India have seen a massive growth in conversions to Christianity.

Some societies and cultures were resistant to attempts to convert them, whereas others were more receptive, but the influence

[11] For a summary of this debate, see Terence Ranger, "Christianity and the First Peoples: Some Second Thoughts," in *Indigenous Peoples and Religious Change*, ed. Peggy Brock (Leiden: Brill, 2005), pp. 15–33.

[12] Heather J. Sharkey, "Christians among Muslims: The Church Missionary Society in the Northern Sudan," *The Journal of African History* 43, no. 1 (2002): 51–71.

of the Christian missionaries was immense almost everywhere. Even in societies where Muslims, Hindus, or Buddhists rejected or shrugged their shoulders at the message of Christian missionaries, it was impossible to be unaffected by their example. In the techniques of proselytization, in the organization of schools and education, in their views on the body and health, in their founding of clinics and hospitals, in their emphasis on social service, and in many other areas, the Christian missionaries presented local cultures with a new worldview.

One example is Thailand, a country with a great political and religious tradition and that was never colonized by Western powers. During the middle decades of the nineteenth century, Protestant missionaries from America were welcomed by King Mongkut (reigned 1851–68) and given support in their work not least because some of them had considerable knowledge of Western medicine and science and acted as teachers and doctors to members of the royal family. The work of these Protestant missionaries had a profound impact on the reconceptualization of the religious sphere in Thailand and the wide-ranging religious reforms under the modernizing government of King Mongkut.[13]

To William Carey, the greatest of all modern Protestant missionaries, the expansion of trade in the empire demonstrated the feasibility of mission on a global scale. Carey wrote that, "commerce shall subserve the spread of the gospel."[14] If traders could overcome the great physical obstacles of traveling for the love of the profits arising from a few otter skins, Christians should have the same love for the souls of their fellow men in distant parts of the world, Carey insisted. There are trading companies working in the places where "barbarians dwell," and so

[13] See, for instance, Edwin Zehner, "The Protestants and Local Supernaturalism: Changing Configurations," *Journal of Southeast Asian Studies* 27, no. 2 (September 1996): 293–319.

[14] William Carey, *An Enquiry into the Obligation of Christians to Use Means for the Conversion of the Heathen* (London: The Carey Kingsgate Press, 1792), p. 68.

providence seemed to invite Christians to the trial of traveling the world for the sake of the true religion, he wrote.[15]

IMPROPER IDEAS OF GOD: MISSIONARIES AS AGENTS OF GLOBALIZED RELIGION

The Protestant Christian missionaries, and the much greater number of indigenous Christian missionaries, were agents of globalized religion laying the foundation for the type of religious and political activities that we call fundamentalism in different religious traditions. There were something like 10,000 missionaries employed by British missionary societies at the turn of the twentieth century, but that figure was, in the words of one scholar, "dwarfed by the legions of missionaries" belonging to local communities all over the empire.[16] The way that the Christian message was received, the degree to which it was understood, and the extent to which it was seen as relevant varied enormously. However, in most places, the encounter with expanding Protestant Christianity had profound long-term consequences for the way that people understood and practiced religion.

The papers of great Protestant missionaries such as William Carey convey clearly the strong impulse that laid the foundation for a new attitude toward religion and new types of religious leadership and organization in Hindu, Muslim, and Buddhist communities in South Asia. Christian missionaries promulgated religiosity and religious leadership based on a particular form of religious authority developed within the tradition of ethical prophecy during the great awakenings in the Protestant West. To most Protestant missionaries, religion was a sincere business

[15] Ibid., p. 67.

[16] Peggy Brock, "New Christians as Evangelists," in *Missionaries and Empire*, ed. Norman Etherington (Oxford: Oxford University Press, 2009), pp. 132–53 at p. 132.

because it was ultimately about sin and salvation, concepts that were alien to many other societies. People in Africa and Asia seldom shared this attitude.

One of the earliest observations William Carey made about the religion of native Bengalis (Bengal is in east India) was their lack of sincerity in their approach to God. In a letter to England written in 1795, a year or so after his arrival in India, Carey noted: "Poor souls, they have need of the Gospel indeed; their superstitions are so numerous, and all their thoughts of God so light, that they only consider him as a sort of Play thing."[17] Childish play is an important aspect of the nature of God in religious traditions of this part of the world, but this side of religion was certainly not appreciated by Carey and his companions.

Sometime in November 1800, Carey was talking to a group of Hindus and Muslims in the marketplace in a village in Bengal. As always, Carey exhorted the listeners to forsake their old ways and trust Christ. Carey wrote: "After preaching and prayer, one man said God had given one Shastri [i.e., religious text] to them, and another to us – I observed that the Shastris were so very different from each other that if one God gave them both he must be a double tongued being, which was a very improper idea of God."[18] Different and incompatible ideas of God were only one of the challenges facing the Christian missionaries working in Asia. The missionary activity in other parts of the world often involved fierce competition concerning ideas about God and salvation, both between Christians and locals and between different Christian denominations sending out missionaries. In this competition, frequent preaching and printing of pamphlets and other written materials was part of the repertoire.

[17] William Carey to Andrew Fuller, 30 January 1795 IN/13 Carey to Fuller. References to the private papers of missionaries are to the files in the Angus Library, Regent's College, in Oxford.

[18] William Carey to John Sutcliffe, 27 November 1800, IN/ 13 1 of 2.

One of the main challenges for William Carey, as he saw it, was to convince people in India that their idols were powerless and that they should stop worshiping images. In the religious practice of Hindus, gods are commonly thought to enter into images, and human beings can come close to divinity by worshiping the image and getting a sight (*darshana*) of the god in the image. The reaction of Carey and many other missionaries was an urge to prove to the locals that the images were powerless. Several times Carey suggested testing the images of gods in front of the Hindus by using a hammer to crush the stone or fire to burn wooden figures. By destroying the image, he wanted to show that the Hindu gods had no power and convince the observers to leave Hinduism and embrace Christ. Carey wrote in a letter to a colleague:

> They wished, as they often do to see a Sign or miracle in confirmation of our mission – I asked them if they had not a guardian God to their town, they said yes – Ramchanan, I asked is he a wooden one? Or made of stone – they said who can tell what god is made of – said I what is the things you worship made of – stone – well if it is God I cannot imagine it – now if the people of the town will agree to it I'll try whether he is God or not – I will bring a large hammer, and if I cannot break him to pieces you are right. If I can, your God is gone and you are undeceived – I had on the road made a similar proposal with respect to Jaggannath but as he was a wooden one I proposed to burn him,[19]

This type of very devoted engagement with people of other faiths in other societies was an element in a large process whereby the attitudes, institutions, and ideas of Christianity were globalized. Protestant Christianity became the model for new ways of behaving religiously. From the end of the nineteenth century, these models had become important in many parts of the world and provided a significant repertoire for a new type of religious leader in Islam, Hinduism, Sikhism, and Buddhism.

[19] Ibid.

GLOBALIZATION AND THE DIFFERENTIATION OF RELIGION

Starting in the early nineteenth century and developing at very different speeds in different parts of the world, the structures of law, science, economics, religion, and other spheres of society became delimited subsystems in the larger system of society. The global expansion of a process of differentiation is perhaps most clearly seen in the expansion of the system of states. In Europe after the Reformation of the 1500s, international politics was gradually separated from other systems of society. The wars between Protestants and Catholics made it clear that politics between nations must be based on principles other than religious identity. At the Peace Treaty of Westphalia, signed in 1648 to finish the Thirty Years War, which was partly a continuation of the religious wars of Europe, the young states agreed that the principle of sovereignty should guide international relations and that states could behave pretty much as they wanted in internal matters. A modern system of states was appearing on the historical scene.

The story of the formation of modern states was very complex, and I have oversimplified matters because I wish to focus on the diffusion of the European political system outside Europe. The system of states – with its concepts, assumptions, ideologies, and practices – has spread to the rest of the world over the last 200 years. The process took place at different speeds and with different local adaptations in the Americas, Asia, and Africa. I am certainly not claiming that there is just one version of modern politics, but some of the key institutions and concepts have clearly become universalized, such as democracy and citizenship, for instance. By the time the colonial period ended around 1950 – in some places earlier and in some slightly later – all societies on the globe had adopted the state system in some form and were organizing themselves according to its peculiar logic.

Today, we all take it for granted that politics is about states with clear borders conducting their internal affairs through elections and external affairs through international organizations like the United Nations and practices such as diplomacy and war.

The global diffusion of a system of religion was in some respects a process parallel to the diffusion of a system of states.[20] The globalization of the process of differentiation laid the foundations for the modern versions of the world religions around the globe. This may sound strange, as most people are accustomed to thinking of world religions as eternal and easily identifiable things that have existed for centuries. However, the idea that mankind may be divided into world religions with comparable organizations, theologies, and rituals is fairly recent.

From the early 1800s, the institutions and ideas of Christianity were globalized through the contacts established by the colonial expansion of Europeans. The differentiation of a religious system, which had taken place in Europe over some time, was replicated in Asian and African countries. Religion as a distinct category was globalized. This made it possible to draw clear boundaries around the religious system and delimit its previous influence in other spheres of society. The academic discipline called the *history of religions* or *religious studies* is part of the causes and consequences of the development of the idea of world religions.

The case of Hinduism is telling in this process. If we read the writings of leading Hindu intellectuals of the late nineteenth century, it is easy to discern the process of differentiation of religion from other systems. Hindu intellectuals of this period were aware that Hinduism always had been a lot more than what was implied in the new English word "religion" introduced to Indian social reality. Hinduism had been a label of geographic origin, a way of life, a system of law, a political ideology, a great

[20] Peter Beyer, "The Religious System of Global Society: A Sociological Look at Contemporary Religion and Religions," *Numen* 45, no. 1 (1998): 1–29.

culture, or even many cultures, as well as rituals and theology. In the late 1800s, Hinduism was reconstructed or reimagined to be a world religion comparable to Christianity. The process of reconstruction or reimagining took place in the dialogue between Hindu intellectuals and Western scholars who were keen to explore the ancient traditions and the living customs of India. The Hindu intellectuals taking part in this dialogue were often educated both in the new European schools and in the traditional institutions of learning. One of the foremost among them, Bankimchandra Chatterji, pointed out around 1880 that Indians before the arrival of the British "did not perceive the independent existence of that object which is understood by the word religion."[21]

In Hindu fundamentalist groups, the mimicry of Christian ways of communicating and organizing religion is evident. Dayanand Saraswati (1824–1883), the founder of the important Hindu revivalist organization Arya Samaj, wanted to strengthen Hinduism by getting rid of premodern ritualism and the caste system and by organizing the Hindu religion along the lines of Christianity. In recent times, the Vishva Hindu Parishad (VHP), or in English the World Hindu Council, a key organization for Hindu fundamentalists in India and globally, has been explicit in its call to develop Hinduism along the lines of Semitic religions. The VHP was founded in 1964 by the lawyer Shiv Shankar Apte. He and his collaborators were very concerned that Hinduism had no real integrated structure, and the VHP was founded in order to unite Hindus. In the 1980s, Hindu nationalists made important advances in the ways they organized themselves. The Hindu nationalists of the RSS and VHP perceived the other religions in India – Christianity, Islam, and Sikhism – to be threats to Hindu culture and decided to emulate the organizing principle of these other religions. They

[21] Bankimchandra Chatterji, quoted in Torkel Brekke, *Makers of Modern Indian Religion* (Oxford: Oxford University Press, 2002), p. 31.

started building an ecclesiastical structure in order to defend Hinduism from outside pressure.[22]

The VHP is an organization that self-consciously mimics the organizational structure, zeal, and unifying religiosity of Christianity and Islam. This mimicry is seen in how the core activists of the VHP, the *pracharaks*, are trained in instruction camps and how they devote their lives to itinerant preaching and organizational work in order to build a Hindu church.[23] But the mimesis is also apparent in the way that Hindu fundamentalists have selected key elements in Hindu tradition and elevated them to the status of sacred symbols and objects. Leaders of the VHP point to the organized prayer and other daily rites of Muslims and Christians as practices that generate unity and strength, and they have insisted that the Hindus need to build the same kinds of collective religiosity if they are to survive what they perceive as fierce competition between the religions of South Asia.

Christianity was the model for the construction of Hinduism as a world religion, as was the case for Buddhism, Islam, and Sikhism, but it is important to distinguish between structure and substance. I am not saying that other religious traditions adopted or accepted the *substance* of Christian doctrines – on the contrary. However, the internal *structure* of world religions, with their priesthoods, schools, rituals, basic doctrines, and, even more importantly, the *structure* of the relationship between the believer and his or her religion were shaped according to Christian models. To return to the parallel of states, just as countries such as, say, Egypt, Burma, or India began to identify themselves as states within a global system of states, religions such as

[22] Christophe Jaffrelot, *The Hindu Nationalist Movement and Indian Politics – 1925 to the 1990s* (London: Hurst, 1996), p. 352.

[23] Christophe Jaffrelot, "A Nationalist but Mimetic Attempt at Federating the Hindu Sects," in *Charisma and Canon – Essays on the Religious History of the Indian Subcontinent*, ed. Vasudha Dalmia, Angelika Malinar, and Martni Christof (Delhi: Oxford University Press, 2001), pp. 388–410.

Islam, Buddhism, and Hinduism defined themselves as religions within a global system of religions.

From the early nineteenth century, Christians, Muslims, Buddhists, and Sikhs became increasingly conscious of the fact that their own tradition was just one subsystem in a global system of religions. The model and standard for what a religion should look like was set by Christianity. Just as Western states were the dominant political powers in the world beginning in the early 1800s, Christianity was the dominant religion. Other religions have, to a significant extent, formed their institutions, organizations, and modes of leadership along Christian patterns. And they have formed their *resistance* to the consequences for religion of globalization and modernization along Christian patterns, too.[24] This is one reason why fundamentalism must be understood in the context of globalization.

Let me give one concrete example of how the organization of religion was globalized along the patterns of Christianity. The Young Men's Christian Association (YMCA) was established in London in 1844 to develop young men spiritually and physically through religious and physical education. Over the next few decades, the YMCA established itself not only in North America and in many European countries but also in all major cities and towns of South Asia, including the colonial hubs of Calcutta, Bombay, and Colombo, as well as in Egypt, China, and Japan.

Following the development of the YMCA as a global Christian organization, there appeared almost identical organizations within other religions as reactions against the YMCA. In Egypt, the Young Men's Muslim Association (YMMA) was established to protect young Muslims against the YMCA and Christian influence. In Sri Lanka, the Young Men's Buddhist Association (YMBA) was created to counter the missionary onslaught and defend local religion. The Young Men's Hindu Association, Jain

[24] I find Peter Beyer's outline of this process useful. See Peter Beyer, *Religion in Global Society* (London: Routledge, 2006).

Young Men's Association, and parallel youth organizations for Sikhs were all established at the end of the nineteenth century with the aim of reviving religion and culture and defending the young generation against Christian influence through various educational activities.

Although the importance of the YMBA for the revival of Buddhism in Sri Lanka is well established, and although scholars have pointed to the role of the YMMA, alongside the Muslim Brotherhood, in Egypt's Muslim revival in the 1930s, I have not seen studies analyzing this new type of organization in several world religions working for the spiritual and physical education of young men, and later women, as a means of cultural survival in a globalized age. These organizations – Muslim, Buddhist, Hindu, or Sikh – were reactions against the YMCA as an organizational manifestation of globalized Christianity in the colonial period, but they were reactions formulated in the same mold as the threat itself.

We can return here by a different route to the problem stated in the introductory chapter. Some scholars argue that the term "fundamentalism" is so tied up with its Christian origins that we may not speak of fundamentalism in other cultures. This position rests on a misunderstanding. Fundamentalism developed in all world religions as part and parcel of the process whereby the world religions themselves developed as comparable entities within a global system of religion. Christianity, Islam, Judaism, Hinduism, Buddhism, and Sikhism developed, in the eyes of both believers and external observers, into world religions through the globalization of a system of religion, and this process was a precondition for the development of fundamentalism outside the West.

GLOBALIZATION AND THE OBJECTIFICATION OF RELIGION

Over the last few paragraphs, I have argued that the idea that the world's peoples may be divided into a clear number of world religions with their different theologies but parallel structures emerged as an aspect of globalization. If we look at how premodern religions work, we see that they are always embedded in, and inseparable from, other elements of culture. Looking at traditional religion, it would be meaningless to ask somebody to describe the essentials of Islam or Christianity or Buddhism without specifying where and when because these world religions have not existed without being shaped in local cultures where the limits between what counts as religion and what counts as other things – such as magic, medicine, law, or even clothing and food – are fuzzy. In such normal situations, most followers of a religion will not spend a lot of energy thinking about what it means to him or her to belong to a particular religious tradition. Religion is part of the culture one is born into, and one takes part in the rituals and festivals of that culture without asking questions, in a bit the same way as one uses a language.

Of course, there have always been exceptions, as when people become aware of belonging to a particular religion by being confronted with followers of other traditions or by seeking out a more self-consciously religious group within the main religion: joining a Sufi teacher or a Hindu guru, or becoming a strict forest-dwelling Buddhist monk, for instance. The point is that most people have not thought of religion as an object that one might separate from other parts of culture, an object that one may choose to relate to in the way one likes or even reject. The spread of this type of consciousness about religion to the minds of very large numbers of people, perhaps the majority in most world religions today, presupposed a process of objectification, which is related to the process of differentiation.

Objectification is the process by which basic questions about religion become important to large numbers of believers, such as "What is my religion?" and "Why is it important to my life?"[25] Such questions are modern queries and contribute to making

[25] I borrow this useful term from Dale Eickelmann and James Piscatori, *Muslim Politics* (Princeton, N.J.: Princeton University Press, 1996), p. 38.

religion a self-contained system that can be clearly distinguished from culture in general and from other societal spheres. The process of objectification takes place all over the world and in all world religions, although starting at different times and developing at different speeds.

In the world of Buddhism, the process of objectification is evident from the nineteenth century in the way that religious leaders (e.g., Anagarika Dharmapala in Sri Lanka) or political leaders (e.g., King Mongkut of Thailand) worked hard to create a new conception of what Buddhism *really* was. They wanted to separate Buddhism from Sinhalese or Thai culture and go back to its fundamentals. They were convinced that Buddhism as a universal and timeless religion could be salvaged from the superfluous trappings of culture and made into an object that every follower could relate to as a believer making a conscious and informed choice to be Buddhist. This is a modern way of being religious.

In the world of Hinduism, the idea of being Hindu as something fundamentally different from Muslim can perhaps be traced back to the sixteenth century in some parts of India in some sections of society. However, in many places in the region that today is India and Pakistan, the lives of Muslims and Hindus were very similar, and many British administrative reports of the nineteenth century describe how the categories of Hindu, Muslim, and Sikh were far from clear-cut in the real world.[26] One caste may contain people from all three religions, and the only occasions when one might get a glimpse of clear religious boundaries between Hindus and Muslims would be when somebody got married, or perhaps on certain festivals, although people would often take part in festivities across religious borders. This would start to change in the twentieth century, as people became more aware of, and more concerned with,

[26] See, for instance, examples given in Rafiuddin Ahmed, *The Bengal Muslims* (Delhi: Oxford University Press, 1996).

belonging to one religion. The awareness was clearly linked to the growing political importance of religious identities, which would manifest itself in many ways, such as the forging of Hindi, Urdu, and Punjabi as "Hindu," "Muslim," and "Sikh" languages. Everybody became more self-consciously Muslim, Hindu, or Sikh, and religious identities became gradually more exclusive while boundaries to other traditions became more important.

In the world of Islam, too, the process of objectification is shaping the relationship of believers to their religion. Both Muslims and non-Muslims talk and write about Islam as a system that may be abstracted out of specific cultures, and Muslims have over the past few decades been asked, even forced, to relate to their religion in new ways, and especially to take a position on questions of radicalism and violence. In the parts of the Muslim world where mass literacy and primary education have penetrated slowly, the objectification of Islam has gained speed only over the past few decades.[27]

The objectification of religion in the consciousness of Muslims is closely connected to new techniques and technologies of communication, such as printing and the Internet. More Muslims today claim the right to read and interpret the textual sources of Islam than ever before, and many of the leaders of the Muslim awakening, such as Amr Khaled and Zakir Naik, are criticized by conservatives because they bypass people with religious education and knowledge, the *ulama*, and approach the basics of Islam directly. In other words, the objectification of Islam is closely linked to questions of religious authority. The process of objectification started as early as the nineteenth century among the new middle classes in colonial cities of Asia and Africa, but it started only long after the Second World War among less educated people in the same regions.

[27] Dale F. Eickelman, "Mass Higher Education and Religious Imagination in Contemporary Arab Societies," *American Ethnologist* 19, no. 4 (November 1992): 643–55.

A different but related global process may be labeled *deculturation.* Deculturation is the development by which religion is separated from culture, and it has some important consequences for the development of fundamentalism in the twenty-first century.[28] Increasing migration is an aspect of globalization that speeded up processes of objectification of religion in most world religions after the Second World War, with large numbers of migrant laborers entering Europe from the Middle East, North Africa, and South Asia. Millions of Muslims, Sikhs, Hindus, Buddhists, and Christians settled in new countries in the period after the Second World War, and this is affecting world religions in profound ways. The migrating groups – the *diasporas* as they are often called – are cut off from the territory and the cultures in which they or their parents were born.

This situation of being Muslim, Sikh, or Hindu but living outside a Muslim, Sikh, or Hindu culture makes many people feel a need to reconstruct their religion in universal terms detached from the particular culture of a past homeland. Islam, Sikhism, or Hinduism then becomes a more general set of rituals, beliefs, and symbols, and in such an environment the individual is free to choose whether to embrace a religion or reject it. The consciousness of belonging to a particular religion increases, and often the visibility of such identity to outsiders increases, too, because the insider is more concerned with the symbols that he or she sees as universal signs of adherence, such as the turban for Sikh men or the veil for Muslim women. The people who do not move to other countries are also affected by the ways in which migrants are reimagining and reinventing religion because new forms of communication create important channels for the global exchange of ideas.

[28] This process is the topic in Olivier Roy, *Holy Ignorance: When Religion and Culture Part Ways,* translated from French by Ros Schwartz (London: Hurst, 2010). It is also discussed in Olivier Roy, *Globalised Islam: The Search for a New Ummah* (London: Hurst, 2006).

Fundamentalists have a highly objectified concept of religion. They see their religion as a timeless universal system of truth that can and should be detached from local cultures. They share the objectified concept of religion with many nonfundamentalists, but they do not share it with people who still experience and practice religion in an "unconscious" way as part of their received culture and worldview. Fundamentalists are at least as conscious of their religion and their religiousness as other modern people, and this fact shows how fundamentalism is a modern phenomenon and differs from traditionalism or conservatism in any normal sense of those terms. The fundamentalist relationship to religion is just as much a product of globalization as the relationship to religion displayed by born-again believers of all faiths.

Fundamentalists are very concerned about what Christianity, Islam, or Buddhism *really* is, and they generally think that they have an answer that is ignored by most of the people who claim to belong to the same religion. Most people who call themselves Christians have a wrong idea of what Christianity really is, according to Christian fundamentalists. The same is the case for Muslim, Hindu, Sikh, or Buddhist fundamentalists. In other words, fundamentalists do not think it is strange at all for people to try to describe what Islam, Buddhism, or Christianity essentially is without reference to a particular place and time because they are convinced, as are many people in the modern world, that such universal and timeless religions exist.

By stressing the universality of religion, its decoupling from specific cultures and from time and place, fundamentalists in all the world religions construct ideas about a pure and true religion that must either be accepted and followed completely or rejected. Those who are lukewarm to such clear demands are outsiders to the fundamentalist cause. This modern consciousness about religion is the basis for fundamentalist criticism of traditional ways of being religious, and traditional structures of religious authority, which is the topic of the next chapter.

3

A Global Shift in Religious Authority

In the last two chapters, I claimed that fundamentalism in the world religions presupposes a process of intense modernization and globalization that has taken place over the past two centuries, and especially since the second half of the nineteenth century. In particular, there took place a process of secularization in the limited sense of differentiation of religions from other systems, such as politics, law, and education. There is no reason to assume that the period of modernization and globalization we are looking at produced secularization in the sense of decline in religious belief, but there is no doubt that differentiation has taken place globally, although with significant local variations. Closely linked to the process of differentiation, there took place a process of objectification through which religion came to be seen as a thing that could be detached from culture. This resulted in a new and self-conscious way of relating to religion.

In the same period, Christianity became a powerful model for the reconfiguration of Islam, Hinduism, Buddhism, and Sikhism as world religions. New religious styles, forms of religious leadership, and types of religious organizations were developed with Christianity as the model. People all over the world came to see themselves as members of religions, just as they belonged to different states. There developed a global system of religions in which the different world religions were defined, both by believers and external observers, in relation to each other. It was obvious to everybody that, say, Islam and Hinduism had somewhat different contents, but at the same time they were thought to be, and made to be, structurally similar.

Most people probably did not reflect on these huge institutional and conceptual transformations in the nature of religion in the modern world, but some did react strongly against the changes. In many cases, the relevant reactions did not come from the traditional religious elites, and there were several reasons why they did not. Traditional elites often did not have the modern education necessary to engage in complex new debates about religion and modernity, and in some places traditional religious elites did not lose a lot from the changes because these elites were supported by colonial authorities as a way to maintain peace and stability. The strongest and most relevant reactions against the globalizing process of differentiation often came from laypeople. Fundamentalism as a global phenomenon is a type of reaction where lay leaders and their organizations are key agents.

PROPHECY AND RELIGIOUS AUTHORITY

To understand the significance of these lay reactions, we need to understand something about the nature of religious authority, and for this purpose it is useful to apply some of the ideas of Max Weber. Weber was an exceptionally erudite and creative writer, and he is among the founding fathers of sociology. At the same time, he has been criticized for being a Eurocentric historian who harbored untenable ideas about the lack of rationality in other cultures.[1] Such criticisms should be taken seriously,

[1] See, for instance, J. M. Blaut, *Eight Eurocentric Historians* (London: The Guilford Press, 2000), chap. 2.

but they certainly do not mean that we should forget the good things about his sociological and historical insights.

One important insight to be found in the thinking of Max Weber is his analysis of religious leadership in the world religions. The three important types of religious specialists discussed by Weber are the priest, the prophet, and the magician. Priests are functionaries of organized and permanent religious enterprises. They have special and exclusive knowledge of fixed doctrines and rituals. Magicians and prophets, in contrast, are individuals who use their *personal* gifts and powers rather than authority as part of an institutionalized hierarchy. Magicians use their powers to exert influence over the physical world and achieve more or less mundane goals, whereas prophets use their individual gifts to proclaim a new doctrine or a new divine commandment.[2]

We can forget the magician here and focus on the prophet. It is the personal call and the opposition to the established order that are the important traits of prophecy. Prophets are key agents of change. Their new and radical message has the potential for starting a process of breakthrough. "Breakthrough" means radical change in the established religion, which is institutionalized and leads to change in society as a whole. Weber looked at religious change as a long process of evolution toward more systematic and rationalized forms. Prophecy and its potential for breakthrough played a key role in his idea of religious and social evolution.

The prophet and the priest are two very different, and often opposing, roles. The priest and the prophet compete, and the relative prominence of the two roles is an important factor in the position of religion in society and in the development and change of the external relations and internal organizations of religious groups. The roles are different because they derive their authority from different and conflicting sources. The personal call is the most important feature distinguishing the

[2] Max Weber, *The Sociology of Religion*, translated from the German by Ephraim Fischoff (Boston: Beacon Press, 1993), p. 46ff. (Originally published in 1922.)

prophet from the priest. "The latter lays claim to authority by virtue of his service in a sacred tradition, while the prophet's claim is based on personal revelation and charisma."[3] Charisma is a key concept in the sociology of religion, and it has been important to several scholars of political leadership.

There are two different types of prophetic roles in Weber's thinking, and they are both closely connected to different concepts of God. Weber observed that different concepts of God in, on the one hand, Abrahamic and, on the other hand, South Asian and Far Eastern religions resulted in very different types of prophetic roles in the world religions. Christianity, Islam, and Judaism emphasize the transcendent and personal aspects of God. The transcendent and ethical God is a Near Eastern concept, Weber asserted.[4]

In the Abrahamic religions, we find the ethical prophet. He is the instrument of God's will and preaches obedience to divine laws and precepts. Old Testament prophets as well as Muhammad and Zoroaster are typical examples of the ethical prophet. In the Indian and Chinese religions, we find the other type: the exemplary prophet. The exemplary prophet is somebody who has found the way to decode the universe and points the way to salvation by sharing his knowledge and techniques with those who care to follow him. He has no divine commandment. In fact, the gods themselves are in need of his special knowledge because they are immanent beings trapped in the same cycle of death and rebirth as other creatures. The typical exemplary prophet is the Buddha.[5] There are no examples of ethical prophets in India or China, and the traditional religions and the classical texts of these high civilizations make it impossible that this type of religious role should appear there, Weber asserted.[6]

3 Ibid., p. 46.
4 Ibid., p. 56.
5 Ibid., p. 55.
6 Ibid., pp. 55–56.

The roots of the idea of prophecy as opposed to priesthood can be found in the historical research on the prophets of ancient Israel. Historians have noted that the prophets of the Old Testament were charismatic laypeople who exercised authority in milieus of pious laity as preachers of morality. The religion of the prophets is the religion of the word. The prophets bring the word of God to man, whereas the priest carries the gifts of men to God through sacrifice.[7] These lay preachers provided a model for religious discourse continued later within Christianity and Islam, and the model of prophecy found in the Abrahamic religions, with its ultimate source in the Old Testament, is important for my argument about the nature of fundamentalism.

I think Weber was right in pointing to the very peculiar nature of Near Eastern prophecy. The concept of God found in the Abrahamic religions leads to a prophetic role with fervent preaching of divine commandments that must be obeyed by humanity. This kind of religious role was absent in other world religions until it diffused during the modern period of globalization. The Hinduism espoused by the Brahmins or the Confucianism that was seen to be the basis of Chinese social order may have been challenged by charismatic and innovative persons, but they would not claim that they were messengers chosen by a transcendent God with a moral message to humanity. This claim is peculiar to Judaism, Christianity, and Islam.

Fundamentalism arose in Christianity, Judaism, and Islam from the late nineteenth through the twentieth century. Wherever it arises, it is characterized by styles of religious leadership, and claims to religious authority, derived from the tradition of ethical prophecy found in these world religions. Fundamentalist leaders all take on great personal responsibility for changing religious and social reality, are mostly outside the

7 I rely here on a discussion of the significance of historical scholarship on Israelite prophecy to the sociology of religion in Peter L. Berger, "Charisma and Religious Innovation: The Social Location of Israelite Prophecy," *American Sociological Review* 28, no. 6 (December 1963): 940–50.

established hierarchies, do not have classical priestly roles, and preach divine messages of moral obligation to their congregations or followers.

So the typical fundamentalist leader acts prophetically at least some of the time, and I believe this is one of the distinguishing features of fundamentalism. At the same time, moving on from Weber's work on prophecy, we should be aware that in modern circumstances prophecy based on individual charismatic authority does not only arise at the margins of society but can develop anywhere, even inside the structures of established order, inside churches for instance. It is also important to notice that modern religious leaders, including fundamentalists, behave prophetically without necessarily ticking all the boxes of charismatic authority as Weber analyzed it.[8]

In Buddhism, Hinduism, and Sikhism, religious authority and leadership styles that owed much of their form to the tradition of ethical prophecy were introduced by Christian missionaries and were adopted by leaders in these non-Abrahamic religions in an attempt to come to terms with and resist modern challenges to their cultures. I spent the last chapter trying to show how the period of globalization starting in the mid-nineteenth century provided the channels through which such communication took place. I pointed out that Protestant missionaries were agents of a great cultural movement through which religious styles and practices, and attitudes toward religion, were globalized. Many of these styles, practices, and attitudes may ultimately be traced back to the religious awakenings of the Anglo-American religious culture starting in the eighteenth century.

All this means that the structures of religious authority and the religious roles that we can see today in movements that we call fundamentalist within Hinduism, Buddhism, and Sikhism are

[8] This and other points are made in a collection of essays that tried to apply Weber's analysis of prophecy to modern conditions. See Jeffrey K. Hadden and Anson Shupe, eds., *Prophetic Religions and Politics: Religion and the Political Order.* (New York: Paragon House, 1986), especially the discussion in chap. 2.

modern hybrid types that borrow elements from the Abrahamic traditions, especially from Christianity. In important respects, the styles of leadership and legitimation employed by fundamentalist movements in Hinduism and Buddhism mimic those of Christianity. A significant element in the spread of fundamentalism after 1850 is the spread of the role of the ethical prophet to new cultures. To specify what I mean by this, I will look at this process in Muslim and Buddhist societies.

LAY AUTHORITY AND FUNDAMENTALISM IN THE MUSLIM WORLD

In the Muslim world, a shift in religious authority has taken place over the past two centuries, and some of the consequences of this shift are evident today in struggles and negotiations over authority, legitimacy, and power between different types of religious actors, in particular between fundamentalists and religious elites, which have often submitted to the power of states in exchange for support and official recognition.

A comparative historical sociologist encounters a problem when he or she wants to compare the religious groups of Islam with those of Christianity. Sunni Islam has no church, and it is incorrect to talk about priests and laity in Islam. There are groups of people with Islamic education occupying various roles in society, and the common term *ulama* refers to all of these groups. Similar problems arise when we want to analyze changes in Hinduism with words and categories taken from a Christian context. In this book, however, I wish to highlight parallel changes in religious authority and in the relative positions of groups taking place in different world religions, and in order to do this it is helpful to use broad categories. Bearing these reservations in mind, I am sometimes going to refer to *ulama* with the broad sociological term *priests* and to common Muslims who are not *ulama* as *laypeople.*

The changes in religious authority started at different times in Sunni Muslim societies, and they have necessarily taken a variety of local forms and produced different consequences. Nevertheless, the broad development has been the rise of a new type of lay authority to challenge established roles and hierarchies. The founders of the original Muslim fundamentalist movements took on roles and responsibilities in society that were traditionally the domain of the *ulama*. They were part of the global movement starting in the nineteenth century whereby religious elites in the world religions were challenged by laypeople who wanted direct and unmediated access to religious heritage and culture. These challenges have mostly come from an emerging middle class of educated professionals such as teachers, doctors, engineers, and civil servants.

The *ulama* had an important function in traditional Muslim society because they held monopolies in key fields of social life, such as jurisprudence and education. They did not have real political power – in many historical situations, Muslim societies would be ruled by a military aristocracy without any religious functions – but the *ulama* did have a very significant degree of economic independence. The foundation of such independence was their role as administrators of charitable endowments (*waqf*); that is, the Islamic institution of land or buildings from which revenues are reserved for religious and charitable purposes, such as the upkeep of Islamic schools and mosques or other public goods.

However, when secular education and secular law, and other secular institutions, were introduced and developed in Muslim societies of Africa and Asia at different times and at different paces between 1800 and today, the authority of the *ulama* started to crumble. Their schools were taken over by centralized states, and governments wanted to tax or nationalize the charitable endowments, which meant the end of financial independence. Very often the consequences were dramatic for the livelihood and status of the religious teachers and scholars, as in Egypt beginning in the early nineteenth century, when the system of Islamic education and scholarship was hit hard by the reforms of Muhammad Ali, as I will explain in more detail later. Muslim fundamentalism is partly a reaction to the destruction of Islamic learning and scholarship by the modern state and to the loss of authority of traditional "priests." Fundamentalists reject the outdated learning and skills of the *ulama* educated at traditional Islamic schools and universities because the fundamentalists belong to the modern world, which places legitimate knowledge in the secular realm, and because they often see the modern *ulama* as far too close to evil, secularizing governments.

Several perceptive studies of modern religious change in the Muslim world have pointed to the great effect of new technologies, such as printing, in this process of change. Printing arrived at different times in different places, but even in the Ottoman Empire, which was close to Europe, printing was not important until the nineteenth century. Perhaps printing was adopted so late in the Muslim world because orality was the heart of transmission of knowledge in Islam and there was always a distrust of the printed word.[9] Orality was important to Christian culture, too, and the role of preaching, singing, and speaking *increased* in Protestant culture even after the spread of printing technology starting in the late fifteenth century. Muslim societies were late in taking up printing because they managed without it until the requirements of modern bureaucracies kicked in during the nineteenth century. However, when printing was employed by religious groups, it had an impact on religious authority that was profound.

Among South Asian Muslims – that is, in the lands that are now India, Pakistan, and Bangladesh – the arrival and use of

9 Francis Robinson, "Technology and Religious Change: Islam and the Impact of Print," *Modern Asian Studies* 27, no. 1 (February 1993): 229–51 at pp. 233–38.

the printed word had the effect of eroding the authority of the *ulama*.[10] There is an irony here because in the short run printing often became a tool to promote the role of the priests as defenders of Islam in a situation where the region was ruled by foreigners. Before the penetration of the British traders and soldiers, and the piecemeal establishment of the British Indian Empire during the eighteenth and nineteenth centuries, South Asia had for many centuries been ruled by Muslims. When the Mughal state fell apart and political control was established by the British in the early decades of the nineteenth century, there was no longer a political superstructure to ensure righteous Islamic rule. This experience was shared by colonized societies elsewhere, too, and for some sections of these societies the new political situation produced a sense of crisis. The *ulama* of South Asia stepped in to take responsibility for the moral guidance of millions of Muslims living under British rule in South Asia, and in order to effectively reach out to the masses with their message, the *ulama* employed the latest technology: printing.

In the long run, however, printing was a disaster for the *ulama* of South Asia. The traditional way of transmitting knowledge of Islam's classical texts and the issues they addressed was person to person. In order to master the language and the correct interpretation of texts, a student aspiring to become a true expert had to spend years in a Muslim school (a *madrasa*) and learn the technicalities and the right mode of interpretation from an established scholar. The considerable skill and knowledge that went into mastering texts was situated in the head of the teacher-scholar. To put it crudely, his body and his brain were indispensable elements in the transmission of knowledge, and this gave him his authority. From the last decades of the nineteenth century and increasingly into the twentieth, the classic treatises of Islam were made available as printed texts and in translation, so that new sections of society had easy access to them *without* the

[10] Ibid., especially pp. 244–45.

help of the religious elite. The bodies and brains of the priests became dispensable. The authority of the Muslim religious elite started a long decline, which has continued through the twentieth century and into the twenty-first.

Exactly where this process of decline in authority will end is hard to predict, but some of the immediate consequences are highly visible. Since the late nineteenth and early twentieth centuries, there have appeared many leaders who have claimed expert knowledge of Islam *without* the traditional education that was crucial to establishing authority in the past. These are the new lay leaders who are central to my argument about the nature of fundamentalism. These lay leaders claimed to have access to ultimate truths without intermediaries. I am not saying that all these new lay religious leaders necessarily should be classified as fundamentalists, but I am saying that this new type of lay religious leadership is one of the defining characteristics of fundamentalism. To illustrate the importance of the new lay leader emerging in South Asia, we may look briefly at the values of Maulana Maududi.

Maulana Maududi was a typical product of modern secular education. He repudiated traditional religious authority, came into sharp conflict with the traditional religious elites, and cast himself as the savior of Muslims by creating for himself the status of a sage with special powers.[11] He saw the *ulama* as hopelessly outdated and unable to address the issues of real importance to the Muslims of South Asia, and his goal was to bring the social, religious, and political issues of concern to new audiences. Maududi wanted to make laypeople committed to the fate of Islam and Islamic values, and for this purpose he created a new style of popular religious discourse in his books. Maududi insisted that every Muslim should have direct access to the holy texts and shun interpretation of religion and tradition offered

[11] Seyyed Vali Reza Nasr, *Maududi and the Making of Islamic Revivalism* (Oxford: Oxford University Press, 1996). See especially chap. 7.

by the *ulama*. He even translated the Qur'an and equipped his translation with footnotes and comments with the very explicit intent of reaching the masses of Muslims – a demanding, modern, and lay-oriented job. Maulana Maududi's understanding of Islam is entirely the product of print culture, and the people who are attracted by Maududi's religious and political visions mostly share his modern perception of their own religion.[12]

The Muslim fundamentalist activist is normally a person with a secular education who reads the works of people like Maududi, and the classics of Islam, without paying any attention whatsoever to the issue of traditions of interpretation. It would be possible to analyze the emergence of jihadist terrorism from the 1990s within the context of crumbling structures of authority. One scholar suggests that the important thing about al Qaeda is not its militancy but rather its great contribution to the fragmentation of traditional structures of religious authority.[13] The lack of any centralizing church and the continuing fragmentation of authority may be among the causes of the globalization of Muslim militancy in recent years.[14]

RELIGIOUS AUTHORITY IN SUNNI AND SHIA ISLAM CONTRASTED

If it makes sense to see the rise of a new type of lay religious authority, and a corresponding decline in traditional forms of religious authority, as essential to the phenomena we call fundamentalist, this will have implications for how we categorize the movement that is often seen as the prime example of fundamentalism: the Islamic revolution in Iran in 1979. The revolution

[12] Roy Jackson, *Mawlana Mawdudi & Political Islam: Authority and the Islamic State*. New York: Routledge, 2011.

[13] Faisal Devji, *Landscapes of the Jihad: Militancy, Morality, Modernity*. Ithaca, N.Y.: Cornell University Press, 2005, p. xvi.

[14] Faisal Devji, *The Terrorist in Search of Humanity: Militant Islam and Global Politics*. New York: Columbia University Press, 2008, p. 175.

was carried out under the leadership of Ayatollah Ruholla Khomeini, and the religious government of the Iranian state is often presented as the most obvious case of religious fundamentalism in the Muslim world. However, if lay opposition to traditional religious authority is a defining trait of fundamentalist movements, as I claim, Khomeini was not a very good example of a fundamentalist.[15]

The struggle between religious and secular ideas of authority in the Iranian revolution had more in common with the conflict between king and pope over political authority during the investiture controversy in medieval Europe than with the struggle between traditional religious elites and the modern lay leader of Muslim fundamentalist movements in the Sunni Islamic world of Egypt and Pakistan. Iran's Islamic revolution was a conflict between the secular state and the church. The similar conflict between state and church in Europe was resolved centuries earlier.[16]

Khomeini and his supporters were *priests* in the general Weberian sense of that term because they belonged to a complex and established hierarchical organization and handled religious authority on the basis of a tradition handed down through generations in the educational centers of Shia Islam, such as the city of Qum. The Shia church was an establishment that retained a certain degree of autonomy from the state until modern times, but in the early twentieth century the Iranian

[15] Martin Riesebrodt's study of fundamentalism makes a comparison between the first wave of Protestant fundamentalism in the United States from 1910 to 1928 and Shia Muslim fundamentalism in Iran from 1961 to 1979. He notes that the "carriers" of fundamentalism in the United States were pastors, evangelists, and lay preachers, whereas in Iran the clergy played a key role. Still, Riesebrodt claims that important parallels exist between the carriers of fundamentalism in the Protestant United States and Shia Muslim Iran. See Martin Riesebrodt, *Pious Passion: The Emergence of Modern Fundamentalism in the United States and Iran*, trans. Don Reneau (Berkeley: University of California Press, 1993), especially pp. 184–86, 148–52, and 71ff.

[16] Said Amir Arjomand, "Iran's Islamic Revolution in Comparative Perspective," *World Politics* 38, no. 3 (April 1986): 384–414 at pp. 388–89.

state began expanding its powers in civil society at the cost of the clergy, and from the 1920s the secularist government really began its attack on the privileges of the priestly class. A number of reforms in education were introduced in order to take control of this important sphere out of the hands of the traditional religious elites. Reforms were introduced that made it illegal for women to wear the veil, which in the eyes of the modernist regime of the Shah was a symbol of attachment to old-fashioned religion. Through the twentieth century, there raged a struggle for power and authority between the priests and the modernizing and secularizing state.

If we use the term "fundamentalism" for both Sunni lay activists and Shiite revolutionary clerics, we include very different phenomena under that label. Shiite clergy can still take the role of a traditional elite defining what it means to be Iranian, whereas traditional elites in the Sunni Muslim world are compromised by their relations with the colonial powers and with secular states on friendly terms with the Western world, as in Egypt.[17] During the Egyptian revolution in spring 2011, several groups, including the Muslim Brotherhood, struggled to position themselves for the new political situation after the resignation of President Hosni Mubarak, whereas the state-sponsored religious elite, the *ulama*, was irrelevant. The leaders who created the Iranian revolution had very little in common with the lay religious prophetic leaders that were important figures in global fundamentalism, such as Hasan al-Banna or Maulana Maududi.[18] To simplify matters, al-Banna and Maududi were lay prophets, whereas Khomeini was a priest.

If we read Khomeini's own writings on Islamic government, we see how significant this difference is. His book, translated into English under the title *Islamic Government*, is a treatise about the foundations of political authority in Shia Islam. The key

[17] Lawrence, *Defenders of God*, pp. 222–24.

[18] See the discussion of parallels and differences in Martin, *Creating an Islamic State*, p. 138.

concept in this regard is, in Persian, *vilayat-i faqih*. *Vilayat* means "government" or "governance." *Faqih* is the term used to refer to a person who has mastered the science of religious law, *fiqh*. Thus, *vilayat-i faqih* means the government of the jurist. The government of the jurist was a religious doctrine that Khomeini expounded as the basis for his own political authority.

The government of the jurist relies on the belief in the doctrine of the Hidden Imam, which is a typical feature of Shia Islam. In Shia Islam, an imam is a person chosen by God to lead the faithful. An imam is infallible and perfect. The first imam was Ali, the cousin and son-in-law of the prophet Muhammad. Most Shia Muslims believe that there have been twelve imams in the past and that the last one has entered a state of hiding, which is called Occultation. This is the Hidden Imam.[19] Ideally, the Hidden Imam is the political leader of the faithful, but in his absence somebody has to take on the duties and responsibilities of governing society. The expectations that the Hidden Imam will return in the figure of the Mahdi has been the basis of a Shia messianism at several times throughout history.

Khomeini insisted that Shia tradition shows clearly that only a jurist of the very highest standing can be the caretaker of political power while the community of believers awaits the return of the Hidden Imam from Occultation. One of the peculiar facts of the revolution in Iran in 1978 and 1979 was the near absence of resistance to this innovation in political and religious authority. In spring 1979, just after the revolution, the Iranians started working out a new constitution, and Khomeini and his supporters managed to enshrine the principle of the government of the jurist in the constitution almost without serious disagreement.

[19] The early development of the theory of the imamate and the idea of Occultation took place in the last part of the ninth century, immediately after the death of the eleventh Imam in 874 CE. It is described, for example, in Said Amir Arjomand, "The Crisis of the Imamate and the Institution of Occultation in Twelver Shiism; A Sociohistorical Perspective," *International Journal of Middle Eastern Studies* 28, no. 4 (November 1996): 491–515.

They did this through a number of clever moves. They managed to establish a constituent assembly (The Assembly of Experts) that was so small – it counted only seventy-three members – that they were able to fill most of the positions with their own people.[20] A handful of liberal, modernist representatives, as well as some critical clerics in the Assembly, did oppose the suggestions for enshrining the principle in the constitution, but the majority in favor of the absolute political authority of the jurist was overwhelming.

What about Iran after Khomeini? Many hoped for reform during President Muhammad Khatami's administration (1997–2005) but were disappointed when Mahmoud Ahmadinejad won the presidential election in 2005. Ahmadinejad is a layperson without formal religious education, but although he is not part of the religious establishment, he seems to have held strong beliefs about the Hidden Imam from his youth. He believes he was chosen to be president of his country by the Hidden Imam and that the return of the Hidden Imam as the Mahdi is imminent, and he has repeatedly vowed to shape policies in order to prepare the country for this millennial event. Such theological opinions are more detailed and concrete than those held by the majority of clerics, and they have brought him into conflict with the religious elite.

Ahmadinejad has used the idea of the Mahdi to strengthen his own political power and weaken the position of the religious elite. The clerics, and especially the Supreme Jurist, will really no longer be needed when the Hidden Imam returns as the Mahdi, so when Ahmadinejad insists that the Mahdi is just around the corner and Iran should prepare itself, he is implying that the priests are not relevant.[21] Ahmadinejad is the lay political leader

[20] Said Saffari, "The Legitimation of the Clergy's Right to Rule in the Iranian Constitution of 1979," *British Journal of Middle Eastern Studies* 20, no. 1 (1993): 63–82.

[21] Said Amir Arjomand, *After Khomeini: Iran under His Successors* (New York: Oxford University Press, 2009), pp. 156–58.

who has seen the divine hand of the Hidden Imam operating throughout his own career, and he feels the support from the Mahdi to be so strong that he can challenge the religious elite. In other words, Ahmadinejad may fit the fundamentalist label better than somebody like Khomeini or his successor as Iran's religious leader, Ayatollah Ali Khamenei.

BUDDHIST FUNDAMENTALISM AND RELIGIOUS AUTHORITY

When we move our focus to the Buddhist world, sociological concepts such as priests and laypeople become less problematic because Buddhist societies have institutionalized the order of monks and nuns, which is called the Sangha. The global shift in religious authority is just as evident in many parts of the Buddhist world as in the Islamic world. Modern times have seen important changes in the role of the laity in most Buddhist societies, and in many parts of the Buddhist world an increasingly vocal and educated middle class has taken on a greater role in the sphere of religion. Some of the new religious movements that have spread from Japan to the rest of the world have started and have been developed by laypeople without the sanction or participation of Buddhist clergy. At the same time, Buddhist clergy in many Buddhist countries have started taking on new social and political roles.

In the Theravada Buddhist countries of Asia, rapid political and cultural changes resulted in the blurring of the boundaries between religious and political roles beginning in the nineteenth century. The changes in the structure of religious authority and in the relative position of elites and lay leaders were faster and more visible in Sri Lanka and Burma than in Thailand, which had never been colonized. In all countries, the Buddhist Sangha, the ancient monkhood, was undermined by expanding states, the centralization of power, and modernization, whether the processes came with colonization or were self-imposed. The social and scientific revolutions of the period led naturally to feelings of national consciousness and responsibility among the Buddhists of the Theravada countries.[22] A new type of culturally and politically aware lay leader produced a revolution in religious authority. The shift in religious authority came with new responsibilities: political responsibilities for monks and religious responsibilities for laypeople.

Sri Lanka is a main focus for our exploration of Buddhist fundamentalism, and in the Sinhalese Buddhist society of that island state the shift in authority must be traced back to the last years of the nineteenth century and the work of Anagarika Dharmapala. He had a strong feeling of responsibility for maintaining and strengthening the religious identity of Sinhala Buddhists. There was an urgent need to create unity among the members of the nation across internal boundaries, and the most obvious strategy was to erase the differences between monk and layman and spread Buddhist culture, which to a large extent had been the property of members of the religious elite. Buddhism is, in Dharmapala's rhetoric, a system uniting laypeople and religious specialists into one religious nation, and he went far in erasing the differences between monk and layman.[23] This was an innovation, as there always was a distinction between the roles of monks and laypeople in Theravada Buddhist societies. Laypeople were not expected to learn the Pali Dhamma (i.e., the body of doctrinal literature composed in the language Pali) to the extent that the monks and nuns were or lead a celibate life devoted to religion, and the door to Nirvana was not open to them.

[22] Heinz Bechert, *Buddhismus, Staat und Geschellschaft in den Ländern der Theravada-Buddhismus.* Erster Band: *Allgemeines und Ceylon* (Frankfurt am Main: Alfred Metzner Verlag, 1966), p. 117.

[23] See, for instance, Anagarika Dharmapala, *Return to Righteousness – A Collection of Speeches, Essays and Letters by Anagarika Dharmapala*, ed. Ananda Guruge (Colombo: The Ministry of Education and Cultural Affairs, 1938), pp. 224–25.

Throughout the history of Sri Lanka, kings have ensured the maintenance of the legal-political community. The Buddhist religion may have formed an ethical basis for the common civic culture of the Sinhalese, but the Buddhist texts themselves take hardly any interest in the affairs of the world. The most obvious reason for this is that Buddhism originated as a salvation technique for those who were prepared to leave the world. Obviously, the early Buddhists could not have foreseen the phenomenal geographical spread of their system from Emperor Ashoka's time (the third century BC), nor could they have had any notion of the vast spectrum of cultures onto which Buddhism was to be grafted. Earlier in the history of Sri Lanka, the silence of the texts on lay ethics was not a problem, but when the institution of Buddhist kingship was discontinued in 1815, the basis for national unity disappeared. In order to unite, the Sinhalese needed a common code of ethics, and Dharmapala wrote the *Daily code for the laity*, in which he gave a number of rules on how laypeople should behave in their daily lives. Monks who espouse similar views have been called Dharmapalite monks, as they take inspiration from Dharmapala, and their work has had a profound impact on Buddhism in Sri Lanka.[24]

In Sri Lanka, the process of transformation in religious authority has continued to change Buddhism up to our own time. One important work of anthropology has showed how new and unprecedented religious roles developed in Sri Lankan Buddhism after the Second World War.[25] In particular, laypeople continue to take on ever newer forms of religious authority. Inspired by Hinduism and free from the authority structures of traditional Buddhist society, laypeople act as possessed mediums. Laypeople have also appropriated practices traditionally associated with the lives of monks and nuns, such as meditation,

[24] H. L. Seneviratne, *The Work of Kings: The New Buddhism in Sri Lanka* (Chicago: University of Chicago Press, 1999), p. 93.

[25] Richard Gombrich and Gananath Obeyesekere, *Buddhism Transformed: Religious Change in Sri Lanka* (Princeton, N.J.: Princeton University Press, 1988).

to serve new ends. There is little doubt that the colonial period changed religious authority in Sri Lankan Buddhism in profound ways and that the consequences are continuing to transform religious structures in the island state.

The transformations taking place in religious authority have great repercussions for the religious roles and status of women. Women have generally had fewer and more limited religious roles than men in the Theravada Buddhist world of Sri Lanka, Thailand, and Burma. According to the monastic rules, a woman can only be ordained as a nun (*bhikkhuni*) by a group of fully ordained male and female members of the Sangha, and when the ordination lineage for nuns disappeared several hundred years ago, the ordination of nuns became impossible and the order of nuns became extinct. This is the common historical explanation given by critics of female ordination for the fact that modern women are barred from entering the Sangha as nuns. Sometimes one also hears arguments about women's inferior spiritual qualities, which would diminish the quality of the Sangha, and some justify this view with reference to the account of the Buddha's initial resistance against establishing an order of nuns.

However, debates and negotiations about the possible religious roles of women are a hallmark of Buddhism in modern times, and there have been several initiatives in Sri Lanka and Thailand at creating new religious roles for women. Again, the founder of Buddhist fundamentalism in Sri Lanka, Anagarika Dharmapala, provides a good example. He was convinced that it was of crucial importance to involve women in his struggle to resuscitate Buddhism and save his religion and culture from destruction at the hands of Christian missionaries. In the 1890s, he worked hard to reestablish the tradition of female renunciation in Sri Lanka, and in spring 1898 he founded a center in Colombo for the establishment of what was to be called the Sanghamitta Order of Nuns. Sanghamitta was the name of the first nun to arrive in Sri Lanka, in the third century BC, according to Buddhist texts, so this was a fitting name for an order that wanted to reinvent the tradition of female renunciation on the island.

Dharmapala received help from a number of resourceful people in his work to revive the tradition of nuns, and the most important of them was an eccentric American woman called Countess Canavarro. They had become friends when Dharmapala visited the United States in 1897, and the countess entered Dharmapala's order of *anagarikas* in a hurriedly invented ceremony in New York in summer of that year. The *anagarika* (literally "the homeless") was the role of the socially engaged renunciate, midway between that of layperson and monk and wearing a robe of yellow or white, invented by Dharmapala in 1891 as part of the transformation in religious authority in Sri Lankan Buddhism in colonial times. Countess Canavarro had a background in theosophy, which had led to an interest in Buddhism and contacts with the activist Dharmapala, and in late 1897 she arrived in Sri Lanka with the aim of helping Buddhist women to revive their own religious heritage.[26] The possibility for women to become nuns, and what kinds of titles and what styles and colors of robes they are entitled to, has been a recurring issue since the time of Anagarika Dharmapala.

In Thailand, we see similar currents in the nationalist ideology that developed in the middle of the nineteenth century. King Mongkut (ruled 1851–68) was very concerned with forging a united Thai people that included both monks and laity. He put great emphasis on scripturalism, tracing all that was important to scriptures (i.e., the Pali canon) and at the same time editing out the elements that did not conform to his rational and antiritualistic stance. At the same time, he created new rituals, which may be seen as the new elements of a civil religion in Thailand. The function of the new rituals was to bring laypeople together and

[26] Tessa Bartholomeusz, *Women under the Bo Tree* (Cambridge: Cambridge University Press, 1994), p. 53ff.

make them take part in and adhere to the same state religion institutionalized in the new and important Thammayut Nikaya (Nikaya means "order" or "lineage"), established by Mongkut in 1833 when he was still a monk. The monks should preach more and create stronger ties between the religious elites and the laity as part of a new activism according to which religion was not merely to be confined to the monasteries but should be propagated and taken to the people in order to strengthen national integration.[27]

One of our examples of Buddhist fundamentalism, the Santi Asoka sect established in Thailand by Samana Bodhirak in the 1970s, displays a break with traditional structures of religious authority that eventually brought it into open conflict with the religious elites (i.e., the Thai monkhood) and the state. Bodhirak is a charismatic religious leader who believes that his own personal insight and experience is much more valuable for a true understanding of Buddhism than traditional training in the classical texts of the Thai Buddhist canon. In his own words, he became a monk through his own revelatory insight, and he insisted that he was a "real monk" even when he was a layman.[28]

In the case of Santi Asoka, the shift in religious authority is perhaps most obvious in its ordination of monks and nuns. In Buddhism, there are strict rules about how people must be ordained to become proper monks or nuns. The key idea is that the Buddhist monkhood as an institution and every Buddhist monk as an individual stand in an ordination lineage that can be traced all the way back to the Buddha. If the local ordination lineage is broken, the only way to reestablish Buddhism is to link up to an unbroken ordination lineage in another Buddhist

[27] Stanley J. Tambiah, *World Conqueror and World Renouncer: A Study of Buddhism and Polity in Thailand against a Historical Background* (Cambridge: Cambridge University Press, 1976), p. 215.

[28] Donald Swearer, "Fundamentalistic Movements in Theravada Buddhism," in Marty and Appelby, *Fundamentalisms Observed*, p. 669.

country. Buddhism has been "saved" in this way in many Asian societies throughout history. In order to include a new person in an ordination lineage and make him a real monk, the newcomer must be initiated in a consecrated area and at least ten ordained monks must be present in order to ensure the continuity of the lineage.

When Bodhirak established his own ordination lineage, this was a challenge to the established monkhood in Thailand and probably the most obvious proof that he disregarded the authority of the traditional religious elites of his country. The highest religious and political authorities in Thailand reacted with dismay to this breach of rules, and in 1989 Asoka members were arrested and charged with a breach of basic monastic rules of Buddhism. Many of the most prominent monks in the country have said that Santi Asoka is a threat both to Buddhism and national security in Thailand, and the government has spent much energy in trying to contain Bodhirak's influence and standing. The sect members claim that the constitution of Thailand guarantees freedom of religion and see the authorities' crackdown as an infringement of this basic right.

The position of women within the Santi Asoka movement is instructive regarding the challenge to traditional religious authority posed by this sect as well as certain other similar movements of modern Buddhism in South and Southeast Asia. The official stance of the Thai Sangha on the position of nuns is that the lineage was broken a long time ago, thus making the ordination of nuns today impossible, but the Santi Asoka movement has created a completely new female religious role without the sanction of the Thai Sangha authorities. This new role is called *sikkhamat* and refers to women who wear brown robes, shave their heads, and go on alms rounds every morning, pretty much like "real" nuns, *bhikkhunis*. These modern nuns lead lives inside the Santi Asoka monasteries much like the monks. They teach religion to lay Asoka members and take part in the everyday deliberations and decisions of the religious community.

PROTESTANTISM AND FUNDAMENTALISM

Sociologist Robert N. Bellah constructed a scheme of religious evolution where he suggested five stages of religious development: *primitive religion, archaic religion, historic religion, early modern religion,* and *modern religion.* When discussing the ideas of Talcott Parsons earlier, I cautioned against the idea of applying biological evolution to society or parts of society. The same comment could be made with reference to Bellah's evolutionism, but what is of interest here is his suggestion that the Protestant Reformation of Europe was a type of reform that in a general sense may take place in other religions as well. The reformers of Europe broke through a hierarchical system of religious authority and declared salvation open to everybody. In Bellah's words: "What the Reformation did was in principle, with the usual reservations and mortgages to the past, break through the whole mediated system of salvation and declare salvation potentially available to any man no matter what his station or calling might be."[29]

When the term "Protestantism" is used in this way, it is disconnected from its Christian context and used to refer to general processes that may affect religious hierarchies and organizations anywhere, regardless of what region of the world we are looking at. Protestantism comes to mean, then, a revolution in religious authority through which a religious elite loses its position in society, its power over people and resources, and its legitimacy in the eyes of laypeople and political elites. Fundamentalism everywhere presupposes changes in religious authority that may be called Protestant in this very general sense because fundamentalism is almost always driven by a new type of leader: the layperson without traditional religious credentials of priesthood but with plenty of personal zeal.

[29] Robert Bellah, "Religious Evolution," *American Sociological Review* 29 (1964): 358–74, reprinted in *Sociology of Religion,* ed. Roland Robertson (Harmondsworth: Penguin, 1969), pp. 262–93 at p. 280.

4

Prophecy and Preaching

Fundamentalists everywhere display characteristic ways of "doing religion." These include public preaching, or preaching in the sense of writing polemic texts, to drive home certain ideas in conflict and competition with other views. Fundamentalism, as an attitude toward religion and as a style of religious participation and leadership, draws on the tradition of ethical prophecy found in the Abrahamic religious traditions. It is in this prophetic tradition that the urgency of the fundamentalist message finds its repertoire, and preaching is among the most important elements in this repertoire.

In Chapter 2, I argued that there took place a global diffusion of specifically Protestant Christian styles of religiousness starting in the nineteenth century, in some places early in the century but in most parts of Asia and Africa toward the end. I looked briefly at the work of the great Protestant missionary William Carey to show some of the attitudes and styles that were part of the new global exchange of religiousness between the Protestant Christian West and the rest of the world beginning in the early nineteenth century. I said I would return to this point, and as an example we may take a look at the changes in religious preaching that have taken place in many parts of the world since the nineteenth century.

THE ORIGINS OF MODERN PREACHING

"Pray for me, that I may be so filled with the Holy Spirit when coming on this platform that men may feel I come with a message from God," urged Dwight L. Moody, a key figure in Christian revivalism, when he preached to crowds in New York at the end of the nineteenth century.[1] Moody was sure he had a message from God, and it was all-important that people listened to him, which was typical of the preacher in the American revivalist tradition. The modern preachers were self-appointed prophets.

Preaching has been an important aspect of religious leadership in several world religions, but it has taken on new forms and functions in modern times. In the Christian world, the great historical divide is the Reformation. The prophetic tradition found in the Old Testament, with its sense of zeal and urgency, was taken as an important model for many Reformation thinkers.

The Reformation has its predecessors in religious figures who were essentially preachers, such as John Hus in Bohemia (part of today's Czech Republic) and John Wyclif in England. At the end of the fourteenth and beginning of the fifteenth century, John Wyclif was preaching sermons challenging important theological points of the church and attracting attention from both church authorities and the laity. Wyclif is best known for his translation of the Bible into English, but his own preaching, and the sermons given by zealous followers, were felt to be more dangerous to the church and the political establishment and were met with tight restrictions starting in the early fifteenth century.[2]

[1] Quoted in Gaustad, *A Documentary History of Religion in America*, p. 278.

[2] Anne Hudson, *The Premature Reformation: Wycliffite Texts and Lollard History* (Oxford: Clarendon Press, 1982), especially chap. 2 and p. 269ff. As an aside,

The Reformation put great emphasis on the religious sermon, and Martin Luther himself was preeminent in the pulpit.[3] He preached, often several times in one day, to the public in the town of Wittenberg, where he worked. In the theology of the reformers, salvation is to be found through the Word, and the Word had to be expounded. Luther preached with passion and penetrating theological insight. He sang, too. He composed hymns and believed that singing was an excellent means of driving off the devil and inspiring strength and determination in the heart of the faithful Christian. The new importance of preaching changed the ways in which the interior of a church was organized, it created a new interest in towering pulpits, and it made a strong, clear voice the primary asset of the new Protestant priests in Northern Europe.[4]

For the sake of simplicity, we can look at the mid-eighteenth century as the next crucial time for the development of modern Protestant Christian styles of religion. Many historians have presented American religious history as a process of cyclical religious revivals, and the most important of these revivals have been given the label *awakenings*. Such religious revivals and awakenings are processes of greatly increased religious activity that can be fixed to a certain period.[5] The religious revival known as the *first great awakening* has often been thought of as a phenomenon belonging to the English-speaking world, but the important developments in the religious landscape of Britain

we could mention that the most important of the modern Christian organizations devoted to Bible translation and the spreading of the Word has taken its name after John Wyclif. It is called the Wycliffe Bible Translators and assists a large number of missionaries with linguistic competence with the aim of reaching new peoples with the Bible.

3 Roland Bainton, *Here I Stand: A Life of Martin Luther* (London: Penguin Books, 2002), pp. 348–50.

4 Diarmaid MacCulloch, *Reformation – Europe's House Divided* (London: Penguin Books, 2004).

5 For a critical look at the idea of awakenings, see Kathryn Long, "The Power of Interpretation: The Revival of 1857–58 and the Historiography of Revivalism in America," *Religion and American Culture* 4, no. 1 (Winter 1994): 77–105.

and America starting in the 1730s had roots in earlier movements in continental Europe. Methodism was the movement that would become the most important of the Protestant evangelical groups that shaped the revival of British and American Christianity beginning in the mid-eighteenth century. Through their two great missionary organizations, one American and the other British, Methodists would play a considerable role in the encounter between Christianity and other religions. This encounter is crucial to my argument about fundamentalism in world religions as a consequence of the globalization of a Protestant Christian conception and practice of religion as zealous lay activity in the defense of faith through preaching, proselytization, education, and social work.

During the middle decades of the eighteenth century, George Whitefield preached in Britain and America. He was the most popular preacher of the English-speaking world at that time. He reached millions through his popular preaching and became the first public Anglo-American religious celebrity. Through extemporaneous, open-air preaching to huge crowds, he transformed the Protestant tradition of preaching into a dramatic event that could compete for public attention far outside the normal arena of the churches.[6] He was inspired by the theater scene and consciously brought a sense of drama into his sermons in order to evoke the emotions of his listeners. Whitefield traveled nonstop throughout America and England and preached wherever he went: from pulpits, in streets, and in the fields.

There is an important lineage of religious preaching starting with Wyclif and Hus, running through Martin Luther and other reformers of the sixteenth century, down to the great preachers of the religious awakening of the eighteenth century, such as George Whitefield and John Wesley, and to the fundamentalist

[6] Harry S. Stout, *The Divine Dramatist: George Whitefield and the Rise of Modern Evangelicalism* (Grand Rapids, Mich.: Eerdmans, 1991).

preachers of Protestant America and Britain of the nineteenth and twentieth centuries. In this history, we can identify an important Protestant style of religious leadership that puts great emphasis on the spoken word and the immediacy and urgency of the message delivered by the preacher to his listener. It is within this Protestant tradition of preaching that the modern popular religious orator is shaped, and to connect this to the argument in the previous chapter, I believe this style of preaching is the heritage of the tradition of ethical prophecy, with its urgent message from God to mankind.

Max Weber pointed out that the role of preaching was an important distinction between, on the one hand, the role of the ethical prophet and, on the other hand, that of religious teachers and founders of philosophical schools, such as Plato or Confucius. Vital, emotional preaching is distinctive of prophecy regardless of whether the preaching is done through shouting in the marketplace or through a literary text. The enterprise of the prophet is closer to that of the popular orator (demagogue) or the political publicist than to that of the teacher, Weber asserted.[7] I am arguing that modern preaching practices are one example of how fundamentalists everywhere have adopted styles of doing religion that originated in the Protestant Christian world.

MODERN PREACHERS IN BUDDHISM AND HINDUISM

Does this mean that preaching was absent from great Asian religious traditions such as Buddhism or Hinduism before their encounters with the modern West and its styles of religiousness? We can take a look at the history of Buddhism in Sri Lanka to illustrate the transformations I am pointing to. There was a tradition of preaching in the Theravada Buddhist society of Sri Lanka starting in the thirteenth century. Buddhist monks composed works about preaching and its benefits to listeners. One

[7] Weber, *The Sociology of Religion*, p. 53.

example is a text called *The Garland of Offerings* (Pujavaliya) composed by a monk named Buddhaputra Thera around 1270 CE.[8] Both the sermons and the texts about preaching that we encounter in medieval Sri Lanka are designed to encourage people to understand the excellent teachings and the example of the Buddha so that they may cultivate Buddhist virtues. Although it is possible that the Buddhist monks who engaged in preaching felt some responsibility for the spiritual welfare of the laity in general, it is obvious from the preaching texts that their focus was on the nobles, and in particular the king and the members of his household. It is also certain that the *practice* of preaching was nothing like that observed in modern times.

In the middle of the nineteenth century, Buddhist preaching in Sri Lanka changed dramatically. A new style of preaching was introduced by Protestant missionaries, and this style of preaching was copied by local religious leaders in Sri Lanka. The first great modern preacher of Sri Lankan Buddhism was the monk Mohottivatte Gunananda. Gunananda first became famous for a great debate against a Christian missionary held in a place called Panadure in Sri Lanka in 1873. What was new about Gunananda's preaching? Traditionally, a monk talking publicly would be seated and shield his face behind a fan to depersonalize his message, but Gunananda stood up on a platform and adopted gestures and other modern techniques of oratory. In the words of one scholar, Gunananda "adopted a style more like Christian evangelical preaching."[9]

The most important novelty was the audience. Thousands of normal Sinhalese people gathered to hear Gunananda speak at Panadure, and later many would listen to his rhetorical attacks

[8] Mahinda Deegalle, "Buddhist Preaching and Sinhala Religious Rhetoric: Medieval Buddhist Methods to Popularize Theravada," *Numen* 44, no. 2 (May 1997): 180–210.

[9] Mark Frost, "'Wider Opportunities': Religious Revival, Nationalist Awakening and the Global Dimension in Colombo, 1870–1920," *Modern Asian Studies* 36, no. 4 (October 2002): 937–67 at p. 944.

on Christianity in other debates. News about his great success as a preacher would reach the United States and Britain not much later through the rapidly expanding network of news agencies and newspapers. The new style of Buddhist preaching featured events that would have been appreciated by the great open-air preachers of Anglo-American Protestantism of the 1800s. Religions on different sides of the globe were starting to look more like each other in their techniques of communication as a result of the contacts brought by globalization and, in particular, by colonialism and missionary activity.

In Sri Lanka, the fundamentalist Buddhist leader Anagarika Dharmapala continued this way of preaching in the late nineteenth and early twentieth centuries in order to insulate laypeople from conversion to Christianity and to make them more morally and religiously committed. In recent times, prominent members of the Sangha have further developed preaching skills and techniques. The most famous Buddhist preacher in Sri Lanka was Venerable Soma (1948–2003), who was extremely popular in many sections of Sinhalese Buddhist society and had several programs on national TV, where he debated contemporary problems and issues, often with a critical stance toward contemporary politicians. Venerable Soma was a religious and political celebrity in Sri Lanka in the late twentieth and early twenty-first centuries and made a huge contribution to the shaping of modern political religion in the country. He was often compared to Anagarika Dharmapala by his followers and colleagues.[10]

In the case of Hinduism, we can see a parallel development of preaching that mimics the styles of Protestant Christian missionaries in India. The greatest of the nineteenth-century Hindu preachers was Swami Vivekananda, and he was deeply influenced by Christian preaching. Vivekananda was a handsome fellow with a very good voice perfectly suited for captivating large

[10] Mahinda Deegalle, "JHU Politics for Peace and a Righteous State," in Deegalle, *Buddhism, Conflict and Violence in Modern Sri Lanka*, pp. 233–55 at p. 240.

audiences with sermons, lectures, and talks about the essence of Hinduism.

Let me be clear that I am not claiming that Buddhism and Hinduism lacked traditions of religious and philosophical discussion before the intense contacts brought about by globalization beginning in the nineteenth century. On the contrary, there were a number of very sophisticated traditions of intellectual debate and disputations in these religious traditions with all their branches and sects. This is reflected in the rich literature on diverse topics that has been preserved in temple libraries, and in unbroken traditions of oral transmission, throughout Asia. My point is that only after the meeting with Protestant Christianity in modern times did representatives of these Asian religions engage in preaching that targeted large lay audiences in order to awaken their religiousness and morality. A number of Buddhist and Hindu leaders in modern times have copied Protestant preaching styles, which we can trace back to the great awakenings in Britain and America and, ultimately, to the Reformation.

MODERN MUSLIM PREACHERS

If we move our focus to Islam, the picture is different, and perhaps more complicated, because Islam shares with Christianity the tradition of ethical prophecy. Muslim history contains varieties of preaching, lecturing, and admonishing by religious elites targeting the laity. The Friday prayer is the most obvious tradition, stretching back to the beginnings of Islam.

However, the point here is that in most Muslim societies, too, the role and functions of preaching have been transformed in modern times, and it is impossible to understand Muslim fundamentalism without realizing the impact of the globalization of modern forms of "doing religion." One important modern movement of Muslim preaching is the Tablighi Jamaat, which was started in India in the 1920s by Maulana Ilyas (1885–1944) and has spread to most corners of the world, including Europe and North America. Maulana Ilyas organized parties of common Muslims to walk around in the country and preach the basic doctrines and values of Islam in a peaceful and nonconfrontational manner. The aim was to awaken Muslims, and if possible non-Muslims, to the truths of the Qur'an and to proper moral behavior. Maulana Ilyas rejected all political activity because he believed that Muslims must reform themselves and be able to lead righteous lives before any political ambition would be legitimate. His idea of proselytism and preaching (*dawa*) was highly influenced by the example of Christian missionaries. Organized Muslim missionary work developed at the very end of the nineteenth century with a transformation in ideas about proselytism and preaching brought about by the contacts with globalized Christianity.[11]

Similar developments have taken place in many Muslim societies, at least partly as a result of the exposure to globalized Protestant religiousness from the nineteenth century up to today. When Hasan al-Banna started the Muslim Brotherhood in the late 1920s and early 1930s, he visited coffee shops and other places where people gathered, and he would preach to the members of the middle classes about their indifference to Islam much like a zealous Protestant pastor. Much of the energy of the Muslim Brothers in the early years was spent on campaigning against Christian missionaries and conversions to Christianity. Al-Banna's lay preaching campaigns in cities and villages brought him into conflict with the religious elites and testify to his role as a lay religious innovator, a typical fundamentalist.[12]

[11] Christian W. Troll, "Two Conceptions of Da'wa in India: Jama'at Islami and Tablighi Jama'at," *Archives de Sciences Sociales des religions* 39, no. 87 (July–September 1994): 115–33. For an interesting account of the functions of preaching in a modern Muslim society, see Richard T. Antoun, *Muslim Preacher in the Modern World: A Jordanian Case Study in Comparative Perspective* (Princeton, N.J.: Princeton University Press, 1989).

[12] Brynjar Lia, *The Society of the Muslim Brothers in Egypt – The Rise of an Islamic Mass Movement* (Reading, Mass.: Ithaca Press, 1998), pp. 32–35.

In Egypt today, the televangelist Amr Khaled is one recent and prominent expression of the way that Muslim preaching has continued to adopt and incorporate globalized religious styles. Amr Khaled rocketed to celebrity status in the late 1990s after he quit his job as an accountant, and he appears on TV shows throughout the Arab world in expensive suits with his depoliticized message of personal development and piousness. Working for a peaceful Islamization from below focused on the individual, Khaled is now regarded by many as one of the most influential religious preachers in the world, and, as a lay preacher with great popular success, he was feared both by the religious establishment and the state in Mubarak's Egypt.

In the South Asian Muslim world, the greatest televangelist at the start of the twenty-first century is undoubtedly Zakir Naik. He operates a media empire, English-language schools, and an organization called The Islamic Research Foundation, and his television preaching is watched by millions of Muslims across the world. He is the typical lay preacher, with a background as a medical doctor and no formal religious education. Speaking in English, he addresses the growing numbers of Muslims who are able to relate to a globalized idea about what Islam should be. Naik is a very controversial figure in liberal circles because of his rhetorical attacks on other religions and on other varieties of Islam, but he is also strongly disliked by many members of the Indian Muslim *ulama* because he blatantly ignores their religious authority, as he insists that everybody can interpret the Qur'an on their own and the mullahs are redundant. This has resulted in intense debates in the Indian Muslim media, where conservative mullahs of the powerful Deobandi *madrasa* have accused Naik of destroying Islam by driving the common Muslim away from the sources of right religious authority.[13]

[13] See, for instance, as an overview, Yoginder Sikand, "Zakir Naik: 'Islamic Media' Mogul Faces New Foes," at http://newageislam.com/NewAgeIslamArticleDetail.aspx?ArticleID=3922.

Changes in preaching and in organizing movements are just examples of what I mean when I say that there developed new ways of "doing religion" in religious cultures exposed to Protestant Christian missionary activity. Other developments were equally important. For instance, new ways of raising funds, drawing in the resources of wealthy laypeople, or new ways of organizing religious schools, doing missionary work, setting up clinics, and thinking about bodily health, would all be candidates for detailed studies of the impact of globalization on the religions of non-European societies. The new ways developed at different points of time in different societies, but the earliest beginnings of serious influence were sometime in the early nineteenth century.

These historical developments constitute that common global history of fundamentalist movements that I mentioned in the introduction. We need to see fundamentalism as a phenomenon that can be found in many religious traditions, including all the world religions, not only because these are movements and groups that resemble each other across cultures but because they share the same history. It is meaningless, in my view, to speak about "fundamentalism" in cases where we cannot identify some of these patterns of religious styles inherited from Protestant Christianity during the modern period of globalization. A fundamentalist group may not have all the traits associated with this way of doing religion, but it must share at least some of the core elements, such as the attitude of urgency, a certain zealousness and gravity in the approach to religious behavior, and the urge to preach in order to communicate an important message about the religious responsibilities of co-religionists.

PART II

FUNDAMENTALIST STRUGGLES

5

The Struggle for the State

We saw in the chapters of Part I that one of the defining characteristics of fundamentalist movements is their wish to halt or reverse the trend that we called *differentiation* so that religion can reassert the influence it has lost in the modern world. All fundamentalist movements, then, will have opinions about the role of religion in one or more of the important societal spheres of modern societies. States wield ultimate power in the modern world, and sometimes fundamentalist organizations and movements with high ambitions work to take control of the state. Some fundamentalist movements have an all-embracing vision of how to establish a state that is guided by the right religious values and laws, and how to mold a nation observing those values and laws. Sometimes these visions have motivated violent struggles against state authorities.

THE ISLAMIC CALIPHATE

I started this book with a brief look at a Kurdish militant leader, mullah Krekar, who in many respects is the embodiment of Muslim fundamentalism as it is cast in modern media. In spring 2003, his organization, Ansar al-Islam, was accused of harboring al

Qaeda fighters and cooperating with agents of Saddam Hussein. The U.S. State Department and other branches of the U.S. government were worried that Saddam Hussein could offer weapons of mass destruction to the fighters and their comrades in the al Qaeda network. This worry seems unrealistic now, as we know that mullah Krekar had his hands full with his military campaign against far stronger Kurdish secular organizations, in particular the Patriotic Union of Kurdistan (PUK). Kurds have been fighting for independence from Iraq for several decades, and the PUK was an ally of the U.S. forces during the invasion that started in March 2003. Thus, Islamist Kurdish organizations like Ansar al-Islam, which from the start enjoyed very limited support among Kurds, lost out and became irrelevant to future political developments.

What did mullah Krekar want? In the short term, he wanted to carve out a piece of Iraqi Kurdistan for the establishment of an Islamic state. In the long run, he wanted this Islamic Kurdish state to be part of a much broader Islamic caliphate that would encompass the Middle East, North Africa, and much of South and Southeast Asia. These goals were made clear in my interviews with the mullah, and they are mentioned in a book he published in 2004. In his book, he writes that modern times have been a tragedy for Muslims: "The Caliphate fell, the beacon disappeared and the prayer-call was silenced."[1]

The way to the reestablishment of the caliphate goes through the individual Muslim, according to Krekar. Islam is not only about faith, he explains. Real Muslims define themselves as members in a social and political community, and they take action to strengthen and defend this community. According to Krekar, they may need to use violence to gain the power needed to reach the goal of an Islamic caliphate. A reform of Muslim lives is also a necessary precursor to the long-term goals, he insists. Justice in the social organization of the future caliphate

[1] Mullah Krekar, *Med Egne Ord* (Oslo: Ashcehoug, 2004), p. 212.

will be guaranteed by the implementation of Islamic law, but Muslims should strive to establish communities based on *sharia* immediately as part of the way toward the larger goal.[2]

Krekar's ideas of history and his political goals are typical of the militant brand of Muslim fundamentalism that developed in the aftermath of the Soviet invasion of Afghanistan in the international jihadist milieus fighting the Soviets in the 1980s. This is where al Qaeda was established. However, the particular understanding of history and the political goals of a future caliphate espoused by leaders like Krekar must be traced back some decades.

Maulana Maududi was the most important Sunni Muslim fundamentalist ideologue and organizer from the 1930s to the 1950s, and his ideas about the Islamic caliphate have had a profound impact on fundamentalist thought and action across the Sunni Muslim world. During his lifetime, Maududi witnessed the establishment of a state for South Asian Muslims – Pakistan – and he had clear conceptions about the ideology that should underpin such a state, although his concrete thoughts on political organization were more vague. He wanted a gradual, rather than revolutionary, establishment of a true Islamic system so that people could take part in the changes and embrace the future state without coercion. "We also want to replace the existing system with the Islamic order by democratic means," Maududi said in a speech held in Lahore in July 1950.[3] At this time, Maududi was disappointed with the lack of religious values showed by the state leaders, such as Muhammad Ali Jinnah, and he worked hard to set Pakistan on a more Islamic track.

The ideal future Islamic state, however, would not be a democracy. Maulana Maududi always saw the adoption of Western political ideals by modern educated Muslim elites as the most

[2] Ibid., p. 57.

[3] Maulana Maududi, *Selected Speeches and Writings of Maulana Maududi*, trans. S. Zakir Aijaz (Karachi: International Islamic Publishers, 1988) p. 100.

basic problem that the young state of Pakistan was facing during its foundational years. A main characteristic of an Islamic state, he said in a speech held in Lahore in 1939, was that human beings would stop placing themselves in positions of authority over each other.[4] The tragedy of all non-Muslim nations in history was always that groups of people set themselves up as rulers and made the rest of society into slaves. This was a fact of modern nations, too, Maududi asserted, pointing to the fascists in Italy, the Nazis in Germany, the capitalist states of Britain and the United States, and the communists in Russia. Everywhere, an elite group asserted their right to rule and make laws regulating society according to their own ideas. Maududi often resorted to this type of historical exposition of the basic differences between true Islamic politics and all other systems.

The most basic principle of the political theory of Islam, said Maududi, was that a true Islamic society and its members must render all authority to God and surrender all rights of legislation and exercise of authority. God alone is the sovereign and lawgiver. No law given by God may be changed or removed. A government running an Islamic society is entitled to obedience only in its capacity as a political agency set up to enforce the laws of God. This is the core of Maududi's concept of Khilafa, which is translated as "representation" or "viceregency." According to Maududi, God has bestowed viceregency to the Islamic society as a whole, so that every Muslim is in fact a caliph. He took the Protestant idea to its limits, then, in both religious and political spheres by insisting that every believing Muslim has a direct relationship to God and that nobody stands between man and God either in a religious or a political sense.

But this is not a democracy in the Western sense, Maududi pointed out, because sovereignty lies not with the people, and laws cannot be made and unmade according to their will. On

[4] Sayyed Abul-ala Maududi, *Political Theory of Islam* (Lahore: Markazi Maktaba Jamaat-e-Islami, 1939).

the other hand, it is not a theocracy in the European sense, he claimed, because, historically, the Western theocracies were characterized by the satanic rule of a priestly class that made laws as they wished and elevated themselves into godhood. In contrast to these failed political systems, the true Islamic society would reject the privileges of a priestly class and give every Muslim with the power of judgment the right to interpret the law of God when necessary. In this sense, the Islamic polity is democratic, Maududi said. At the same time, it is a theocracy, as only God is sovereign and his legislation is absolute and binding on everybody. In Maududi's words: "If I were permitted to coin a new term, I should describe this system of government as a 'theo-democracy', that is to say, divine democratic government because under it the Muslims have been given a limited popular sovereignty under the suzerainty of God."[5]

Maududi's ideas about the nature of an Islamic state developed during the years leading up to the creation of the state of Pakistan in 1947, and during the first years after the birth of the new country his ideas were worked out in speeches, books, and debates addressing the political and judicial organization of the new state. To Maududi and other Muslim leaders, the creation of a Muslim homeland in Pakistan was an event of mythic proportions, and in the carnage following the partition of British India in 1947, thousands of Muslims (as well as Hindus and Sikhs) had lost their lives for the realization of this dream. It was of paramount importance to Maududi that the sacrifices should not be wasted by establishing a secular state instead of the promised Muslim land. In particular, Maududi spent much energy working for an Islamic constitution for Pakistan, and in his views on the ideal shape of this foundational legal document his fundamentalist stance was clear. We return to the struggle for an Islamic constitution in the next chapter, about fundamentalism and law.

[5] Ibid., p. 32.

The founding fathers of influential fundamentalist ideologies in Egypt and South Asia who have called for the reestablishment of an Islamic caliphate have something in common: a lack of specificity and detail. They do talk and write about the same concepts – caliphate, imamate, *shura*, and *sharia* – but they never get down to specifying the practical everyday working of the state. Therefore, we often end up with a clear impression of what this Islamic state is *not*: it is not capitalism, imperialism, communism, fascism, or democracy.

Fundamentalist ideas about the Islamic caliphate in Pakistan, Egypt, and other important Muslim countries have a number of modern features. In fact, the fundamentalist idea of establishing a state where religion, politics, and law are one is to a very large extent an invented tradition, although it is presented as a return to the basics. There is a lively academic and political debate about the relationship between religion and politics in Islamic history, and the popular perception seems to be that in Islamic civilization religion and politics have always been inseparable. This idea is eagerly supported by Muslim fundamentalists, too, such as Sayyid Qutb of the Muslim Brotherhood and Maududi, as well as more recent actors. Their project is to merge religion and politics, and they always turn to history to demonstrate that this is the norm in Islam. If one looks at the Qur'an, as both Muslim fundamentalists and Western critics tend to do, one can certainly find verses that can be interpreted to the effect that religion and politics are one, but any serious reading of Islamic history will show that religion and politics were in fact separated shortly after the death of the prophet Muhammad, and there are a number of modern Muslim leaders who say that Islam in fact has a long tradition of separating political and religious spheres.[6] Islam is not fundamentally different in this respect from other world religions, although one gets that impression from current debates in the media.

[6] Eickelmann and Piscatori, *Muslim Politics*, chap. 3.

THE STRUGGLE AGAINST PAGANISM

Many Muslim fundamentalists believe that the disestablishment of Islam in modern times has a historical precedent in the state of affairs in Arabia at the time of Muhammad. *Jahiliyya* is an Arabic term that is often translated as *paganism* or *barbarity* and refers to a state of affairs in which men and women forget God and build their societies and institutions on laws made by humans and legitimized by secular philosophies. In *jahiliyya*, people dominate each other through secular systems, such as capitalism and nationalism, and forget that the eternal religious law, the *sharia*, is the only true authority in worldly matters.

The ideologues who made the concept of *jahiliyya* central to Muslim fundamentalism were Maulana Maududi and Sayyid Qutb, a revolutionary member of the Muslim Brotherhood. It was Maududi who first discussed this idea and influenced Qutb through his writings and personal contacts.[7] They both said that the modern barbarity that could be observed in many societies in their own time, the 1940s and 1950s, was essentially the same kind of barbarity that existed in Mecca and the rest of the Arab world when Muhammad received his message from God.

The barbarity of modernity, then, is not something qualitatively new, according to Muslim fundamentalist thinkers, although the specific forms of organization and technology certainly are novel. Qutb was a radical thinker, and his use of the concept of *jahiliyya* was quickly and decidedly refuted by the authoritative sections of the Egyptian religious establishment. They believed that his ideas were dangerous and rejected his description of contemporary political rule as barbarism comparable to that of Muhammad's Arabia, as well as his call for jihad,

7 Emmanuel Sivan, *Radical Islam: Medieval Theology and Modern Politics* (New Haven, Conn.: Yale University Press, 1985), p. 23.

or holy war.[8] Qutb's thoughts have had a significant impact on the moral reasoning about violence in extremist sections of Muslim fundamentalism: documents or manuals belonging to the group of terrorists who carried out the 9/11 attacks construed their mission as a raid on contemporary paganism and barbarity along the lines of Muhammad in Arabia.[9]

Nationalism is the greatest barbarism, in the eyes of many Muslim fundamentalists. Nationalism is an ideology that demands obedience to a state existing on a narrowly defined territory and asks each individual to bow before the state and to work, and even die, for the welfare of a restricted group of people, the nation. This was exactly the kind of narrow-minded barbarism that Muhammad struggled against when he rejected the tribalism of the Arabs in his own time, according to thinkers like Qutb.

Such hostility has led some observers to stress what they see as an inherent contradiction between Muslim fundamentalism and nationalism. The attempts by modern states to demand loyalty from inhabitants on the basis of territorial and racial belonging may be perceived as an affront to the universalism of world religions, and looking at the history of the Middle East we recognize that the enmity between secular nationalists and fundamentalists has been a significant factor in the political history of the region. Modern states such as Egypt and Turkey have mostly been ruled by leaders who wanted to build strong states on the basis of secular nationalism, and these leaders have cracked down hard on fundamentalists. In the Muslim world, secular nationalism arose as "a derivative or mimetic reaction to colonial rule," in the words of one scholar.[10] However, in the cases of American Protestant, Hindu, or Buddhist fundamentalism

[8] Gilles Kepel, *Muslim Extremism in Egypt: The Prophet and Pharaoh* (Berkeley: University of California Press, 2003), pp. 43ff and 60. This study of Egyptian fundamentalism was first published in French as *Le Prophète et pharaon* (Paris: Editions La Decouvérte, 1984).

[9] Hans G. Kippenberg, "'Consider That It Is a Raid in the Path of God': The Spiritual Manual of the Attackers of 9/11," *Numen* 52, no. 1 (2005): 29–58.

[10] Lawrence, *Defenders of God*, p. 87.

there is no inherent contradiction between fundamentalism and nationalism, as we shall see.

The ideology of Qutb found practical expression in the book *The Neglected Duty*, written by the young Muslim revolutionary Muhammad Faraj (1954–1982) just before the assassination of Egyptian president Anwar Sadat in October 1981. *The Neglected Duty* was the ideological statement of the circle planning the assassination of the president, and its main point is that a ruler who does not govern according to the *sharia* is an apostate who should be killed. The book explains that the caliphate disappeared definitively in 1924, by which it means the Ottoman caliphate, the last great Islamic polity, which was transformed into the modern secular state of Turkey in the 1920s. The globalizing forces of Western expansion, including the adoption of Western law codes in all of the most important Islamic states from the late nineteenth century onward, have caused the disestablishment of Islam as a political system. As part of the process of disestablishment, the laws of Islam were removed in their entirety and substituted by laws imposed by infidels, the author explains, and it is the duty of any believing Muslim to change this situation.[11]

In other words, *The Neglected Duty* describes a grave crisis in Islam in the modern world and places the origins of the crisis in the process of globalization and change that started at the end of the nineteenth century. The establishment of an Islamic caliphate was predicted by Muhammad, it is the command of God, and every true Muslim agrees on the obligatory character of this command, the author says.[12] The establishment of an Islamic caliphate must start from a territorial nucleus and spread through the effort of true Muslims, and people who die without exerting themselves to this end are not true Muslims, according to *The Neglected Duty*.

[11] Johannes Jansen, *The Neglected Duty: The Creed of Sadat's Assassins and Islamic Resurgence in the Middle East* (New York: Macmillan, 1986), pp. 167–75.

[12] Ibid., pp. 162–66.

How exactly should Muslims do this? *The Neglected Duty* discusses several options. One might consider establishing benevolent societies in order to make people perform their prayers and carry out good works. This in itself is very positive, but it is never enough, as such societies would be subject to the infidel state. One might consider concentrating on education and acts of devotion, avoiding politics altogether, but this is really the position of the coward. One might consider founding a political party, but this will be counterproductive, as it means collaboration with the pagan institutions of modernity. A number of such initiatives, which are all good in themselves, might be thought of by some Muslims as paths toward the improvement of society, but in the end the only effective means is holy war. Jihad is required by all Muslims, and the neglect of this duty is the cause of the humiliation and division of the Muslims today, *The Neglected Duty* asserts. "Jihad [struggle] for God's cause, in spite of its extreme importance and its great significance for the future of this religion, has been neglected by the '*ulama* [leading Muslim scholars] of this age.... There is no doubt that the idols of this world can only be made to disappear through the power of the sword."[13]

Qutb's ideology was radical and violent, and his views were not representative of the mainstream of Muslim fundamentalism. Hasan al-Banna, the founder of the Muslim Brotherhood, was ambivalent about the use of violent means to establish the Islamic state. The Muslim Brotherhood developed a military wing of trained cadres in the mid-1930s, with the aim of preparing for armed struggle against the British colonial power.[14] However, the ideology that al-Banna developed for the organization in the 1930s was a vision where Egypt, and later the rest of the world, would join the Islamic brotherhood and order life according to the all-encompassing system of Islam by their own

[13] Ibid., p. 161.

[14] Lia, *The Society of the Muslim Brothers in Egypt*, p. 177ff.

free will. It was the duty of all Muslims to work toward the goal of establishing a true Islamic political and social system, according to al-Banna, but he did not subscribe to revolutionary methods for reaching that goal. The radicalization of sections of the Muslim Brotherhood developed later, in response to political turmoil and state repression starting in the late 1940s. Hasan al-Hudaybi, who led the Muslim Brotherhood from 1951 to 1973, was also very clear in his demand for an Islamic state where the complete *sharia* could be implemented, but at the same time he was careful to distance himself from the radical zealousness of Qutb and his followers.[15]

In recent times, the Muslim Brotherhood in several countries has changed into a movement that wants to play by normal political rules and be part of a democratic system. The transformations in the behavior of the Muslim Brotherhood in Egypt started in the 1980s, continued through the 1990s, and at the beginning of the twenty-first century the organization has taken part in the electoral politics of Egypt in a nervous relationship with the government of Hosni Mubarak. Although it still has Islam as the great solution and still wants to remake the system of law in accordance with *sharia*, its day-to-day political work in Parliament has often focused on more pressing problems, such as the disregard for basic liberties shown by state authorities.[16] During the Egyptian revolution in spring 2011, the global media was brimming with speculation about the possible role of the Muslim Brotherhood, but at the time of writing it remains to be seen how the Islamists will position themselves in the political field of Egypt and other Arab societies.

The change in the Muslim Brotherhood from a secretive and hierarchical fundamentalist organization to a flexible political party talking the language of democracy is linked

[15] Barbara Zollner, *The Muslim Brotherhood – Hasan al-Hudaybi and Ideology* (London: Routledge, 2009).

[16] Mona El-Ghobashy, "The Metamorphosis of the Egyptian Muslim Brothers," *International Journal of Middle East Studies* 37, no. 3 (August 2005): 373–95.

to the development in Islamic political theory spearheaded by important contemporary Muslim fundamentalists such as the influential mufti Yusuf Al-Qaradawi. The most important among these thinkers are educated in jurisprudence and put a lot of emphasis on the place of law in the Islamic state. They believe that it is possible to shape a true Islamic society within the context of a constitutional democracy and assert that the application of elements of Western-style democracy with Islamic modifications is the only way forward for Egypt and for Muslim societies in general.[17]

The Islamists who are formulating the framework for an Islamic democratic system have a number of ideas that are modern and that make their political ideas converge with those of liberal Western political philosophy on several points. For instance, they assert that the political authority of rulers derives from the people and that the people have a right to choose holders of office through free elections. They believe that a system with many competing political parties is good because it allows for greater plurality of viewpoints, and they are of the opinion that a modern parliament is the best institution for framing laws. In the worldview of these modern Islamists, an ideal democracy would also safeguard basic liberties, such as freedom of speech, freedom of assembly, and freedom to practice religions other than Islam. However, they also believe that certain modern Western freedoms are fundamentally opposed to an Islamic state. In particular, they do not believe that freedom of religion should entail freedom to *change* religion from Islam, and they insist that a parliament cannot frame laws on that limited number of issues on which unambiguous Qur'anic verses lay down laws, such as the prohibition against adultery and alcohol consumption. It is on modernized ideas like these that the Muslim Brotherhood has shaped its political platform.

[17] Bruce K. Rutherford, "What Do Egypt's Islamists Want? Moderate Islam and the Rise of Islamic Constitutionalism," *Middle East Journal* 60, no. 4 (Autumn 2006): 707–31.

CHRISTIAN DOMINION

In order to understand American Protestant fundamentalist attitudes toward the relationship between religion and politics, we need to take a look at the ideas about theology and history that are dominant in these communities. In the 1820s, there took place a theological innovation in a circle of Christians in Ireland and England. A key figure behind the innovation was John Nelson Derby (1800–1882), a clergyman in the Church of Ireland. (The Church of Ireland is part of the Anglican Communion, the international association of autonomous Anglican churches.) Derby broke with the church in 1828 and was a main speaker at a series of evangelical conferences held in Dublin in the last years of the 1820s. In the early 1830s, Derby teamed up with English Evangelicals and contributed to the founding of the Plymouth Brethren. This group was an important source of inspiration for later American fundamentalists. They adhered to the belief in the centrality of the layperson and were skeptical of what they saw as laxity and arrogance among religious elites.

During the evangelical gatherings in Ireland, Derby presented novel and powerful ideas about the history of the world. He believed that history is divided into distinct periods of time called *dispensations*. This view is called *dispensationalism*. In the Scofield Reference Bible, which has been very important to Protestant fundamentalists' interpretation of the Bible ever since its publication in 1909, seven such dispensations are described. These are Innocence (the Garden of Eden), Conscience (Adam to Noah), Human Government (Noah to Abraham), Promise (Abraham to Moses), Law (Moses to Christ), Grace (Christ through the present to the judgment of the world), and finally the Kingdom or Millennium.[18]

[18] Ernst Sandeen, "Toward a Historical Interpretation of the Origins of Fundamentalism," *Church History* 36, no. 1 (March 1967): 66–83 at pp. 67–68.

The significance of this new theological reading of history to fundamentalist ideas about politics, and law in particular, becomes clearer if we compare the last two dispensations in this system. In the period called Law, stretching from Moses to Christ, man must obey the Mosaic laws, whereas in the dispensation called Grace, man must repent and turn in faith to Christ. In other words, each dispensation requires different things from mankind as it marches toward the final judgment and the Millennium. John Nelson Derby and the other British Evangelicals in his circle shared the view with many of their American counterparts that Jesus would return to earth *before* the establishment of the Millennium, the thousand years in which faithful Christians would reign with Christ before the final battle against Satan at Armageddon.

The combination of dispensationalism with this *premillennialism* would shape a very particular attitude toward history and toward political activity among large sections of American fundamentalists. In fundamentalist milieus of the 1920s and 1930s, this worldview was dominant, and there seems to have been a boost in millenarian expectations starting in the late 1960s and 1970s, when a number of novels about the last days and the second coming of Christ hit the best-seller charts in the United States. In this period, dramatic events in world politics were often interpreted in the light of premillennial dispensationalism. In particular, events in the Middle East were seen in this light because Christ was expected to return to the Holy Land and the Jews were expected to have a key role in the last dispensation. During the final phases of the Cold War in the 1980s, when the Moral Majority launched its campaigns for a strong America, it was also easy to associate natural fears of nuclear confrontation between the superpowers with apocalyptic images from millenarian Christianity. Moral Majority leader Jerry Falwell himself did this in his famous pamphlet on nuclear war and the second coming of Jesus Christ.

However, some Protestant fundamentalists do offer a total fundamentalist vision of an American polity. The movement of religious activists known as *reconstructionists* has taken a strong interest in the application of God's law in modern American society. This movement is made up of a number of highly educated people who work to spread their views about the reconstruction of society along true Christian lines. The most important of them are Rousas J. Rushdoony and Gary North, both prolific writers with ambitions of influencing Christian thinking in America. They would shun the label fundamentalist because they see mainstream fundamentalists as badly confused in their refusal to listen to the reconstructionist arguments. There are several issues separating the worldview and theology of reconstructionists from *mainstream* U.S. fundamentalism, but for an analysis of fundamentalism as a global phenomenon, the Christian reconstructionists are indeed fundamentalists because they react against the same global trends that I presented in Part I of this book.

In 1965, the Orthodox Presbyterian pastor Rousas John Rushdoony (born 1916) founded the Chalcedon Foundation in Vallecito, California, as an organization devoted to research and education and the promotion of Christian reconstruction of society.[19] The Orthodox Presbyterian Church was established by conservative Presbyterians in the 1930s as a revolt against modernist theology. Chief among these theologians was John Gresham Machen, a conservative professor of New Testament studies at Princeton Theological Seminary, who devoted his life to the struggle against modernist ideas about theology, Scripture, and science. Reconstructionism, then, grew out of Calvinist Protestant Evangelicalism, and the influence of Calvinist ideas

[19] Molly Worthen, "The Chalcedon Problem: Rousas John Rushdoony and the Origins of Christian Reconstructionism," *Church History* 77, no. 2 (June 2008): 399–437.

about law and society is evident in the title of Rushdoony's most important book, *The Institutes of Biblical Law.* The title is a pun on John Calvin's book *The Institutes of Christian Religion* (1536), one of the key texts of the Reformation era.

In terms of philosophy and theology, reconstructionists are postmillennialists. They reject the widespread idea among mainstream fundamentalists that Christ will appear *before* the Millennium. No, the reconstructionists say, Christ will not return until Christians themselves have worked to bring about the Millennium. In other words, postmillennialism calls for an active role in politics for Christians. Christians must take dominion over the earth, according to reconstructionists, or nothing will happen. From this idea, their worldview is often called *dominion theology.*

Another important reconstructionist stance is rejection of state intervention in society. They believe the modern state has invaded private life and local communities with ungodly ideas and institutions. In particular, public schools are dangerous, according to Rushdoony, because they perpetuate un-Christian ideas about society. Children learn to identify with the poor and criminals instead of learning true Christian principles of justice, which demand punishment, a flat tax system, and minimal state intervention. Economic policy is another key issue where reconstructionists have produced a lot of material partly because Gary North, the second leader of the movement, is a trained economist. The reconstructionists believe any state intervention in the market is bad. The free market is grounded in the Bible, and taxing citizens for the purpose of redistribution is a grave sin.

Dominion theology, which combines fundamentalism with clear ideas about federal politics and national identity, shows us why it may be unreasonable to set up sharp boundaries between fundamentalism and nationalism. Some of the aggressive nationalist movements in American history have had memberships that overlapped with fundamentalist movements. For instance, in his authoritative survey of modern American religious history,

Martin E. Marty places the Ku Klux Klan at the center of the interpretation of American religious culture in the 1920s. The Ku Klux Klan is often understood purely as a racist and nationalist movement that menaced and murdered Catholics, African Americans, and Jews in parts of the United States in the conflict-ridden era between the two world wars. However, the Ku Klux Klan was a thoroughly Christian movement with many church-going members and, Marty observes, it was Protestant enough to satisfy the most out-and-out fundamentalist.[20] The Klan was a symptom of the struggle for continued supremacy of white Protestants in a situation where immigrants from Europe and Asia were challenging the identity of the U.S. nation and modernist culture was undermining the fundamentals of Christian belief.

In order to get a better understanding of the relationship between reconstructionism and mainstream fundamentalists, I went through articles about dominion theology in fundamentalist and evangelical magazines from the Fundamentalist Files at Bob Jones University.[21] I looked at eighteen articles of more than one page in length addressing the issue of theonomy from the magazines *Moody Monthly, FrontLine, Biblical Perspectives, The Family in America, Voice,* and *Israel My Glory* between 1990 and 2007. All the articles are critical of reconstructionism and theonomy, and they carry titles like *Dominion Theology: Tried and Found Wanting* and *The Lure of Reconstructionist Theology.* Most of the articles criticize reconstructionists and dominionists on theological grounds and are particularly critical of the postmillennialist position on history.

Why are mainstream fundamentalists eager to distance themselves from reconstructionism or dominion theology? From my fundamentalist magazine articles, it seems that many observers

[20] Marty, *Modern American Religion,* vol. 2, p. 90. Marty discusses what he calls "the spirituality of the Ku Klux Klan" on pp. 88–102.

[21] I thank their library staff for excellent help in searching for material.

believe that dominion theology is gaining considerable influence among Evangelical and fundamentalist leaders in the United States. That makes some of them uneasy. However, one important reason why fundamentalists and Evangelicals spend energy analyzing or refuting reconstructionism is that they are in fact quite able to identify with elements of the reconstructionist worldview. Some admit that the tenets of dominion theology have a certain attractiveness, and several of the articles argue that reconstructionism is gaining ground because it is offering a comprehensive view of the world with clear norms in key areas like education, economy, and criminal justice. As one article concludes, reconstructionism may prove to be "an alluring alternative to many Christians" if fundamentalists and Evangelicals are not better at constructing "an all-encompassing world view and life-view."[22]

Reconstructionism has had a considerable impact in the radical milieus of Protestant fundamentalism in the United States, and several of the important mainstream leaders seem to draw some of their inspiration for political activity from dominion theology. Pat Robertson and other fundamentalist and Evangelical leaders are clearly influenced by Rushdoony and North's thinking and find inspiration for political activity on issues such as economic policies and education in their writings.[23] In the next chapter, I will look at how a prominent dominion theologian applies his thinking to the field of jurisprudence, ending up in defense of a harsh penal code where the death penalty is applied for many moral offenses.

I can see two main reasons why reconstructionist views may gain influence. First, it offers theological legitimacy – with its

[22] Jarl K. Waggoner, "The Lure of Reconstructionist Theology," *Voice* (July/August 2000): 19.

[23] See Worthen, "The Chalcedon Problem." Mark Juergensmeyer explains how people within the militant Christian Right in the United States are inspired by dominion theology. See Mark Juergensmeyer, *Global Rebellion: Religious Challenges to the Secular State, from Christian Militias to al Qaeda* (Berkeley: University of Calfornia Press, 2008), p. 182ff.

postmillennial vision of history – for the kind of political activism pursued by the social movements that are part of the Christian right. Second, it offers a rather simple and very comprehensive worldview where biblical principles can be applied to all spheres of social and public life. This is attractive to fundamentalists in a broad sense because their goal is a de-differentiation of society so that religion may guide the principles on which to build the other important societal spheres, as discussed earlier. Fundamentalists everywhere want more religion in education, in science, in the economy, in jurisprudence, in family affairs, and in politics, and to some the reconstructionists offer a robust defense of this position.

HINDU NATIONALISM AND FUNDAMENTALISM

In the late 1990s and early 2000s, Hindu fundamentalists gained political power in India. In later chapters, I will discuss how they shaped new policies in fields such as science and education, but here our focus is on the Hindu fundamentalist vision of a state governed according to Hindu values and customs, embodied in the concept of dharma.

During the last decades of the nineteenth century, there took place great changes in the way religious and political leaders in India understood Hinduism as a historical religion. British officers and administrators had taken interest in the history of India since the eighteenth century, and the colonial government instituted research and teaching in historical subjects in the Indian colleges that were established in the early nineteenth century. In the dialogue between British and Indian scholars, a new image of ancient India developed. In this image, Hindu India appeared as a great ancient civilization that had gradually declined and now existed in a degenerate state of poverty and superstition. From 1000 BC to the early period of the common era, India flourished. The decline was effected by several factors. External threats from Muslim invaders had made it difficult for

Hindu kings of medieval times, many scholars asserted, while the mystical and inward-looking tendencies of Hinduism had made Hindus less able to organize themselves politically. Many of these opinions were unfounded, but they shaped the views about both the past and the future of Hinduism among members of the colonial administration and Indian elites.

Under colonial domination, many Hindus started looking for a new basis for national unity and strength, and a nationalist movement was born that made demands for independence. The most important nationalist currents were secular, but there were also very significant religious visions of the Hindu nation. The important religious organization called the Arya Samaj, established by Swami Dayananda Saraswati in 1875, created new ideas about what it meant to be Hindu, and several other religious and political organizations were established in the same period with the aim of solving some of the pressing problems of the time, especially the political impotence of India when faced with British world dominance and the perceived lack of unity among Hindus divided by caste, geography, and the lack of an all-embracing church.

The center of gravity of Hindu fundamentalism in the twentieth century is the organization called the Rashtriya Swayamesevak Sangh (RSS), or National Volunteer Organization. The RSS was founded in 1925 by K. B. Hedgewar (1889–1940) to promote Hindu national consciousness and action. During the turbulent times of the 1920s and 1930s, when large sections of the Indian elite were engaged in a struggle for independence from British rule, the RSS mostly stood on the side because they did not share the vision of an inclusive nation envisaged by leaders such as Mahatma Gandhi and Jawaharlal Nehru. Hedgewar and the Hindu fundamentalists of his organization saw nationalism based on secular democracy as a greater threat to a future Hindu state than British colonialism.

The RSS became markedly more political when M. S. Golwalkar (1906–1973) succeeded Hedgewar as its leader in

1940. Golwalkar was a dynamic and religious person who was initiated into the influential neo-Hindu organization Ramakrishna Mission as a student. He held the view that India belonged to the Hindus and that Muslims and Christians had through the centuries threatened the Hindu nation. Golwalkar formulated a concept of race that was inspired by German writers of the 1920s and 1930s and emphasized ethnic kinship and blood relations. In a book published in 1939, he also commented in a positive tone on Hitler's treatment of the Jews.[24]

From Hedgewar's period as RSS leader, the organization had adopted a highly authoritarian style and military-style khaki uniforms, and this has led many observers to conclude that the RSS is a fascist organization.[25] However, Golwalkar's notion of Hinduness was in some respects quite different from the nationalism based on race developed in Germany and from the fascism of Mussolini's Italy. Golwalkar believed that the essence of Hinduness was culture rather than blood, and that the ancient high-caste Hindus of the golden past developed a supreme culture that was the heritage of modern Hindus but could not be shared by Muslims or other minorities. He envisaged an organic society in which the individual was fulfilled by immersion in the larger whole.

To describe this organic Hindu society, Golwalkar used the term *Hindu rashtra. Rashtra* may be translated into English as "people" or "nation" when emphasizing culture or as "country" when the emphasis is on political matters. To Golwalkar, what united this Hindu *rashtra* was their common dharma, an important Hindu concept comprising culture and worldview as well as social duties and position in the community and society.

[24] Golwalkar's mention of Hitler in the book *We, Our Nationhood Defined* has been quoted in many works. See especially Jaffrelot, *The Hindu Nationalist Movement and Indian Politics*, p. 55.

[25] See, for instance, the discussion in Tapan Raychaudhuri, "Shadows of the Swastika: Historical Perspectives on the History of Hindu Communalism," *Modern Asian Studies* 34, no. 2 (May 2000): 259–79.

Golwalkar would explain how the Hindu *rashtra* was a historical fact, and he would exhort his listeners to work to realize it, a unified and strong Hindu country.[26] In several speeches, Golwalkar would stress the importance of manliness and the readiness to use violence when necessary to protect the nation against threats, although he never tired of pointing out that Hinduism was in essence tolerant and peaceful. He would often quote from the Hindu epics, the Ramayana and the Mahabharata, where his favorite gods, Rama and Krishna, used every means available to crush evil opponents. In his expositions of legends and myths, the Hindu gods and heroes were the models for the Hindu leaders of the present, whereas the evil demons were clearly mirrored by the modern non-Hindu minorities that threatened the well-being of the Hindu *rashtra*.

Golwalkar believed the Christians in India worked with their co-religionists internationally to create Christian political rule in India, and he asserted that Christians had made a pact with Muslims to divide India between them.[27] Golwalkar insisted that Muslims had behaved as enemies of the Hindus since they came to India a thousand years earlier. In 1947, they created Pakistan, and they would continue to amass weapons and create more mini-Pakistans inside India unless they were stopped, Golwalkar claimed. Worst of all, he said, the Indian government supported Muslim and Christian efforts to undermine the integrity of the country, and they always branded the RSS as troublemakers and put their cadres behind bars whenever there was a clash between Hindus and Muslims. The secularist and nationalist Congress Party dominated politics during Golwalkar's long period as head of the RSS, and he was deeply critical of what he perceived as the party's participation in a conspiracy to undermine the culture and political independence of the Hindus. The basic

[26] See, for instance, his discussion in M. S. Golwalkar, *Why Hindu Rahstra?* (Bangalore: Kesari Press, 1962).

[27] M. S. Golwalkar, *Bunch of Thoughts*, 3rd edition (Bangalore: Sahitya Sindu Prakashana, 1996), p. 191.

problem with the minorities, according to Golwalkar, was that both Christians and Muslims had no loyalty to India and refused to see the country as their homeland.

From the 1940s to the 1970s, under the leadership of M. S. Golwalkar, the RSS continued to organize devoted and disciplined Hindus throughout the country. The ultimate goal was a Hindu state that could tackle what Golwalkar perceived as the internal threats represented by the minorities and reintroduce true Hindu culture in all spheres of society. Like fundamentalists in other cultures, they believed that an important reason for the political and cultural impotence of their group was a consequence of differentiation. Golwalkar and later leaders of the RSS all observed with disdain that most key societal spheres, such as law, economy, education, science, and politics, had been differentiated from the culture and religion of Hinduism. Part of the solution was to de-differentiate.

The RSS has always insisted it is an organization devoted to culture, not politics, but the fact is that Golwalkar worked systematically to influence the politics of India during his three decades as head of the organization. The strategy behind the long-term work toward de-differentiation can best be seen in how the RSS over considerable time has established a number of associated organizations, each devoted to a particular societal sphere. In fact, the RSS activists have created a veritable family of Hindu fundamentalist organizations, and scholars often call this family the Sangh Parivar, which means "the family of the Sangh (RSS)." For instance, the RSS has created student organizations in order to make students conscious of their Hindu nationality and counter Western influence on the young. Two of the most important student organizations are the Akhil Bharatiya Vidyarthi Parishad (ABVP) and the Vidya Bharati.

In order to de-differentiate the economic sphere, the RSS has created organizations such as the Swadeshi Jagaran Manch that are devoted to the promotion of Hindu economic ideals. These ideals include the rejection of Western-style capitalism and a return to what the RSS sees as an organic Hindu economy where local communities and families are at the center of production and consumption. The RSS has also established purely religious organizations in order to teach their idea of Hinduism and work actively to promote it in the public sphere. The most famous of these religious members of the Sangh Parivar, or the fundamentalist family, is an organization called the Vishva Hindu Parishad (VHP), which was given a prime role in campaigns in the 1980s and 1990s to destroy Muslim holy places in order to make room for Hindu temples.

Through its strict, centralized, and authoritarian organization, the RSS controls a host of sister organizations devoted to the infusion of Hindu culture and values in different spheres of Indian society. The other side of this strategy of Hinduization is the aggressive stance against minorities who do not fit into the vision of Hindu society. The RSS and its leaders have always been motivated by hatred against Muslims and Christians, and they have created several terrorist organizations devoted to attacking members of these minority groups in different parts of India. Best known among the terrorist groups controlled by the RSS is the Bajrang Dal, the youth wing of the VHP, which specializes in violence against Muslims and Christians and has been involved in large-scale atrocities in India.

A recent addition to the family of militant organizations calling for a Hindu state is the lesser-known Abhinav Bharat. Abhinav Bharat was established in 2007 in order to defend Hinduism against what its founders and members perceive as Muslim aggression. The leader of Abhinav Bharat – Himani Savarkar – is very explicit in her rejection of all Indian traditions that do not belong to the Hindu majority. She is married to the nephew of Veer Savarkar, the man who formulated the notion of Hinduness, or *hindutva.* In 2008, the Indian magazine *Outlook* interviewed Savarkar about her views. She said: "We must declare ourselves a Hindu rashtra where everyone is a Hindu. Anyone who isn't should be declared a second-class citizen and denied voting rights. Those who have problems with this should leave and settle in other countries."[28]

The RSS has managed to get into national politics, and between 1999 and 2004 they were able to take the reins of the state and fill the government offices in Delhi with its trusted members. How was a fundamentalist organization able to take control of a large state like India through democratic means? After the 1948 assassination of Mahatma Gandhi by an RSS activist, the organization became a political pariah and it lacked the self-confidence to work actively for real political power. Instead, it concentrated on building its grassroots network of groups or branches (*shakhas*) of volunteers, who gather throughout India to do paramilitary training or engage in yoga and prayer. For decades, the RSS concentrated on building an organization from the bottom up, and it focused on cultural work and raising consciousness of belonging to a Hindu nation among its members. This reluctance to get involved in party politics, and the ambivalence toward the political field, is one difference between the RSS and the typical fascist groups in Europe.

However, the low-key work of the RSS changed after the period in Indian history known as the emergency. In the years 1975–77, Indian prime minister Indira Gandhi asked President Fakhruddin Ali Ahmed to declare a state of emergency, thereby curtailing civil liberties in order to defend national security. Indira Gandhi's short emergency rule is generally seen as a spout of dictatorship, but it had a profound long-term impact on the further development of Hindu fundamentalism in India. The leaders of the RSS were sent to jail, and after the emergency was lifted and Indira Gandhi was voted out of office in 1977, the RSS labeled the struggle against Indira Gandhi a second freedom struggle, comparing it to the long fight against British colonial rule. Leaders of the RSS have pointed out that their organization stood up against a tyrannical government and united the Indian

[28] November 17, 2008, http://www.outlookindia.com/article.aspx?238939.

people against it. This is depicted as a struggle for democracy, in which the RSS had a decisive role. The RSS exaggerates its role in the emergency, but the story has become a myth that the RSS needed in order to gain political respectability.[29]

In the 1980s, the newly gained respectability and self-confidence of the RSS started to have a real effect on its role in Indian politics. The RSS was no longer seen as the fundamentalists who killed Mahatma Gandhi because he befriended Muslims but rather as the guys who resisted the tyranny of Indira Gandhi and her Congress Party. The political wing of the RSS is the Bharatiya Janata Party (BJP), which was created in 1980. The party was established by members of the RSS, such as Atal Bihari Vajpayee and Lal Krishna Advani, who later would play key roles in national politics. However, in the early years of its existence, the new party was often criticized by the RSS because its politicians launched a watered-down version of the Hindu fundamentalist program with little reference to Hindu culture. In the beginning, the BJP even tried to woo Muslim voters and enlisted a few Muslim politicians. The RSS supremos were not pleased.

During the 1980s, however, it gradually became easier to float exclusivist and aggressive political views in India. There were several reasons for this, but the most important factor was that the Congress Party, the biggest political party and originally the defender of secularism in India, started using religious divisions to further its own political ends. In the early 1980s, there was a severe conflict between Sikh militant fundamentalists and Indian authorities in the state of Punjab. In 1984, the Indian armed forces cracked down on the Sikh militants who had fortified themselves inside the Golden Temple in Amritsar. The attack on the Golden Temple was codenamed Operation Blue Star, and it left the holiest building of the Sikhs in ruins. In revenge, the two Sikh bodyguards of Prime Minister Indira

[29] Arvind Rajagopal, "Sangh's Role in the Emergency," *Economic and Political Weekly* 38, (July 5–11, 2003): 2797–98.

Gandhi assassinated their boss in 1984. The assassination of Mrs. Gandhi in turn led to pogroms against innocent Sikhs in many parts of India, and these massacres left several thousand people dead. Congress politicians were implicated in the atrocities, and the police and armed forces did little or nothing to prevent the killings. In the eyes of many Sikhs, what happened in 1984 was proof that the Congress Party is really a Hindu chauvinist party and that the Indian state is a state for Hindus.

In the same period, relations between the Congress Party and the Muslim minority became strained. Throughout the 1980s, there were a number of riots between Hindus and Muslims in north Indian cities, and in these events the police forces consistently took the side of the Hindus. Where local police took part in riots against Muslims, the central government did little to punish the crimes or reintroduce a minimum of state neutrality toward the different religious communities of the country. On the whole, then, India experienced an erosion of secularism during the 1980s, and this made it possible for the BJP to work toward political power in cooperation with extremist groups such as the VHP beginning in the late 1980s.[30]

During this period of heightened communal tensions and radicalization of politics, the destruction of a temple at the birthplace of the god Rama in the city of Ayodhya became the great symbolic case for the RSS, the BJP, the VHP, and several other members of the Hindu fundamentalist family. They claimed that the Muslim ruler Babar, the founder of the Mughal Empire in the early 1500s, had destroyed a temple to Rama in Ayodhya to make room for a mosque called the Babri Masjid. The activists demanded that the judiciary and the government allow Hindus to take control of the land and build a temple to Rama to redress what they saw as a historical injustice. The use of history in this campaign had several parallels to similar disputes over territories and buildings in other parts of the world, such

[30] Jaffrelot, *The Hindu Nationalist Movement and Indian Politics*, p. 330ff.

as the Middle East or Kosovo. By staging large processions and mobilizing Hindu holy men (*sadhus*), the RSS, the BJP, and the VHP wanted to unite Hindus against Muslims and, in December 1992, the campaign ended with the destruction of the mosque by Hindu activists.

DHARMARAJYA AND INTEGRAL HUMANISM

From the late 1980s, the combined efforts of the mother organization RSS and its two affiliates, the political party BJP and the religious movement VHP, started to have an impact on the voting behavior of Hindus in large parts of northern India. In the parliamentary elections in 1991, the BJP got 20 percent of the votes and gained 120 seats in the Parliament. The Congress Party created a minority government, which lasted for five years. In the parliamentary elections of 1996, the BJP got about the same percentage of national votes but gained 161 seats and became the largest party in the Indian Parliament. This was the first time that a party other than Congress was the largest in Parliament, and the BJP leader A. B. Vajpayee was invited to form a government. Vajpayee spent two weeks trying to get the support of other parties in Parliament but failed. In 1998, the BJP increased its support again, gaining almost 26 percent of the votes and 182 seats in Parliament. At this stage in Indian history, it was clear that Hindu fundamentalists had gained a respectable place in the largest democracy in the world. The 1998 government of the BJP and its coalition was short-lived, and a new general election was called in 1999. In this election, the BJP was able to stabilize a coalition of parties, and it headed a government for five years under Prime Minister A. B. Vajpayee.

On the official Web pages of the BJP, the philosophy of integral humanism formulated by Deendayal Upadhyay (1916–1968) is identified as the guiding philosophy of the party. In four lectures given in April 1965, Deendayal elaborated the issue of integral humanism to an audience of members and workers of the Bharatiya Jana Sangh, the political forerunner of the BJP. The point of departure for Deendayal was the crisis India was facing. The cause of the crisis was that Indians had forgotten their own culture during the colonial period because they started mimicking British and European culture and values. There is nothing wrong in adopting the technology of advanced nations, he pointed out, but it is very bad for a people to try to adopt basic norms and worldviews from elsewhere, such as Western-style economic liberalism, democracy, or socialism. These ideologies are all closely linked to their Western origins, and India is fundamentally different from the countries where these ideologies and worldviews developed.

Deendayal said that Indians needed to find the essence of their own culture and to shape personal and national life according to it. "The first characteristic of Bharatiya [Indian] culture is that it looks upon life as an integrated whole. It has an integrated view point."[31] This is in contrast to the Western worldview and culture, he asserted, because the West typically thinks in sections, dividing the world into pieces and then trying to put the pieces back together. This is the source of the confusion haunting the West, he said. The lack of integration in the Western worldview is clearly seen in the key Western philosophers and scientists, he continued, such as Hegel, Marx, and Darwin. They all looked on life as competition between different units of the social system or in nature, and the result has been that the West cherishes unhealthy competition and conflict.

The basic principle of integration rests on dharma, Deendayal said. Dharma is an ancient and extremely important concept in Hinduism, and its basic meaning is the natural law of the universe and the norms, duties, and privileges of individuals according to their social standing. Deendayal translated dharma

[31] Deendayal Upadhyay, *Integral Humanism* (Delhi: Bharatiya Janata Party Publication, 1965), p. 18.

as "law," and he saw it as the foundation for an integrated life for the individual and society in India.

The important point for Deendayal, and for his system of integral humanism, was the fundamental correspondence between the individual and society. He rejected what he saw as the Western view of society as arising from the mutual agreement between many individuals. He said: "In our view society is self-born. Like an individual society comes into existence in an organic way. People do not produce society. [...] In reality, society is an entity with its own 'SELF', its own life; it is a sovereign being like an individual; it is an organic entity."[32] In fact, Deendayal continued, society has its own body, mind, intellect, and soul, like individuals, but the feelings and thoughts of groups cannot be known directly from observation of the feelings and thoughts of individuals.

According to Hinduism, individuals are born with souls, and these souls are reborn in new bodies when the individual dies. Deendayal said: "Similarly a nation too has a soul. There is a technical name for it. [...] The word is Chiti."[33] According to Deendayal, all elements of society have as their goals the realization of this soul. An individual is an instrument in bringing forth the Chiti, the soul, of the nation. The same is the case with all institutions, including the state. The state has no value in itself, Deendayal asserted, as it is an instrument for running society in accordance with the natural law or dharma, and thus bringing forth the soul of the nation. The correct way to run the state with the aim of realizing the soul of the nation is summed up in the concept of *Dharmarajya*, Deendayal said.

What is *Dharmarajya*? "*Rajya*" means simply "political rule" or "government," so "*Dharmarajya*" should be translated as "Government according to dharma." Deendayal was vague as to the exact nature of a modern state that conforms to the Hindu

[32] Ibid., p. 32.
[33] Ibid., p. 37.

ideals of *Dharmarajya*, but he was clear that the Western model of democracy, with its emphasis on the will of the people, was not sufficient for India. Democracy in a true sense, he asserted, is for the good of the people and not for serving the changing will of the people. Often, the majority would not know what is for their own good, and under such circumstances dharma must still guide politics. *Dharmarajya* would include basic freedoms but would never abandon dharma to please a majority of the people.[34]

Deendayal's thoughts on how his integral humanism would be put into practice as a political program were rather vague, although he often talked about issues such as a decentralized economy and universal free education. It was only after the creation of the political party BJP from the milieu of the Bharatiya Jana Sangh and the RSS that the politics of integral humanism and Hindu *Dharmarajya* would become important to national politics. In 1985, a working group of the BJP made a report to its president with a mandate to review the party's performance over its first five years and suggest the course for the next five years. The report built on interviews and questionnaires designed to measure the moods and opinions of regional branches of the party and its supporters. Eight out of forty-two pages in the report were used to explain why the integral humanism of Deendayal should be officially adopted as the ideological basis for the BJP in the future.[35]

The Hindu fundamentalists in the RSS and its extended family of organizations had slowly, over several decades, worked its way toward the center of Indian politics. With the new political landscape appearing in the 1980s, in which the traditional power of the Congress Party was on the wane, and with the mounting tensions between religious communities

[34] Ibid., p. 59.

[35] *Working Group Report*, presented to National Executive Bhopal, July 20, 1985. New Delhi: Bharatiya Janata Party Central Office.

and between the state and religious communities, this old authoritarian grassroots movement got its chance. By manipulating Hindu symbols and playing on interreligious fears and stereotypes, the BJP built itself up as the political wing of the fundamentalist movement. Between 1999 and 2004, the democratic system ensured that the BJP enjoyed government power, and its leaders immediately initiated policies to make India more Hindu.

The Hinduization of the sectors of society does not seem to have been very successful. For instance, in economic policy, it was very difficult for the BJP to return to ideas about organic Hindu self-sufficiency and anticapitalism that the RSS and the Hindu fundamentalists of the past had talked about. In fact, the BJP never really attempted to reverse the process of economic liberalization that had begun in the early 1990s. In the field of law, too, a real fundamentalist policy of de-differentiation was not possible. The higher levels of the Indian judiciary, especially the Supreme Court, have always asserted their independence from government, and a Hinduization of the system of law was not high on the agenda of the BJP.

Perhaps India proved too modern. The differentiation of Indian society had come so far that the only fields in which the fundamentalists could hope to achieve a de-differentiation were education and science; in these fields, there were strong attempts to achieve a real and lasting Hinduization, as we will see in later chapters. The political system itself proved to be a challenge to the long-term success of the Hindu fundamentalists: in 2004, they lost the parliamentary elections to their great surprise, and the Congress Party returned to power in Delhi. The establishment of a Hindu *rashtra* in India proved difficult, although in one part of the country the fundamentalists have penetrated the state apparatus to the extent that we may reasonably talk about a fundamentalist state. This is Gujarat in Western India, a federal state with more than 50 million inhabitants, where the

BJP government has supported a policy of Hinduization and violence against minorities.[36]

DHARMARAJYA – THE BUDDHIST STATE

The year 2004 was a watershed for politics and religion in Sri Lanka and in the entire Theravada Buddhist world. In April of that year, a political party called the Jathika Hela Urumaya (JHU) succeeded in getting nine candidates elected to Parliament. The party had originally fielded over 200 candidates to contest the 225 parliamentary seats of the country, and their organization as a party, and their focused campaigns for the election, had only started two months before the elections.[37] The JHU is a party consisting entirely of Buddhist monks.

The first recorded attempts by monks to stand for elections to political posts in Sri Lanka are from the 1940s. In 1946, the famous monk and scholar Walpola Rahula published a book called, in its English translation, *The Heritage of the Bhikkhu*, in which he argued that the monk (*bhikkhu*) of Buddhism really had an important heritage of social and political engagement that had been forgotten and needed to be revived. Most observers believe that Rahula's ideas about politically active monks are modern and that the members of the Theravada Buddhist Sangha in the past generally avoided political roles, but his book had a profound impact on the self-image of many Sinhalese monks, and it made political involvement seem more natural than before.

There were several reasons why the monks of the JHU decided to run for election in 2004. They believed the war between the state and the guerrillas of the Liberation Tigers of Tamil Eelam

[36] See, for instance, Nikita Sud, "Secularism and the Gujarat State: 1960–2005," *Modern Asian Studies* 42, no. 6 (2008): 1251–81.

[37] Deegalle, "JHU Politics for Peace and a Righteous State."

(LTTE) was not handled the right way by the government, and they wanted to have a greater say in shaping the peace process, where they feared that weak and corrupt politicians might sell out on issues of national integrity. They also perceived a growing threat from what they call "unethical conversions," evangelical Christian movements converting Buddhists to Christianity by unjust means, such as gifts of money.

There was also the case of the death of the famous monk Venerable Soma.[38] As I mentioned in Chapter 4, Venerable Soma was a very famous Buddhist monk, with his own TV programs and enjoying a wide audience for his preaching in Sri Lanka. He preached about the relevance of Buddhism for contemporary political issues and was highly critical of Christian missionary activity in the country. When Soma died while on a tour of Russia in 2003, it was seen as the result of a conspiracy, and at the funeral a prominent monk-politician insisted publicly that Soma was murdered by "Christian fundamentalists."[39]

The long-term political goal of the JHU is *Dharmarajya*, a righteous and religious state that takes proper care of the Buddhist heritage of the country. The party is committed to safeguarding the sovereignty and integrity of the country, endorsing Sinhalese as the national language and national culture, and protecting Buddhism as the national religion of Sri Lanka. In their conception of *Dharmarajya*, the JHU shows its wish to roll back modernity and its negative consequences for religion and the standing of the monks, as well as for the politics, economics, culture, and morality of the Sinhalese people. The documents presenting the JHU election platform describe how Sri Lanka was once ruled according to righteous Buddhist standards, and the party points to the Indian Buddhist emperor Ashoka of the third century BC as the ideal ruler.

[38] Mahinda Deegalle, "Politics of the Jathika Hela Urumaya Monks: Buddhism and Ethnicity in Contemporary Sri Lanka," *Contemporary Buddhism* 5, no. 2 (2004): 83–103.

[39] Deegalle, "JHU Politics for Peace and a Righteous State," pp. 239–40.

In their insistence on the primacy of Sinhalese culture and the Sinhalese language, the JHU monks are Buddhist nationalists, but in their insistence on the rollback of modernity and modernism they display typical fundamentalist ideas and values. A good Buddhist ruler should look at his subjects as his own children and should ensure that the economy and politics of the country are based on Buddhism, not on modern ideologies, the JHU insists. Politics should be based on the rule of the village (*grama rajya*) rather than centralized rule, and the economy should be of a Buddhist type, empowering the local farmer and entrepreneur. In the field of education, the monks of the JHU want to introduce a curriculum that fits Buddhist culture and teaches children about Buddhist morality and about the duties that come with different roles in society, such as monk and layperson, husband and wife, and child and parent.[40] The reintroduction of religion in all spheres of society, a de-differentiation of Buddhism, is the priority, although the details often remain diffuse.

One may discuss to what extent the designation fundamentalism really is suitable for the politically active Buddhist monks of the JHU or for other movements and organizations concerned with Buddhism and its relationship to society and politics in the country. Some scholars find the description useful, whereas others do not.[41] In the conception of fundamentalism that I offer here, the greatest difference between the JHU and fundamentalist groups in other religions is the nature of the religious authority of the activists. I have argued that fundamentalisms are movements generally initiated by lay leaders in places where traditional religious elites have been sidelined by modern developments, as I discussed in Chapter 3. However, in the case of

[40] Ibid., p. 247ff.

[41] In one collection of essays, the editors and authors make a strong argument for the use of the word "fundamentalism" in a Buddhist context. See Tessa J. Bartholomeusz and Chandra R. de Silva, *Buddhist Fundamentalism and Minority Identities in Sri Lanka* (New York: State University of New York Press, 1998), pp. 1–4.

the JHU, the activists are monks: they belong to the established religious elite.

At the same time, the new political role taken by monks in Sri Lanka is the result of the great shifts in religious authority structures parallel to those that have been found in many other societies beginning in the late nineteenth century. The traditional priesthoods and their institutions were sidelined in Sri Lanka, too, and the position of the Sangha in society has been questioned and completely new roles invented, such as the *anagarika*, which I explained in Chapter 3. Certain sections of the monkhood have responded by actively inventing and developing their own modern role: the monk-politician. This role is between that of the traditional monk and the modern lay politician, and although the political monks draw on old religious symbols and concepts for their authority, they also need to tap into modern and secular sources of authority to make their idea of *Dharmarajya* credible to a modern audience.

The *Dharmarajya* espoused by Buddhist fundamentalists in Sri Lanka is not a new concept and is not only found in Buddhism, as we saw in the discussion of Hindu fundamentalist political ideas. In Sri Lanka and Thailand, and indeed in many other Buddhist societies in Asia, political power has for centuries been closely associated with Buddhism. Before the new and intensified contacts with the Western world starting in the nineteenth century, Buddhist societies such as Sri Lanka and Thailand were governed according to what has been called a *galactic* polity.[42] This means that the political realm would contain a number of chiefs, each ruling with much autonomy in their own spheres. The Buddhist king in the center of the realm (in royal cities such as Kandy in Sri Lanka or Ayutthaya in Thailand) would demand symbolic subordination but did not exert great political influence over matters in the peripheries. With the appearance

[42] The concept of galactic polity was suggested by Stanley J. Tambiah. See Tambiah, *World Conqueror and World Renouncer.*

of modern states in the nineteenth century, power became centralized and borders with other states were drawn much more sharply than in premodern times.

The monks in their monasteries were the religious elite who handled the great tradition of the Buddha. Ideally, the monks did not get involved in economic activity, but laypeople donated the material needs of the monks, and over time the monasteries grew rich. Laypeople needed to donate from purely rational and selfish motives because this was the best way to assure a good rebirth for themselves or for their loved ones. The king was the foremost layperson, and, because he wielded military power, he was the only one who could ensure that the monasteries were defended and that rogue monks were taken out and disrobed, thus preserving the purity and status of the monkhood in the eyes of society. So the premodern social and political organization of Theravada Buddhist societies (such as Thailand, Sri Lanka, and Burma) was based on a symbiotic relationship between the king, the monks, and the laypeople.

In the societies that were colonized, such as Sri Lanka and Burma, the close relationship between religious and political power was broken when the institution of Buddhist kingship was discontinued in the nineteenth century. This produced a crisis in Buddhist culture and politics that was the background to the work of many of the religious reformers and leaders of the nineteenth and twentieth centuries. The state-building processes of centralization and standardization had great impact on the relationship between Buddhism and politics. In Sri Lanka, both monks and laypeople started social or political movements that were critical of the government and the state both before and after independence from Britain in 1948.

In Thailand, many of the revolutionary consequences of the fundamental challenges to traditional structures of religious authority played themselves out considerably later, in the mid-1970s, when a large number of monks started to take political initiatives outside the traditional hierarchical structures of the monkhood and without the support of the government. The most famous of the new breed of activist political monk was the militant Kitivuddho, who called for the killing of communists in the mid-1970s. Some of the modern movements had leaders who were clearly opposed to the traditional religious authority of the monkhood and had ambivalent or hostile relations to the religious power structures. The most controversial of them is Santi Asoka.

Santi Asoka is a Buddhist fundamentalist sect established in the mid-1970s by Bodhiraksha Bhikkhu. Bodhiraksha was born in 1935 and brought up a Christian. He started out as a singer and TV producer, but he quit his job and was ordained as a monk when he was thirty-six. He spent periods within the established monkhood, but he was thrown out because he made grandiose claims of having become an Arhat (a being of great religious accomplishment close to the Buddha in insight) and because he completely disregarded the traditional structures of religious authority in the Thai Buddhist establishment.[43]

Santi Asoka arose in the mid-1970s when the politics of Thailand was changed by a number of secular ideological movements on both the left and right sides of the political divide. Disappointed with secular politics, a large number of religious activists, most of them monks, started to take political initiatives on their own. The model for political and religious reform for most of these activists was provided by the golden age of modern Thai politics under the reign of King Mongkut in the mid-nineteenth century. The religious activists in 1970s Thailand demanded a return to the fundamentals of the Buddhist tradition, and they had great visions for a future in which a focus on

[43] J. L. Taylor, "New Buddhist Movements in Thailand: An 'Individualistic Revolution,' Reform and Political Dissonance," *Journal of Southeast Asian Studies* 21, no. 1 (March 1990): 135–54. See also the discussion of Santi Asoka in the context of changing roles of monks and laypeople in Donald Swearer, *The Buddhist World of Southeast Asia* (New York: State University of New York Press, 1995), pp. 136–40.

the individual and his or her moral Buddhist action would transform all spheres of society. These new visions and movements amounted to a revolution in Buddhist politics in Thailand.[44]

Typical of modern revivalist and fundamentalist groups, the Santi Asoka makes much higher demands on its followers than mainstream Thai Buddhism. Followers are expected to organize much of their life around their membership and are expected to strive for simplicity and moral order through discipline and asceticism. Santi Asoka members are expected to be vegetarians and eat very little, and even married members are asked to abstain from sexual activity. The sect demands that religion should embrace all aspects of life and, before the government crackdown on its key members in 1989, it had high political ambitions. These ambitions were channeled into support for a political party called the Palang Dharma Party (PDP) and its leading candidate, a retired Major-General by the name of Chamlong Srimuang. Chamlong has played a significant role in Thai politics since the mid-1980s, and he has received much criticism from political opponents for his membership in the Santi Asoka sect.

So, both in Sri Lanka and Thailand, and probably in other Buddhist countries, the last decades of the twentieth century and the beginning of the twenty-first witnessed Buddhist groups that worked hard to merge religion with politics and to gain real political power by taking part in elections on different levels, including parliamentary elections.

[44] Charles F. Keyes, "Buddhist Politics and Their Revolutionary Origins in Thailand," *International Political Science Review* 10, no. 2 (1990): 121–42.

6

The Struggle over Law

Some years ago, I interviewed evangelical and fundamentalist leaders in Norway because I was writing a book about the relationship between religion and politics. Scandinavian societies – Norway, Denmark, and Sweden – are often seen as prime examples of secularized nations, and the people I interviewed were all extremely concerned about the gradual erosion of belief and morals among modern Norwegians. As a response to the decline of religion, Protestant Christian fundamentalists founded a political party called the Christian Unification Party (Kristent samlingsparti) in 1998. Its vision was neatly summed up in an article published in the magazine *Ny framtid* (New Future) in 1999: "We want to stop the de-Christianization of Norway and contribute to the re-Christianization of Norway. We want a law code that is not in conflict with the Bible and the Constitution."[1] The party is still active, and in the parliamentary elections of 2009, it got roughly 5,000 votes, which was around 0.2 percent of the total. In other words, this is a small party, but certainly not the smallest in Norwegian politics.

[1] *Ny framtid*, 1999, no. 1, p. 4.

The Christian Unification Party is very concerned with law, constitutional law in particular. Norway got its constitution in 1814 as part of the settlement after the Napoleonic Wars, and the Christian Unification Party believes that the constitution was a gift from God to the Norwegian nation. However, according to Norwegian fundamentalists, the Norwegian Parliament passes laws that are in conflict with the letter of the Bible and the constitution, and the king has been stripped of his powers to intervene. According to the Christian Unification Party, the most glaring examples of such unconstitutional and un-Christian legislation are laws that legalize abortion and gay marriage, issues that are of concern to Christian fundamentalists everywhere. The abuse of power by Parliament is also seen in the liberal immigration laws that let Muslims into the country, thereby diluting Christian culture, according to the party. The solution to this hijacking of the political system by a modernist and liberal Parliament is the abolishment of the parliamentary system and the reestablishment of true respect for the king, the divine constitution, and the Bible.

To connect this to the larger themes in Chapter 1 about secularization, the differentiation of religion from law is an important element in the process of modernization in all parts of the world. Fundamentalists see the differentiation of law from politics as a grave threat to religion in society, and they often focus their struggle on the institutions that make laws (i.e., parliaments or, in the United States, the Congress) and on the highest levels of the judiciary, which set the standards for the interpretation of laws: the Supreme Courts.

BIBLICAL LAW IN AMERICA

The struggle to influence lawmaking was a hallmark of the second wave of Protestant fundamentalism, which rose during the late 1960s. When Jerry Falwell organized the Moral Majority in

1979, the movement quickly gained support from substantial sections of Evangelicals and fundamentalists in the United States. Through the 1980s, the Moral Majority continued its campaigns to influence presidential elections and Supreme Court decisions on key issues such as abortion, gay rights, and prayer in public schools. Soon Pat Robertson's Christian Coalition followed suit with a large organizational apparatus for influencing the political views of Christian America.

In the last chapter, I pointed to reasons why many Protestant fundamentalists are ambivalent about getting too engaged in politics. Premillennial dispensationalism can make involvement in politics seem unnecessary: if Christ can return any time, what is the point in doing anything apart from purifying one's own thoughts and behavior? What's more, dispensationalist fundamentalists believe that the time in which Old Testament laws were relevant has passed. Fundamentalists would say that several laws in the United States are bad or un-Christian, but in our dispensation the focus is really on something else – on faith and grace. On this issue, there is an intellectual and theological confrontation between mainstream fundamentalists and the conservative Calvinists that I referred to as *reconstructionists* or *dominion theologists.*

In a massive book called *Theonomy in Christian Ethics,* first published in 1977, the prominent reconstructionist theologian and philosopher Greg L. Bahnsen sets out the principles for the application of biblical law to modern society. Bahnsen starts out with a detailed criticism of other Christian theologians. All the branches of modern Christianity, whether Catholic, Lutheran, or Reformed, have joined hands with Enlightenment philosophers in their insistence that the individual and the state are free from biblical law. The law of God is no longer taken to be valid by Christians, and this has resulted in lawlessness and social breakdown, Bahnsen writes.

Fundamentalists, too, are confused about the real meaning of the Bible, Bahnsen asserts. The main reason is that fundamentalists have adopted the dispensationalism of the Scofield Reference Bible, which divides time into seven unequal periods.[2] Fundamentalists dismissed the law of God in Christian ethics, Bahnsen writes, and they ended up in statism, meaning submission to the tyrannical laws of the modern state. For the fundamentalists, the relevance of Mosaic law was restricted to a previous dispensation. In sum, all modern Christian denominations have made the law of God redundant, with catastrophic results, and the only way to infuse society with Christian ethics is to establish theonomy, which means, in Bahnsen's words, "that verbalized law of God which is imposed from outside man and revealed authoritatively in the words of Scripture."[3]

What does this mean in practice? As with many religious fundamentalists who look for legal principles in sacred texts, the actual program turns out to be lacking in detail and rather diffuse, but the reconstructionist vision certainly entails the introduction of biblical punishments for the crimes listed in Scripture. Homosexuality is the most important example of a serious crime for which modern society has succumbed to the humanism of the Enlightenment, according to Bahnsen's work. "When God says homosexuality (for instance) warrants capital punishments, then that is what social justice demands; that is how heinous with respect to social relations the crime is in God's judgment."[4] Bahnsen goes on to list other serious crimes, such as adultery and unchastity, sodomy and bestiality, rape, incest, incorrigibility in children, kidnapping, witchcraft, and blasphemy. They all qualify for the death penalty, he asserts.

This view of biblical law is not representative of Protestant fundamentalists in the United States, or anywhere else for that matter, but the reconstructionists are not alone in their work to infuse U.S. law with biblical moral concepts. The Christian

[2] Greg L. Bahnsen, *Theonomy in Christian Ethics*, 3rd edition (Nacogdoches, Tex.: Covenant Media Press, 2002), p. 21ff.

[3] Ibid., p. 35.

[4] Ibid., p. 427.

Identity movement, too, wants to biblicize U.S. law in quite similar fashion, and they envisage a future where biblical law is sufficient for upholding justice and order. The Christian Identity movement bases itself on peculiar ideas about history, asserting that white Protestants are the real descendants of Israel and that they are engaged in a cosmic struggle against evil Jews and African Americans.[5]

ISLAMIC LAW AND MODERNITY

In the last chapter, I looked at fundamentalist visions for a religious state. For most Muslim fundamentalists, the reestablishment of an Islamic caliphate is first of all about the restoration of Islamic law, *sharia*. Many of the fundamentalists who work for the restoration of *sharia* believe it is an easily identifiable system that was marginalized first by colonialism and then by post-colonial states in the Islamic world. They also believe it is a system that can be restored, reintroduced, or applied more consistently, with the right political will. The transplantation of Western legal systems onto other societies was perhaps the most obvious sign of the globalization of modernity in much of Asia and Africa. Legal transplants in Muslim, Jewish, Hindu, Buddhist, and Sikh societies were the result of the diffusion of Western law, and this diffusion would not have taken place without the expansion of European power since the early nineteenth century. In most of the Islamic world, Western codes and standards of law were adopted during the late nineteenth and early twentieth centuries, and in most places the remnants of Islamic law exist only in areas of family law.

The abandonment of Islamic law in most legal areas apart from family law since the late nineteenth century was one aspect of the crumbling of traditional relationships between political

[5] Michael Barkun, *Religion and the Racist Right: The Origins of the Christian Identity Movement* (Chapel Hill: University of North Carolina Press, 1995), p. 200ff.

elites, legal experts, and laypeople in many societies of Asia and Africa. In pre-colonial Muslim societies of the Arab world, a symbiotic relationship developed between the holders of political power (the caliphs) and the experts on Islamic law (the jurists). There are a number of different titles within the group of jurists, but the most important distinction here is that between the jurist (*faqih*) with knowledge of the science of jurisprudence (*fiqh*) and the judge (*qadi*) appointed by the caliph.

Already a century after the death of Muhammad (632 CE) there developed a new and very clear distinction between the jurists and the wielders of power, and the jurists came to have an important role in society as civic leaders.[6] In their capacity as judges, the jurists gave their legal verdicts, but they also solved disputes outside the courts, were tax collectors, supervised charitable trusts, and oversaw public works. The jurists became a distinct religious and legal class that were intercessors between the masses and the rulers. The rulers depended on the jurists for the religious and legal legitimation of their policies, and the jurists depended on the political power for support, protection, and for enforcing their legal decisions.

The caliphs were God's superintendents on earth, but they were subject to the religious and legal authority of the jurists, like everyone else. The rulers generally knew that they had to comply with the religious law as expounded by the jurists in order to maintain political legitimacy and garner the approval of the people. History certainly has many cases where rulers tried to manipulate jurists to further their own interests or simply disregarded their judgments, but the general tendency was for caliphs, sultans, and governors to respect the jurists and their opinions.

So the Muslim world entered the nineteenth century with a long and complex history of religious law as a societal sphere

[6] For the early development of political-legal relations, I rely on Wael B. Hallaq, *The Origins and Evolution of Islamic Law* (Cambridge: Cambridge University Press, 2005), especially chap. 8.

with great influence on other societal spheres, such as politics and economics. During the nineteenth century, most Muslim societies were subject to great transformations in their legal systems as a consequence of colonization, or as a result of explicit imitation of Western culture and politics by local rulers, as in Turkey and Iran. European colonial authorities differed in their treatment of law in colonized societies, but they generally took a cautious approach. In most parts of the British Empire, the colonial authorities would attempt to make a working system of laws and courts by applying local customary law with a modern British approach. The result was that Islamic law was gradually made subordinate to civil law, and it was gradually standardized and codified according to the ideals of modern European legal practice.

For instance, in South Asia, the British never had any intention of completely scrapping Islamic law, or Hindu law for that matter. In 1772, The British East India Company claimed jurisdiction over Bengal, the large lands of eastern India where Muslims were a majority. British Bengal is today divided between India and Bangladesh. At the same time, the East India Company, the most powerful private enterprise in the world at the time, replaced the Muslim judges (*qadis*) with British magistrates. The British magistrates' task was to administer Islamic law, and in order to do this well the magistrates had local muftis, specialists on Islamic law, to assist them. Over time, many magistrates were recruited from the Bengali Muslim population, but the judiciary was trained in English law. The result was the development of a unique blend of Islamic legal content applied according to English principles – a mix of Islamic law, non-Islamic customary law, and English law – which became known as Anglo-Muhammedan law, or Anglo-Muslim law to use a less old-fashioned term.

In Islamic societies of Africa, too, the British colonial authorities wanted to leave existing customs as they were, but they standardized procedures and codified laws. At the other end of the empire, in Malaysia, legal reforms took the same general direction. The British would set up a system of secular courts, but they would not demolish the existing structure of *sharia* courts. Before the British colonization of the Malay Peninsula in the nineteenth century, the legal tradition of the area was an amalgam of Islamic law and non-Islamic customary law. There were several sultanates on the Malay Peninsula, and they operated with different systems of law. The British often found it convenient to leave many areas of jurisprudence to the established Islamic and customary laws. This was particularly true of family law. As a result of this pragmatic approach, there developed a dual system of courts, one Islamic and one secular. The important change in colonial Malaysia was the subordination and regularization of *sharia* courts and the codification of Islamic laws.[7]

In Egypt, the system of *sharia* courts was not abandoned completely or suddenly. Instead, Egypt and several other states in the Arab world constructed a system of civil courts that constituted an alternative to the traditional legal system. The new courts existed side by side with *sharia* courts, and there developed a division of labor between *sharia* courts and the emerging state courts. The British colonial power did not attempt to replace the religious law and its experts, although they were often critical of its standards. Thus, the *sharia* survived the legal reforms in the Middle Eastern societies in the nineteenth and early twentieth centuries, but the introduction of civil courts and civil law codes would over time make Islamic law less relevant.

There is perhaps some irony in the fact that the secular attack on Islamic law was often harder in Muslim societies that were not colonized, such as Turkey. In the Ottoman Empire, the modern reform of law started in the nineteenth century, when Ottoman rulers looked to Europe to create a new system of courts and

7 Donald Horowitz, "The Qu'ran and the Common Law: Islamic Law Reform and the Theory of Legal Change," *The American Journal of Comparative Law* 42, no. 2 (Spring 1994): 233–93.

codified laws. The transplanting of European law and the rejection of traditional Islamic law was part of the policy for making a new state carried out by Mustafa Kemal Ataturk, the secularist nationalist founder of modern Turkey, and his circle, the Kemalists. They wanted to make Turkey a modern nation as thoroughly and quickly as possible, and an important step in the right direction, in their opinion, was the complete abandonment of Muslim law and the adoption of law codes borrowed from European states.

In the fields of commercial law and criminal law, the Kemalist government borrowed freely from European states in the 1920s to construct a completely new legal tradition. However, their ambition to change culture and society is most visible in that area of law where defenders of traditional religion and custom have struggled the most to keep modernity at bay: family law. In the field of family law, the Kemalists adopted the Swiss Civil Code in 1926 as part of their effort to put legal matters firmly in the hands of the secular state and weed out the remains of religious tradition. Of course, people generally do not abandon traditional religious customs overnight when told to do so by a secular government, and in Turkey many religious traditions, such as Muslim marriage customs, have survived and thrived in spite of the secularizing project of the elites.[8] Veiling is a powerful issue that has divided Turkish society over the position of religious customs over the past few decades. Since the late 1980s, Islamist women have started covering their heads with the traditional head covering, and this was met with strong opposition by the secularist state. Islamist women were banned from entering schools and universities, and they were not allowed to carry out their work in public spaces if they kept their head covering on.[9]

8 Ihsan Yilmaz, "Secular Law and the Emergence of Unofficial Turkish Islamic Law," *The Middle East Journal* 56, no. 1 (Winter 2002): 113–31.

9 Aldikacti Marshall Gul, "Ideology, Progress and Dialogue: A Comparison of Feminist and Islamist Women's Approaches to the Issues of Head Covering and Work in Turkey," *Gender and Society* 19, no. 1 (February 2005): 104–20.

So it was the growing ambitions of modern states that would eventually result in the marginalization of Islamic law in the modern period, just as states would marginalize other religious and customary systems of law. In the Muslim world, the realm of law was colonized by modern states through codification, centralization, and control, and by taking over the religious endowments that were the jurists' independent source of wealth and power.[10]

ISLAMIC LAW IN EGYPT

The reactions against the colonization of the realm of law and the gradual marginalization of *sharia* were generally not very strong during the nineteenth century because the changes were piecemeal and slow.[11] If we look at Egypt, the birthplace of much of Sunni Muslim fundamentalist ideology and organization, the struggle over the *sharia* has raged in phases. Egyptian society toward the end of the nineteenth century was deeply influenced by institutions and ideas brought by the Europeans, and large sections of Egyptian society believed that Islamic law was outdated and should be replaced by civil law codes after the French model. The Egyptian authorities adopted the Napoleonic code, which became the dominant civil code in many of the Arab states. At the same time, many Egyptians felt that Islam was such an important part of their society and culture that an adequate legal system should be based on the *sharia*, and a few wanted to scrap the French and European legal and cultural influences altogether. But what exactly would that mean? How would a legal system based on the *sharia* look in a modern Muslim society? In the answer to this question we find some of the key ideas of

[10] Wael B. Hallaq, "Can the Shari'a Be Restored?" in *Islamic Law and the Challenges of Modernity*, ed. Yvonne Y. Haddad and Barbara F. Stowasser (Walnut Creek, Calif.: AltaMira Press, 2004), pp. 21–53, especially p. 23.

[11] Nathan J. Brown, "Sharia and State in the Modern Muslim Middle East," *International Journal of Middle East Studies* 29, no. 3 (August 1997): 359–76.

Islamic fundamentalism as it developed since the early twentieth century. In Egypt, there developed several modern approaches to the question of putting *sharia* into the legal system of the modern state.

The religious elite, the *ulama*, developed their own vision of the modern application of *sharia*, and, not surprisingly, they were of the opinion that only their own group of classically trained jurists were in a position to interpret Islamic law. The problem for the *ulama* in Egypt in the late nineteenth and early twentieth centuries was that their institutions of learning were changing so fast, and the sources of their academic, financial, and social independence from the state were undermined so thoroughly, that they in effect were cut off from the classical tradition of law. Their attempt to restore their own priestly authority and convince their countrymen to implement their version of *sharia* can be distinguished from traditional theories of law by the label *neo-traditionalism.*

Neo-traditionalism was not successful, and Egyptian fundamentalists trace their origins to very different sources of authority. In the early years of the twentieth century, the Egyptian intellectual Rashid Rida proposed a new and revolutionary theory of Islamic law that would become central to Muslim fundamentalists' struggle to restore *sharia.* Rida had many things to say about the application of *sharia* in modern times, but the essence of his ideas was that Islamic legal thought was primarily about the goals that the laws were made to achieve. Rida found in the Qur'an and selected hadith a general utilitarian principle commanding people to act in the service of public good. The *sharia* was made by God to promote social justice, and for this purpose human reason and the observation of facts were often the best guides. In fact, Rida asserted, scriptural rules may be set aside in the interest of total welfare.[12]

[12] Clark B. Lombardi, *State Law as Islamic Law in Modern Egypt: The Incorporation of the sharia into Egyptian Constitutional Law* (Leiden: Brill, 2006), p. 83ff.

Rida's utilitarian principles of modern Islamic law became far more popular than the *ulama*'s neo-traditionalism. The *ulama* wanted to restrict *sharia*-reasoning to the educated, the priests, but Rida's general utilitarian principles opened the door of *sharia* to laypeople. From Rida's principles, almost anybody could speculate about the application of law in modern society. Rida's method appealed to a new generation of Muslim intellectuals who had secular educations but lacked the religious training of the *ulama*, and it took root in the new urban middle classes.[13] This is where we find the Muslim fundamentalist movements such as the Muslim Brotherhood.

The Muslim Brotherhood was deeply influenced by the utilitarianism of Rida. Its founder, Hassan al-Banna, and the other key figures in the organization were mostly vague about how they thought *sharia* could be reintroduced and applied in their own time. However, they were generally of the opinion that the times had thrown open the gates for independent interpretation of the Qur'an and hadith as long as one had the general intentions of Islam in mind. They also strongly believed that Egyptian society should be ruled by an Islamic state. An Islamic state is, in their opinion, one where *sharia* is the law.

Egyptian political culture in the 1950s and 1960s was dominated by Egyptian president Gamal Abdel Nasser's secularism and the pan-Arab struggle against Western political dominance in the region. Islam was not part of Nasser's vision, and he had no patience with Islamists. During Nasser's presidency (1956–70), the Muslim Brotherhood was banned and many of its leaders imprisoned. This was the period when Sayyid Qutb wrote his influential books and formed his negative views about the secularism of modern Egypt and his revolutionary ideas about how to change the state of affairs. These would have an important influence on extremists among the Muslim fundamentalists, as mentioned in the last chapter.

[13] Ibid., pp. 91–92.

However, during Anwar Sadat's presidency (1970–81) there was a change in the government's relations with the Islamist movement, which would have consequences for the debate about the place of Islamic law in the country. After the humiliating defeat in the Six Days War against Israel in 1967, large sections of the Egyptian population, and Arab people in general, felt that their culture and politics had lost their moral strength. The Islamists believed that Egypt needed to return to Islamic values, and the clearest expression of such values would be a commitment to the implementation of *sharia.* President Sadat realized that he needed to accommodate his policies to the popular call for more Islam in society, and in order to broaden the support for the government, he started a process to make Egyptian law more Islamic. In 1971, the government introduced a new constitution, which stated that Islam was the religion of the state and that the *sharia* was an important (but not the only) source of legislation.

In sections of the fundamentalist milieus, these signs of a new government commitment to Islam were received with happiness. The early 1970s seemed to open a new era for the Islamization of Egyptian law, and a number of legislative proposals to enforce elements of *sharia* were introduced in the Egyptian Parliament by members sympathetic to the Muslim Brotherhood. Such private bills suggesting new laws would typically focus on criminal law, moral issues, or the banning of interest in economic transactions. For instance, there were introduced bills calling for the prohibition of alcohol production and consumption, a bill to make it a criminal offense to break the fast in public during Ramadan, bills to restrict contacts between the sexes, and a bill to introduce Qur'anic punishment for theft – cutting off the hand of the culprit.[14]

Most of these private bills were never seriously discussed by Parliament, but they show the popular interest in Egypt from

[14] Rudolph Peters, "Divine Law or Man-Made Law? Egypt and the Application of the sharia," *Arab Law Quarterly* 3, no. 3 (August 1988): 231–53.

the early 1970s in reintroducing *sharia* in the modern law code of the country. The fundamentalists most committed to Islamic law soon realized that Sadat was never seriously devoted to a broad Islamization of Egyptian law, and out of the opposition to Sadat two of the most notorious modern militant fundamentalist organizations emerged, Egyptian Islamic Jihad and Al- Gama'a al Islamiyya, both part of the extended al Qaeda network.

ISLAMIC LAW IN PAKISTAN

During the years following the creation of Pakistan in 1947, the fundamentalist leader Maulana Maududi was the most important voice castigating the government for not creating an Islamic state. He shared the disappointment with many other Muslim leaders and intellectuals who felt that they had been promised a religious state by the leaders of the Pakistan movement. The basic characteristic of an Islamic state, in the eyes of the fundamentalists, would be the rule of Islamic law and the placement of the *sharia* above the constitution and all other legal documents, so that no law would be enacted that was repugnant to Islam. The fundamentalists met with strong resistance from the modernists of the country, and the national newspapers during the years after independence contain many critical comments and editorials about the backwardness of the Islamists.

Maududi's ideas about Islamic law were set out in several speeches and articles, and among the most famous statements are two speeches he gave at the Law College in the city of Lahore in 1948.[15] In the two speeches, Maududi started by describing the nature of Islamic law and then went on to the practical problems surrounding the establishment of Islamic law in Pakistan. According to Maududi, the object of the *sharia* is to base human life on virtues and to clean it of vices, and he explained the way that

[15] Both are included in Syed Abul Ala Maududi, *Islamic Law and Constitution*, ed. Khurshid Ahmad (Karachi: Jamaat-e-islami, 1955).

sharia divides acts into the different categories of virtues and vices. "The sharia is a complete scheme of life and an all-embracing social order – nothing superfluous, nothing lacking."[16] Moreover, the *sharia* is an organic whole that must be applied and enforced in its entirety if it is to serve its intended function.

The source of Islamic law is God and the revelation he has given to humankind through his messengers, the last of whom was Muhammad. By surrendering his will to God, a person becomes a Muslim and effectively enters into a contract with God, Maududi claimed. Being a Muslim, and being part of Muslim society, is a deliberate choice, he asserted, and when people make such a choice, they also accept God's classification of good and evil, right and wrong, and the laws God has made: the *sharia*. If an Islamic society adopts any system of life other than the *sharia*, the contract with God is broken.

There is something utopian about a vision that presents every person's religious identity as the result of a conscious choice. This utopian streak is an aspect of the worldview of a modern ideologue, a true fundamentalist, rather than a traditional religious leader. It is the same type of utopian yearning for a perfect state that one can see in other ideologies of the period, such as fascism and communism, and Maududi often mentioned these systems as contrasts to his own Muslim fundamentalism. The utopianism is also apparent in Maududi's discussion of punishments in accordance with *sharia*. He often felt the need to defend accusations of barbarity leveled at the Islamic punishments for crimes such as stealing and adultery, and his main argument was always that these punishments were intended for a future society. In such a society, Islam would make stealing unnecessary by distributing resources justly, and adultery was highly unlikely because men and women were kept apart, marriage was easier, and perverted sexual images would be banned from books and cinemas.

[16] Ibid., p. 27.

But how was Pakistan going to become such a society? How should Pakistanis get rid of the Anglo-Muslim law they inherited from the British and "return" to a pristine Islamic system of law? Maududi did not yearn for a sudden revolution but realized that a transformation of Pakistan into a truly Islamic state would take some time. The introduction of Islamic law in Pakistan would require a complete demolition of the legal and political structure built by the British over a long time. Such a change could not be achieved through a simple official proclamation or a parliamentary bill, he said. However, he was certain that the collective life of the country could be completely changed within the course of ten years if one had a righteous group of people with a solid plan and wielding the power of government.

The concrete discussions about the application and enforcement of Islamic law in Pakistan came to revolve around the issue of the constitution. When Pakistan became independent, a Constituent Assembly was set down to make a draft constitution, but this proved difficult because the Muslim modernists and the Islamists or fundamentalists had very different ideas about what the basic legal document of the state should say. For the modernists, it was sufficient to take the earlier "constitution" of British India, the Government of India Act of 1935, as the point of departure and adjust it to fit the young state. The fundamentalists, foremost among them Maududi, strongly believed that one had to scrap the colonial documents and traditions, start from scratch, and build an Islamic constitution based on Islamic documents and ideals.

Maududi and his Jamaat-e-Islami were engaged in a heated national debate about the new constitution during these early years of independence. In a speech in 1948, Maududi demanded that the Constituent Assembly make the following statement:

1. That we Pakistanis believe in the supreme sovereignty of God and that the State will administer the country as His agent;

2. That the basic law of the land is the Shari'ah which has come to us through our Prophet Muhammad (peace be on him);
3. That all such existing laws as are in conflict with the Shari'ah will be gradually repealed and no such law as may be in conflict with the Shari'ah shall be framed in future;
4. That the State, in exercising its powers, shall have no authority to transgress the limits imposed by Islam.[17]

Maududi insisted that the constitution of Pakistan should be based on four sources: the Qur'an, the Sunnah (the exemplary stories about the Prophet and his times), the stories about the first four caliphs, and the rulings of great jurists.[18] He also wanted to appoint a group of Islamic scholars and experts of modern legal thought and to "entrust to them the task of a clause-wise codification of Islamic Law according to the modern pattern."[19] The modernist Muslims of Pakistan strongly disagreed, and they had the upper hand in terms of political and military power. However, because of these strong disagreements in society, the Constituent Assembly of Pakistan had a difficult task, and the new constitution was not adopted until 1956. It was abrogated only two years later, after the military coup that brought General Ayub Khan to power.

Pakistan got new constitutions in 1962 and 1973, but neither of them entailed that complete Islamization of Pakistan's constitutional law that the fundamentalists were struggling to achieve. However, when General Zia ul-Haq carried out a coup d'etat and installed himself as military ruler in 1977, he inaugurated a period of Islamization of Pakistan that laid some of the foundation for the extremist politics that has ravaged parts of the country since the late 1980s. The superpowers were also heavily

[17] Ibid., pp. 54–55.
[18] Ibid., pp. 100–1.
[19] Ibid., p. 62.

involved in this development, as neighboring Afghanistan was invaded by the Soviet Union in 1979 and the United States decided to fight a proxy war with the help of Afghan guerrillas and their Pakistani allies. Islamization also created much hostility between the ethnic and religious groups, and it legitimized repression of religious minorities, such as the Ahmadis, the Christians, and the Shia Muslims.

The fundamentalists were obviously correct when they said that Pakistan was created as a state for Indian Muslims in 1947, but its founding father, Muhammad Ali Jinnah, never wanted a religious state and never called for the kind of Sunni Muslim chauvinism that many of the fundamentalists want to make into state policy. When General Zia took power, Islamization became a political goal and a tool to enable the dictator to install some measure of unity on a divided country. In his first televised speech to the nation, he said: "Pakistan, which was created in the name of Islam, will continue to survive only if it sticks to Islam. That is why I consider the introduction of an Islamic system an essential prerequisite for the country."[20]

General Zia would remain in power from 1977 to 1988 and throughout this time would continue to paint a picture of Pakistan's founders as staunch defenders of an Islamic state. Some of this was pure rhetoric to appease the Islamists, who were never content with the speed and depth of Islamization in the country, but Zia was also personally devoted to realizing the Islamic nature of Pakistani society. In 1979, General Zia announced his large-scale program of Islamization, which included the creation of an institution called the Federal Shariat Court. This court had the task of examining whether laws were "repugnant to the injunctions of Islam." General Zia also introduced Islamic criminal law following, at least in theory, the classic *hudud* punishments for theft, murder, and other crimes. The

[20] Quoted in Ian Talbot, *Pakistan – A Modern History* (New York: St. Martin's Press, 1998), p. 251.

enforcement of Islamic punishment for sexual crimes like rape and adultery was particularly controversial.[21]

Taking in the larger picture of the struggle by Muslim fundamentalists to reinstate the *sharia*, then, we can reasonably say that they are facing a difficult task. The system of Islamic law was not scrapped overnight by colonial powers, but beginning in the nineteenth century, a long process of legal reforms would make Islamic law marginal in many Muslim societies. There developed new structures of civil courts alongside the *sharia*-based courts in most Islamic societies during the colonial period, and this development continued in most states once these societies became independent in the aftermath of the Second World War. The secular states backed the civil courts and let them encroach on the areas of law and custom where Islamic and customary law previously had dominated. In stark contrast to pre-colonial Islamic societies, the new political power had no need for religion. Neither the colonial authorities nor the post-colonial governments in Asia or Africa needed the legitimacy of the Muslim jurists. As a consequence of these state-initiated legal reforms, which took place starting in the late nineteenth century, the jurisdiction and authority of *sharia* courts gradually diminished.

However, the gravest threat to Islamic law as a societal system may have been the gradual erosion of the institutions on which it had always built its competence and authority: the schools. Traditional Islamic centers of learning had to compete for students and funding with schools and universities based on Western models. Often the religious schools were weakened or closed, and the *ulama* witnessed a rapid undermining of the institutions needed for reproducing their own knowledge and authority. There took place a shift in religious authority away from the traditional jurists and their institutions to new types of lay leaders, or rather leaders who did not have a traditional

[21] Ibid., pp. 275–76.

religious education but based their authority on personal qualities, on charisma.

HINDU LAW

At independence in 1947, India inherited a complex system of law called Anglo-Hindu law (alongside the Anglo-Muslim law discussed earlier) that had been constructed starting in the late 1700s by British administrators and lawyers of the East India Company, the private enterprise that gradually colonized India from the 1600s until the British possessions on the subcontinent became a Crown colony in 1858.

As their Indian empire expanded in the 1700s, the British experienced difficulties in applying traditional Hindu law in a consistent fashion because it never was anything like a unified and universalized system of legislation. It was rather a range of different local customs and a variety of religio-legal texts expressing the ideologies of individual Brahmins over the centuries. Such customs and texts were interpreted differently by the learned pundits the British talked to, and sometimes the Indian subjects of the East India Company used the confusion of the British to their advantage by paying local pundits to interpret Hindu legal tradition in their favor in British-Indian courts: by extracting and interpreting opinions from the right texts, any number of different legal positions could be defended as "Hindu." To counter such effects, the British started compiling codes and digests of Hindu law so that legal principles could be applied with some consistency in court. This process was parallel to the codification of Islamic law in India and other parts of the British Empire. In India, the result was the invention of Anglo-Hindu law, a mix of British legal principles and processes and Hindu concepts and norms chosen more or less randomly from a large body of legal literature in Sanskrit and other Indian languages.[22]

[22] See Werner Menski, *Hindu Law – Beyond Tradition and Modernity* (New Delhi: Oxford University Press, 2003), especially chap. 4.

When India became independent in 1947, its new leaders had to decide what should be done with the complex system of Anglo-Hindu law. The leaders of early independent India were secularists. They wanted India to be governed by laws modeled on the British system and wanted to get rid of many of the Hindu customs that the British had incorporated into Anglo-Hindu law.[23] During the 1950s, there was an important process in Indian politics to reform Hindu law, and these reforms met with resistance among conservative Hindus. In particular, the leaders of Hindu nationalist parties, such as Bharatiya Jan Sangh and the Hindu Mahasabha, fiercely opposed proposed changes in laws concerning divorce rights, bigamy, and daughters' inheritance rights. The Hindu Mahasabha was the nationalist party associated with the important Hindu fundamentalist and nationalist ideologue V. D. Savarkar, and it was the springboard for the establishment of the Bharatiya Jan Sangh, which would later develop into the political party BJP, whose rise to power we looked at in the last chapter. The politicians of these early nationalist and fundamentalist parties believed that their supporters, Hindus belonging to high castes, would not accept the legal changes.[24]

In spite of the broad reforms of Hindu law, modern Indian law has not been completely purged of religious content. The system of personal law in India has both kept some of the laws established under the British and added new Hindu norms and concepts in some areas. For instance, in the Hindu Marriage Act, enacted in 1955, the Indian state recognizes that ancient customs regulating marriage are still authoritative. Section seven of this act says that a Hindu marriage may be solemnized

[23] For a discussion of the constitutional debates about reform of Hindu law and women's rights, see Torkel Brekke, "The Concept of Religion and the Debate on the Rights of Women in the Constitutional Debates of India," *Nordic Journal of Religion and Society* 22, no. 1 (2009): 71–85.

[24] Narendra Subramanian, "Making Family and Nation: Hindu Marriage Law in Early Postcolonial India," *The Journal of Asian Studies*, in press.

in accordance with the local customs and rites of the husband or wife, which implies that the Indian state has left the legal regulation of marriages to family, community, and caste customs.[25] Similar continuities can be found in other areas of personal and family law. In other words, there is considerable divergence between the secularist rhetoric used by Indian political and academic elites and the realities in Indian courts on matters of personal law. In fact, some form of Hindu law is still applied to Hindus in India.

But who is a Hindu? This question has been a major issue of conflict because the constitution of India defines several big minorities – such as Sikhs, Jains, and Buddhists – as Hindu in legal terms, and many members of these minorities resent being put into this category.

THE QUARREL OVER A UNIFORM CIVIL CODE

As we saw in the last chapter, the fundamentalists of the RSS, the VHP, the BJP, and several other related organizations want to establish a Hindu *rashtra*, a Hindu nation governed by laws that safeguard Hinduism as the dominant culture and religion in India. In later chapters, we will see how this vision was put into practice in the fields of science and education. However, Hindu law as such has not been a main concern of Hindu fundamentalists since the great political transformations of the 1980s that eventually brought them to power in Delhi in the late 1990s. Instead, important controversies about religion and law in India have raged over conceptualizations of secularism and multiculturalism, particularly with regard to Muslim law.

Hindu fundamentalists have been arguing for decades that the official secularism of the Indian state is a pseudosecularism because it lets Muslims apply their *sharia* in the area of personal law, whereas Hindu laws have been reformed since

[25] Menski, *Hindu Law*, p. 297ff.

the period right after independence. To Hindu fundamentalists, the fact that India does not have a uniform civil code that includes Muslims is the most important proof that the government has never been seriously committed to a consistent policy of secularism.

The uniform civil code is the common name applied to a code of family law regulating matters of marriage, divorce, inheritance, and other areas that would be applicable to all Indians irrespective of religion. In other areas of law, such as criminal law, the British had brought the population under one system of legislation, but they had always been afraid to tamper with religious customs and sentiments on issues regarding the private lives of their subjects. Politicians and ideologues of the early independent era looked at the field of legislation they had inherited from the British and searched for ways to bring the two most important systems of religious law – Anglo-Hindu and Anglo-Muslim law – under one framework to make everybody equal in those areas that were covered by the religious laws and customs related to family matters. The reform of Hindu law was one of the key legal issues of early independent India, as I mentioned earlier, and this was one step toward a uniform civil code.

By the reform of Hindu law, Hindus, Sikhs, Jains, and Buddhists were brought under a more secularized and uniform personal law code, whereas Muslims, Christians, and Jews were left with their own religious codes. Christians and Jews are tiny minorities in India, but Muslims constitute an important group, with around 15 percent of the total population, and from the perspective of electoral politics they are a substantial vote bank. Many Muslim organizations and political parties in India have protested loudly against attempts to change Muslim law, and the Congress Party has been careful in its approach to this issue because they have feared interreligious conflicts and loss of votes.

The Shah Bano case, which reached the Supreme Court in 1985, is the most famous symbol of the clash between the idea of a uniform civil code and Muslim demands for minority rights in the area of family law. Shah Bano was an Indian Muslim woman from the city of Indore. In 1978, Shah Bano's husband wanted a divorce. According to Muslim personal law, men have the right to get a divorce without much ado, and the man is then obliged to pay his divorced wife alimony during three months of separation after the breakup. Shah Bano approached the lower civil court and demanded more alimony from her ex-husband than she could expect to get according to Muslim family law. She and her lawyers argued that a different law should be applied that would ensure her maintenance until death or remarriage. The other law is Section 125 of the Criminal Procedure Code (CrPC) and is part of India's secular laws, not part of Muslim personal law. In other words, the Muslim divorcee had a right to maintenance according to civil law but not according to Muslim law.

Shah Bano won her case in the lower and higher civil courts, but finally her ex-husband decided he wanted to try the case in the Supreme Court of India because the decisions in the civil courts were opposed to Muslim personal law, in his opinion. In 1985, the Supreme Court decided that Shah Bano was entitled to alimony from her husband after divorce according to the CrPC, and they disregarded the limitation on the period of maintenance in Muslim personal law. The Supreme Court went further and claimed that a reading of the Qur'an really supported their view that husbands should pay their divorced wives alimony longer than the three months stipulated by Muslim personal law, and the court's decision contained rather blunt statements about the need of Indian Muslims to modernize their ideas about family law. The court also argued in their decision that to avoid similar cases India should introduce a uniform civil code.

Conservative Muslim organizations reacted strongly against the decision, and the government feared the religious tensions that resulted from the case. In response to the protests, the Indian Parliament, which was controlled by the ruling Congress

Party of Prime Minister Rajiv Gandhi, passed a law in 1986 called The Muslim Women (Protection of Rights on Divorce) Act (MWPRDA). This law was passed to annul the Supreme Court decision and said that Indian husbands were *not* required to pay alimony for more than the three months after separation. However, the act also said, rather ambiguously, that husbands were required to pay within those three months a fair amount for future maintenance of their divorced wives. The ambiguity was probably intentional, and courts in India have interpreted it in different ways in divorce cases: some have ruled that husbands must pay alimony indefinitely, whereas others have decided that no requirements can be made after three months.

The Shah Bano case became a symbol of great importance to Hindu fundamentalists during the increasing political and religious tensions in the late 1980s and early 1990s. Their call for a uniform civil code has been a strategy for both criticizing what they saw as a pseudosecularist government biased against the Hindu majority and for driving a wedge between the Hindu and Muslim communities. Hindu fundamentalists claim that the Congress Party in government has granted the Muslims preferential treatment for decades. To outside observers, this claim sounds strange, as it has been established beyond doubt that Muslims in India are generally poor and underprivileged.[26]

However, Hindu fundamentalists have found support among liberal intellectuals, and a number of women's groups have found themselves siding with the fundamentalists in their call for a uniform civil code as part of a movement for Muslim women's liberation. At the same time, a Muslim Indian feminist movement has emerged that demands changes to Muslim personal law. The Muslim feminists refer to the Qur'an and the hadith to justify their call for more gender equality, and they reject the

[26] See the report *Social, Economic and Educational Status of the Muslim Community of India*, normally referred to as the Sachar Committee's report, which can be downloaded from the Indian Ministry of Minority Affairs at http://minorityaffairs.gov.in/newsite/sachar/sachar.asp.

religious authority of the traditional elite, the *ulama*, as part of that broad challenge to traditional religious authority.[27]

The fact is that Muslim personal law relating to divorce and alimony has changed over time in spite of conservative Muslim organizations' attempts to hinder reform and in spite of the Hindu fundamentalists' claim that Muslim law has been treated as immune to all modernization. The clearest signal that Muslim personal law has been changed for good, although in a piecemeal fashion rather than by sudden reform, came with the Danial Latifi case of 2001. In the decision in this case, the Supreme Court ruled that all Muslim men were obliged to pay their divorced wives alimony indefinitely. The Supreme Court bench in the Latifi case referred to the earlier Shah Bano decision and to the MWPRDA and the Indian constitution, but it also referred to the Qur'an and to Muslim personal law as applied in other Muslim societies, such as Tunisia, Jordan, Malaysia, and Indonesia.[28] The realization that change is happening to Muslim law, just as it happened to Hindu law, is probably the reason why the Hindu fundamentalists did not make the lack of a uniform civil code into a big issue once they gained government power, as I described in the last chapter.

BUDDHISM AND LAW

In Buddhist societies, law has traditionally been divided into two separate spheres. On the one hand, there is the Vinaya, which is the ecclesiastical code used by the monks to regulate life in the monasteries, and on the other hand there was the law of the land regulating the affairs of normal people. The Buddhist king

[27] See, for instance, Sylvia Vatuk, "Islamic Feminism in India: Indian Muslim Women Activists and the Reform of Muslim Personal Law," *Modern Asian Studies* 42, nos. 2–3 (2008): 489–518.

[28] Narendra Subramanian, "Legal Change and Gender Inequality: Changes in Muslim Family Law in India," *Law & Social Inquiry* 33, no. 3 (Summer 2008): 631–72 at p. 648.

had an important role in both legal spheres. He would be the one to enforce the law of the land as he believed necessary, but often the reach of the law became limited as one moved away from the center. At the same time, the king was the only person who could guarantee enforcement of the Vinaya, the law code of the monks and nuns, because he was the one in control of military power. The monkhood for their part could have an important role as advisors and ideologues in the court of the king in Theravada Buddhist societies. In the countries of Southeast Asia (e.g., Thailand), they would share such roles with Brahmins (i.e., Hindu priests). In the northern regions of Asia – in societies such as China, Japan, and Korea – the relationship between Buddhism and political power has always been fundamentally different, as Buddhist institutions and persons have generally occupied more marginal and less important roles. Our focus in this book continues to be on Sri Lanka and Thailand.

In premodern Thailand, the royal law of the land was known as the *Dhammathat*, whereas the monks had their Vinaya.[29] The difference between the two systems of law has little to do with a distinction between religious and secular law, but the first part of the word Dhammathat – *dhamma* – gives a hint that the law applied to the population in general had Buddhist sources, too: *dhamma* is the Buddhist religion and its values. At the same time, the Dhammathat had incorporated numerous local norms and rules that were not strictly religious at all but part of traditional legal and moral thinking and practices. In this sense, the Buddhist law of premodern Thai society incorporated both religious and nonreligious elements, as did premodern Islamic or Hindu law. To a Buddhist Thai or Burmese in the eighteenth century, it would have made little sense to ask exactly where the line might be drawn between the Buddhist and non-Buddhist elements of the law code, and we can remind ourselves that the

[29] Frank E. Reynolds, "Dhamma in Dispute: The Interactions of Religion and Law in Thailand," *Law & Society Review* 28, no. 3 (1994): 433–52.

conceptualization of such boundaries was a key element in the process of secularization.

The legal sphere in Thailand would start to change rapidly in the nineteenth century. In the previous chapter, we looked briefly at the modernist reforms introduced by King Mongkut. Mongkut made reforms to the legal framework of the Vinaya, the monastic code, to bring it closer to what he believed was original and pure Buddhism, and Mongkut's son and successor, King Chulalongkorn (reigned 1868–1910), replaced the non-monastic law, the Dhammathat, with a new code of secular laws based on a Western model. The reformist king realized that a complete replacement of traditional law was necessary in order to give Thailand the administrative and bureaucratic overhaul that would enable the country to relate to the modern world in general and to withstand Western imperialism in particular. In order to negotiate and make treaties with Western powers and be taken seriously as a state, Thailand needed a modern code of laws.

The adoption of modern law was also part of a transition from a galactic polity, mentioned in the last chapter, to a radial polity, which means that all parts of the country were now controlled directly from the center, Bangkok. The invention of modern states in Southeast Asia, with modern law codes and modern bureaucracies, began in the nineteenth century and continued at different paces into the twentieth century. One consequence of the development of the state in Thailand was the submission of the once powerful Buddhist Sangha, the monkhood, to the political will of modern governments, a process with parallels in other world religions. However, although transformations in traditional conceptions of religious authority started in the period of reform in the mid-nineteenth century, Thailand did not produce full-fledged lay-initiated Buddhist fundamentalist movements like the Santi Asoka before the 1970s. When such movements appeared, they had all the signs of anger and frustration with a trajectory of modernity and modernism that was taking society further and further away from what many saw as real Buddhist values.

In Sri Lanka, in contrast to Thailand, modernization of the law was imposed from outside by a colonial power. When the British occupied the Kandyan state (the Buddhist state with its capital in the highland city of Kandy) in 1815, they found a society without written laws but with legal customs that were mostly based on orality and aimed at dispute settlement not according to strict codes and generalized legal principles but according to context. As in the case of Hindu India, then, the British met a society in Sri Lanka without law in the European sense of the term, and the only way they believed they could deal with this was to construct law out of the customs and textual evidence they came across. The British authorities' attempt to interview monks and experienced village leaders in order to collect and codify Kandyan law really amounted to an invention of customs and of a new code of laws grounded in a different social ideology and a different view of human nature.[30]

An important change arising from colonialism in Sri Lanka was the disestablishment of Buddhism. In other words, the traditional link between the king and the monkhood, between state and religion, had been severed by the British, although the colonial authorities did try to find modern ways to deal with the conflicts internal to the monkhood, such as the ownership of land. In the decades following independence in 1948, debates took place about the place of Buddhism in relation to the state, and this was an important issue when Sri Lanka created its own constitution in the early 1970s. Sri Lanka's constitution was adopted in 1972, and in Chapter 11 it states that "Buddhism shall be given the foremost place." The unprecedented autonomy experienced by the Buddhist monkhood in Sri Lanka as a

[30] Steven Kemper, "The Buddhist Monkhood, the Law and the State in Colonial Sri Lanka," *Comparative Studies in Society and History* 26, no. 3 (July 1984): 401–27.

result of disestablishment was an important cause for the growth of political Buddhism and the activity of political monks.

We can take a brief look at an issue on which Buddhist fundamentalists and nationalists have had an impact on discussions about law and religion. In Sri Lanka, there have been strong initiatives from Buddhist activists to make laws that would prohibit what they call "unethical conversions." Unethical conversions are conversions of Buddhists to Christianity in which immoral means are used to make people leave their old religion and embrace the new one. A substantial number of Buddhists in Sri Lanka are of the opinion that several hundred Christian organizations, often disguised as NGOs or charitable or educational organizations, offer gifts of money in exchange for conversion, and for this reason Christianity is spreading among the poor sections of society. Several Evangelical Christian organizations do in fact operate in Sri Lanka, as in other parts of Asia, and some work aggressively to gain followers. The Evangelicals come from many different places, because Pentecostalism and the wider charismatic movement are thoroughly global, but many hail from the United States or South Korea.

Concern about Christian conversion strategies has been significant among Buddhists in Sri Lanka since colonial times, but it exploded at the beginning of the twenty-first century to become the most important issue addressed by Buddhist fundamentalists. When the monk party called the Jathika Hela Urumaya (JHU) got nine members elected to Parliament in 2004, one of their key causes was a law against unethical conversions, as I mentioned in the last chapter. Their most important inspiration, the Venerable Soma, who died in 2003, was extremely concerned about the conversion strategies employed by Christians, and he made this very clear in his preaching.

The JHU presented a bill to the Parliament in May 2005 that suggested up to five years in prison for anyone convicted of attempted conversion, and just a month later the government of Sri Lanka presented its own anticonversion bill that suggested fines and up to seven years' imprisonment for any action that was meant to "indirectly influence" people to change their religion. The government bill built on the research and recommendations made by a report called the Sinhala Commission Report that gave details about the organizations engaged in unethical conversion and their modes of operation in Sri Lanka. The debate has continued, and in 2009 a more substantial report about unethical conversions was finished by the All Ceylon Buddhist Congress. This report offers large quantities of material about the history of unethical conversions and about the attitudes of Buddhists toward the practice, and it gives details about 384 centers and organizations engaged in unethical conversions and more than 400 places where such conversions have taken place.[31]

The debate was intense in the Sri Lankan media, and there was massive support for a law against unethical conversions in sections of the monkhood and from large sections of lay Buddhist society through the first decade of the twenty-first century. The debate has caused tensions between religious groups in the country, and in the mid-2000s Buddhist Sinhalese carried out violent attacks on Christian churches and persons in Sri Lanka, and some of those who were attacked belonged to the old Catholic community of Sinhalese rather than the new Protestant groups who are active in proselytization.[32] In light of the recent history of Sri Lanka, it is possible to understand the anxiety of many Buddhists about what they see as a sustained Christian assault on Buddhist religion and culture. At the same time, it seems that some of the material presented by the local commissions is biased against Christianity, and Buddhist fundamentalists have

[31] For the debate about unethical conversions, I have relied on a forthcoming article by Mahinda Deegalle, and I am very grateful to the author for sharing his information with me. See Mahinda Deegalle, "Contested Religious Conversions of Buddhists in Sri Lanka and India," forthcoming.

[32] Neil DeVotta, "Sri Lanka in 2004: Enduring Political Decay and a Failing Peace Process," *Asian Survey* 45, no. 1 (January–February 2005): 98–104.

certainly used the fear of unethical conversions to gain votes and attract supporters.

The passion of Buddhist activists in the campaign to ban unethical conversions shows the extent to which many Sinhalese Buddhists see themselves as a minority fighting for cultural survival. In reality, of course, Buddhism is the majority religion in Sri Lanka, but the sense of being a minority arises from a sense of threat posed first by global Christianity, which is sometimes construed as a continuation of colonialism, and second by Hindu culture, which is the culture of a large minority in Sri Lanka and of its giant and very close neighbor, India. The emphasis on conversions also shows the extent to which modern religious activists have internalized a concept of religion according to which the world religions inhabit the same global sphere and compete for the same prize: converts, and eventually power through numbers.

In Thailand, the issue of abortion has been very important to some groups of Buddhist fundamentalists, such as the Santi Asoka. In the 1980s and 1990s, the controversial politician and Santi Asoka member Chamlong Srimuang was engaged in political work to stop attempts to make abortion legal in Thailand. The Santi Asoka and other Buddhist groups campaigning against more liberal legislation on abortion believe that the demand for such a right is a symptom of immorality in society. To their minds, good Buddhist citizens would abstain from having sex if they did not want children, and their position on this matter is not unlike that taken by a large number of Protestant Christian fundamentalists.

Although Buddhist societies have had serious issues concerning the relationship of Buddhism to law, it is fair to say that the issue of religious law has greater symbolic significance in modern Muslim or Hindu societies than in Buddhist ones. An important reason for this is that Buddhism as a religion has put far less emphasis on the legal and moral issues of laypeople than many other religious traditions. Both Hinduism and Islam have always been religious traditions intertwined with great traditions of law and ethics, which is not the case with Buddhism. The important legal and moral issues that have preoccupied Buddhist thinkers through the ages are almost exclusively about the affairs of monks and nuns and their lives devoted to religious affairs. Buddhist societies outside the monasteries have been regulated by laws and norms that may or may not have some relationship to Buddhism. These laws and norms may to some extent express a Buddhist ethos, but when we call premodern Thai, Burmese, or Sri Lankan law "Buddhist" we must be clear that law codes in these societies are Buddhist in a more diffuse sense than Muslim or Hindu law has generally been.

GOD'S LAW AND REAL FREEDOM

This is the place to return to what I said earlier about modernity producing and universalizing a set of reference points, a set of concepts, a *language*, that everyone has to use if they wish to take part in debates about matters concerning politics and society. This language includes references to ideas such as equality, justice, freedom, and autonomy. The concept of freedom is central to the Western tradition of political philosophy. In the United States, ideas about freedom have been particularly important since the founding of the nation. In a narrow sense, laws are restrictions on people's freedom. Sometimes, restrictions on somebody's freedom are necessary in order to safeguard the freedom of others. Very few people want to live in a society without laws.

A look at different conceptualizations of freedom might make it easier to understand what fundamentalists are up to in the legal sphere. Let us for a moment contrast the different ideas about freedom held by libertarians and religious fundamentalists in the United States. Libertarians are people who want a minimal role for the state in society. One might say that fundamentalists and libertarians share the ideal of freedom in a very general sense, but they have very different conceptualizations of freedom. It means different things to them. Libertarians are keen to restrain government intervention in private lives because they believe that people have radically different ideas about the good life and they should be left alone to pursue those ideals as they see fit, as long as they do not limit other people's right to do the same. So libertarians want as few laws as possible.

Fundamentalists, too, are keen to restrict government intervention in private lives, but for completely different reasons. They believe people in fact will have the *same* ideas about the good life if they only open their eyes and understand the message of the Bible. It is human weakness and confusion that make many people pursue goals that are inconsistent with the message of God, fundamentalists would say. Real freedom is about submitting to God's will and living according to His plan. Therefore, if the government uses laws to help people avoid sin and get on the right track of Christian life, this produces more, not less, freedom on the whole.

In other words, the libertarian and the fundamentalist share the ideal of freedom in a very general sense, but they see the relationship between freedom and laws in a different light. To the libertarian, real freedom is achieved by having as few legal restrictions as possible. To the fundamentalist, real freedom is achieved by blocking sinful practices through the use of laws, thereby helping people onto the right path.[33] Fundamentalist educators teach children to be free by severely restricting their exposure to the corrupting influence of the fallen world outside and by working hard to shape the minds of pupils and students in one mold.[34] Fundamentalist educators would generally

[33] To the reader interested in political philosophy, I should mention that this brief discussion draws on the important essay "Two Concepts of Liberty" by the philosopher Isaiah Berlin. Ideas about true freedom in fundamentalist thought are also discussed in John H. Garvey, "Fundamentalism and American Law," in Marty and Appleby, *Fundamentalisms and the State*, pp. 28–49.

[34] Alan Peshkin, *God's Choice: The Total World of a Fundamentalist Christian School* (Chicago: University of Chicago Press, 1986).

say that it is a misunderstood conception of freedom that leads liberal public educators to value autonomy and critical, independent investigation of different worldviews and traditions.

Let us look at an example from the Christian reconstructionists who want to establish literal biblical law in the modern world. It is a main issue for Greg Bahnsen, in his massive book on theonomy in Christian ethics, that it is a misunderstanding to hold that autonomy produces freedom in a real sense. He returns time and again to the position that "true Christian freedom is found in service to God's holy will."[35] In a recent defense of reconstructionism, or dominion theology, one pastor explained that many critics seem to believe that dominion theology would turn God's Word into a burden, whereas the fact is that "these critics fail to appreciate that God's law liberates whatever it touches, unchaining all things from sin and releasing them to freely serve and glorify their Author and Maker."[36]

Can we find similar disagreements about the nature of freedom in Muslim fundamentalism? In his book about the political theory of Islam, Maulana Maududi explained why the political system of Islam is completely different from Western democracy. The main reason is that mankind has no right to make their own laws in Islam, Maududi said. Muslims living under a true Islamic government would never make or abandon laws according to the wish of the people, but they would all be entitled to give their opinion on matters of interpretation, provided they are qualified to do so. Maududi extended such legal and political authority to the whole of the Muslim community, in a radical departure from classical doctrine. Thus, Maududi asserted, the Islamic polity is a democracy in the sense that all Muslims take part in government, but it is a theocracy in the sense that Muslims are never allowed to make any independent

[35] Bahnsen, *Theonomy in Christian Ethics*, p. 467.

[36] Martin G. Selbrede, "The Blessings of Dominion Theology," *Faith for All of Life* (March/April 2008): 13ff. at p. 17.

judgment on matters where an explicit command of God or His Prophet exists.

Being very widely read, Maududi understood well that his view of government would strike most Western (and many Muslim) readers as unfree, and he explained why he believed that these restrictions had been placed on popular sovereignty in Islam, as opposed to the West. Some might say, Maududi wrote, that God has taken away the liberty of human mind and intellect instead of safeguarding it. Maududi responded: “My reply is that God has retained the right of legislation in His own hand not in order to deprive man of his natural freedom but to safeguard that very freedom. His purpose is to save man from going astray and inviting his own ruin.”[37]

Maududi then went on to discuss the place of freedom in the Western democracies. In the democratic systems, people make their own laws. That might look like freedom, but it is not, he said. First of all, people in the West have to delegate their sovereignty to representatives so that an elite makes laws for the whole people. The deep problem is that secularization in the West has led to a divorce between ethics and legislation on the one hand and religion on the other. As a result, the laws that are passed are often purely in the interest of the lawmakers and have no benefit for the people, Maududi asserted.

However, Maududi's argument is really about human nature and freedom in a deeper sense. Even when people can get directly involved in legislation, they cannot become free by the process because they are in fact made unfree by their own passions and emotions. Maududi used the American prohibition of alcohol as an example. First, the American people realized the destruction brought by alcohol and demanded prohibition, and later their thirst for alcohol made them scrap the ban. This kind of example, Maududi asserted, proves that man is simply not competent as legislator. Even if he frees himself from other

[37] Maududi, *Political Theory of Islam,* p. 23.

lords, "he becomes slave to his own petty passions and exalts the devil in him to the position of supreme Lord."[38] This is why limitations on human freedom are good. God has laid down limits, divine limits, that may not be overstepped, Maududi explained, and he gave the details about these limits (the *hudud*) in spheres such as economics, gender roles, and punishments for theft and alcohol consumption. These limits to human conduct make for real freedom, according to Maududi. He told the reader to think of a path through mountainous regions where the sides of the road are blocked to prevent the traveler from falling and asked: "Are these barricades intended to deprive the wayfarer of his liberty?"[39]

[38] Ibid., p. 25.
[39] Ibid., p. 28.

7

The Struggle for the Sciences

Historian Paul Johnson begins a popular book about modern times by stating that the modern world began on May 29, 1919.[1] On that day, scientists were able to confirm Albert Einstein's general theory of relativity by close observations of a solar eclipse, and, as a consequence, the classical Newtonian worldview had to be modified. Johnson fittingly calls his first chapter "A Relativistic World." Johnson's statement is a way of saying the obvious: that there is no simple way of dating modern times that everybody would agree to, so one might as well choose a date that fits one's purpose. Relativism is indeed one of the aspects of the modern worldview that fundamentalists everywhere react against, but for some reason Einstein's mathematical calculations have not attracted much attention from fundamentalists. I have never heard of a fundamentalist challenging the famous equation $E=mc^2$. This is simply because the relativity of physics has little to do with the status of revealed religious truths. The relativity that hurts for many fundamentalists is the one that questions the status of sacred scripture and its contents.

[1] Paul Johnson, *Modern Times: The World from the Twenties to the Nineties* (New York: Perennial Classics, 2001), p. 1.

Modern biology's view of human evolution has been a major issue of conflict between conservative and liberal Christians in Europe and America since Charles Darwin's work *On the Origin of Species by Means of Natural Selection* was published in 1859. Today, the conflict between fundamentalist Christians and secularist scientists is getting hotter in several countries, and there is reason to expect that human evolution will become even more of a contentious subject in the future in Muslim societies, as we shall see. Thus, it is difficult to agree with the authors of the book *Strong Religion* when they expect that the less triumphal demeanor of contemporary science will take the wind out of the sails of fundamentalism.[2] On the contrary, the conflict between biological science and religion is rather likely to get hotter.

EVOLUTIONISM IN THE PULPIT

Visiting Charles Darwin's pretty and peaceful house in the south of England, and witnessing the care with which he treated everybody, from his children, his servants, and his guests to the plants in his hothouses and fields, one cannot help wondering how such a gentle man could create such a scandal. In 1859, Charles Darwin published his most famous work, *On the Origin of Species*, where he presented his theory of evolution by natural selection in prose as elegant as one finds in any of the great Victorian novels. It immediately became the topic of heated debates in England. In *Origin of Species*, Darwin did not really write much about human evolution, but the implications of his theory for the origins of mankind were evident. Several years later, Darwin spelled them out in the book *The Descent of Man*. The main conclusion in this work, Darwin wrote, was that humans have descended from some less highly organized form, and this would

[2] Gabriel A. Almond, R. Scott Appleby, and Emmanuel Sivan, *Strong Religion: The Rise of Fundamentalisms Around the World*. Chicago: University of Chicago Press, 2003, p. 224.

necessarily mean that we should stop thinking about humans as the result of a separate act of creation.[3] Humans had descended from other species, Darwin maintained, and he was supported in his view by several notable scientists of his day.

Darwin met strong reactions from the Church of England. The most famous attack on his views came from Samuel Wilberforce, the bishop of Oxford, during a debate in 1860 in the University Museum in Oxford. Exactly what was said during this debate is not clear, but there seems to have been a quarrel between Wilberforce and Darwin's most staunch defender, Thomas Henry Huxley. Darwin himself was not present. It was the status of humans in the worldview presented by Darwin that was most offensive to the religiously minded people of England. If Darwin's ideas were to be accepted, it would entail a rejection of the story of creation in the Old Testament. Christians have always placed human beings in a special position in God's creation, as they were created in the image of God, and they share this belief with Muslims and Jews.

However, there were other elements in Darwin's theory that were offensive and unfamiliar to most Christians of the mid-nineteenth century, such as his views about the age of the earth. People living in the twenty-first century are mostly used to thinking about the earth as a very old planet. Most of us do not have a ready answer as to its exact age, but at least we have a vague idea that the earth came into existence several billion years ago, that the dinosaurs went extinct a few hundred million years ago, and that we – *Homo sapiens* – have been around for a short time, perhaps 200,000 years or so. If we are asked to explain why we hold these views, we might refer to the fossil record as proof.

This way of thinking and arguing is modern. Until Darwin's time, most people had no idea that the earth was more than a few thousand years old. Without the early development of the

[3] Charles Darwin, *The Descent of Man and Selection in Relation to Sex* (London: John Murray, 1871).

science of geology, Darwin would not have been able to conceive his ideas, which relied on tiny changes over very large stretches of time. Before the early nineteenth century, most Christians believed that it would be possible in principle to count a certain number of generations back and reach Adam and Eve and the beginnings of history. However, during the late eighteenth century, this worldview, and this conception of history, had been challenged by scholars who observed geological strata and made completely new assertions about the age of the earth. In 1795, the Scottish scientist James Hutton published a book called *Theory of the Earth*, in which he argued that the geological strata of the earth proved that it was much older than previously assumed.

This was the origin of what is often called *deep time*. In the course of the nineteenth century, geologists developed Hutton's ideas further, and by the time the end of the century approached, the conception of time and earth's history among the educated classes of the Christian world had been completely transformed by science. A breakthrough was made by Charles Lyell, who published his work *The Principles of Geology* in three volumes between 1830 and 1833. Darwin's life spanned this period of radical change in conceptions of time. He grew up with the Christian tale of creation, but his fascination with natural science put him in touch with some of the eminent scientists of his day, and he soon started questioning the traditional view about the origins of life. Darwin read Lyell's books on geology while traveling around the world on the ship *H.M.S. Beagle* from 1831 to 1836 in order to collect geological data and keep the ship's captain company, and he was convinced that Lyell was right in his assertions about geological change. On this long journey, Darwin collected a lot of data about geology and biology, and many of his observations became important in his formulation of the theory of evolution by natural selection. His observations of rock formations were really inspired by Lyell's view of the earth as undergoing an extremely slow process of change over a very long time, and this perspective of change was fundamental to Darwin's own theory. There simply could not be evolution by natural selection without plenty of time for selection to work, and Darwin insisted that a reader who did not realize that Lyell had been right about the immensity of past ages could not understand the theory of evolution and should not bother reading his own book at all.

Thus, the Christian reactions against Darwin were reactions against the demolition of the traditional ideas about time and the history of the earth, and against the undermining of the special place that humans occupied in this history according to the Christian worldview. The theory that all species, including humans, were always undergoing a slow process of change was hard to swallow not only for the representatives of the church. Charles Lyell, who became Darwin's friend, refused to accept the idea for many years, and Darwin's teacher at the University of Cambridge, Professor of Geology Adam Sedwick, reacted against his pupil's theory because he found it impossible to believe that species would change by the process Darwin suggested. Species had always remained the same, Sedwick wrote in a response to Darwin, and if new species could enter the world, that could only happen through creation. Everything in the natural world proves "design and purpose," Sedwick insisted, and the adaptation of life forms is proof of a "prescient and designing cause."[4] In other words, many of the scientists of Darwin's time were used to thinking of divine creation in nature and found it implausible, or impossible, that species were "created" through evolution.

So if many of the scientists of Darwin's day had problems accepting the new worldview, so did most conservative Christians. However, if one reads the writings of the American Protestants who called themselves fundamentalists and fought to defend

[4] Adam Sedgwick, "Objections to Mr. Darwin's Theory of the Origin of Species," in *Darwin*, ed. Philip Appleman (New York: Norton, 1979), p. 265. (Article originally published in 1860.)

what they saw as the core of Christianity against modernism in the 1910s, it is rather surprising how little most of them have to say about the theory of evolution. Although their writings contain a large number of defensive articles about the evils of higher criticism, as I will explain, only a few of these original fundamentalists address the question of human evolution.

We can take a brief look at two rhetorical attacks on Darwinism and the theory of evolution included in the important collection of essays called *The Fundamentals, a Testimony to Truth.* In a piece called "Decadence of Darwinism" from 1912, the reverend Henry H. Beach attacks the idea of natural selection for the reasons that it is immoral, false, and self-contradictory.[5] Beach demonstrates familiarity with many of the core concepts in the theory of evolution as it was understood in his time and employs the language of science and quotations from scientists, including Darwin, to demonstrate that the theory of evolution is untenable or, at best, uncertain. He rounds up his article with a warning to avoid spreading the "wretched propaganda" of Darwinism in schools.

A more learned and balanced article about evolution was written by George Frederick Wright, professor of geology at Oberlin College, with the title "The Passing of Evolution."[6] Theories of evolution have come and gone throughout the ages, from the ancient Greeks and Egyptians until Darwin, Wright points out, and the present theory will also pass. Wright shows that he knows a lot about the present state of evolutionary theory, and he is able to criticize those who take Darwin's ideas to imply a rejection of religion. Wright's main concern is to show that both life in general and the peculiar characteristics of humans presuppose divine creation. The special status of mankind is Wright's main concern, and he insists that there is nothing in science

[5] Henry H. Beach, "Decadence of Darwinism," in *The Fundamentals, a Testimony to Truth*, ed. A. C. Dixon, L. Meyer, and R. A. Torrey (Chicago: 1909–1915), vol. 4, pp. 59–71.

[6] George Frederick Wright, "The Passing of Evolution," in Dixon, Meyer, and Torrey, *The Fundamentals*, vol. 4, pp. 72–87.

that should make us believe that humans could enter the world "without the intervention of the Supreme Designing Mind."[7]

Intervention is a keyword. The problem with evolution in the study of both history and nature is that it has no room for the intervention of God. Both historical and geological time are emptied of divine intervention. If the history of the Bible and the history of mankind can be explained with references to laws of historical or biological progress, God is marginalized.

A less sophisticated article included in *The Fundamentals* is entitled "Evolutionism in the Pulpit." It was originally published in the magazine *Herald and Presbyter* in 1911, and its anonymous author refers to himself as "an occupant of the pew," thus casting himself as the critical layman. The main criticism in this article is not directed against the scientists who have formulated and defended different aspects of the theory of evolution. It is rather an attack on the Christian ministers who have adopted this "new philosophy" and readily given up large portions of Holy Scripture because they could not be reconciled with Darwin's theory. These Christian ministers defend themselves by saying that the Bible was not intended to teach science. However, this is a half-truth that is more misleading than a lie, as "the evolutionary theory was conceived in agnosticism, and born and nurtured in infidelity," and it is also the backbone of the "destructive higher criticism which has so viciously assailed both the integrity and authority of the Scriptures," the writer laments.[8] The story of creation in Genesis was set aside and the Bible discredited – not by scientists but by Christian ministers. It is not the outspoken scientists who are the gravest threat to morality and religion, according to this writer, but ministers who use the pulpit to propagate materialism. The Christian layman must react against these treacherous thoughts preached from the pulpits in the Christian world and stop the ministers from

[7] Ibid., p. 83.

[8] Anonymous, "Evolutionism in the Pulpit," in Dixon, Meyer, and Torrey, *The Fundamentals*, vol. 4, p. 92.

deliberately sowing seeds of unfaith in the hearts and minds of their hearers.[9]

Here we are at the ideological source of fundamentalism as I described it in earlier chapters, especially in the discussion about religious authority. The laymen attacking liberal Christian ministers during the rise of fundamentalist Protestantism in America in the early twentieth century perceived their own religion as being under attack from modernism and science. The most dangerous attack came not from outside Christianity; it did not arise in atheistic or scientific milieus. It came from liberal Christian ministers propagating modernism from the pulpit. The natural reaction would be to reject the authority of such ministers and start searching for new leaders with sources of religious authority other than formal education and positions in the hierarchy of the churches and denominations. These new leaders, the lay preachers and pastors who are the hallmark of fundamentalism, would be the defenders of true Christianity against the relativizing forces of evolutionary theory as well as against higher criticism.

Today, there is a strong movement of American Christian fundamentalists who claim that the world was in fact created in six days. This is often called six-days creationism, and the origins of this movement can be found in the work of the Creation Research Institute, established by Henry Morris in 1929. The reason why some fundamentalists insist that the world was created in six days is simple: the Old Testament says so. Many Christian fundamentalists believe that the Bible must be understood in a literal sense. When the Bible says six days, it really means six days.

CHRIST OR CRITICISM: THE STRUGGLE WITH THE SCIENCE OF HISTORY

"It is quite foolish to think that the world was created in six days or in a space of time at all," wrote the philosopher Philo

[9] Ibid.

of Alexandria.[10] Philo was a contemporary of Jesus Christ, although there is no reason to believe he knew about the man from Nazareth. Philo was a Jew, well versed in both the Jewish and Hellenic thought of the city of Alexandria. This was the period and the culture where early Christianity was shaped, and Philo would have considerable influence on many of the great figures in the Christian church of later times. In Philo's opinion, it would be a violation of simple logic to think that the words of Scripture really were about the creation of the world in six days. Time is measured by the movement of the sun. It is meaningless to talk about days and nights, or about time in any sense, before the creation of the sun. Time is more recent than the universe. Thus, the universe cannot have been created within a certain span of time. *Six days* in the story of creation means something completely different, Philo asserts. Six is a perfect number, he explains, and in the story of creation *six* refers to all things earthly, in contrast to the number seven, which refers to heavenly things. In other words, Philo employs what we call *allegorical* interpretation of Scripture. The words of Genesis were certainly inspired by God, but they must not be read as simple statements about the creation of the world and its inhabitants. Words have a deeper, hidden meaning, and it is the task of a serious thinker to discover it. So when Genesis tells us that God made Adam sleep and took away one of his ribs to create Eve, the words of Scripture in their literal sense "are of the nature of a myth."[11]

Philo's allegorical interpretation of the Old Testament would become important to many Christian thinkers of later periods, such as the theologians and church leaders Clement and Origen, who lived in the late second and early third centuries AD. Some scholars have seen Philo's imaginative uses of Scripture as the

[10] Philo, *On the Creation. Allegorical Interpretation of Genesis II, III*, English trans. F. H. Colson and G. H. Whitaker (Cambridge, Mass.: Harvard University Press, 1929), vol. 1, p. 147.

[11] Ibid., pp. 238–39.

beginning of a school of interpretation where literal and allegorical senses of the text are clearly distinguished and the latter are often seen to be the more important.[12]

There were a number of ways to read the Bible during medieval, early modern, and modern times in the Christian world. Scripture was seen to have several senses, and much of the energy of medieval monks went into analyzing and discussing the right interpretations of the text. I have spent some time stressing this point here in order to avoid what seems to be a common misunderstanding: it is not the case that Christian theologians had always read the Bible in a literal sense and that this was suddenly challenged by a modern approach to the study of ancient texts like the Bible. On the contrary, it is reasonable to say that the most literalminded of modern fundamentalists have reverted to one very narrow position in their view of the Bible, which should not be considered the dominant Christian position in premodern times.

During the Middle Ages, it was common to see in the Bible both a literal and a spiritual meaning, and the task of the interpreter of the text was to say something important and meaningful about both levels of meaning.[13] The literal meaning is simple to understand for modern readers. It meant that words signified things. The word "fish" signifies a certain type of creature that lives in water. The spiritual sense of the text was that in which the things in the text in turn signified other things. The word "fish" signifies the creature in water, but the fish itself can signify other things, and perhaps more than one thing. Such spiritual senses of Scripture are probably more difficult to understand

[12] Beryl Smalley, *The Study of the Bible in the Middle Ages* (Oxford: Blackwell, 1952).

[13] Joseph W. Goering, "An Introduction to Medieval Christian Biblical Interpretation," in *With Reverence for the Word – Medieval Scriptural Exegesis in Judaism, Christianity and Islam*, ed. Jane Dammen MacAuliffe, Barry D. Walfish, and Joseph W. Goering (Oxford: Oxford University Press, 2003), pp. 199–200.

for modern people because we are not used to this way of reading. We often see literal meaning as the only legitimate sense of a text. There took place an important shift away from spiritual readings of the Bible around 1300. In the 1320s, the English theologian William of Ockham attacked the pope's uses of allegory to interpret the Bible in his own favor in arguments about politics.[14] Ockham did not deny the usefulness of these kinds of interpretations in the spiritual striving of Christians, but insisted that they could not be valid in difficult arguments over important matters. Thus, he was part of a trend in Christian theology that would place more emphasis on literalism.

With the revolution in the study of ancient texts that developed from the Renaissance and Reformation, in the philological work of figures such as Erasmus of Rotterdam, the views on the status of the Bible entered a process of change that would end in what is sometimes called the "historical-critical method," the modern, scientific approach to historical texts. Christian fundamentalism started as an intellectual crusade against the historical-critical method applied to the Bible, but our brief look at the complexities of biblical interpretation in premodern times shows that fundamentalists are *not* going back to a more authentic Christian way of reading the Bible.

The historical-critical method applied to the study of the Bible matured in the eighteenth and nineteenth centuries in universities in the Western world. Germany was a leading nation in the development of historical research, and the Germans led the way in the critical study of the Bible. The German professor Albert Eichhorn (1752–1827) was a famous representative of the modern, academic approach to the Bible. If one reads the numerous critical articles by fundamentalists attacking the relativization of biblical authority by modern historians, Eichhorn

[14] A. J. Minnis, "Material Swords and Literal Lights – the Status of Allegory in William of Ockham's Breviloquium on Papal Power," in Dammen MacAuliffe, Walfish, and Goering, *With Reverence for the Word*, pp. 292–308.

is often among the main suspects. Eichhorn wrote a study of the Lord's supper in the New Testament where he considered aspects of the historical context of the text. He insisted that theology and doctrine could not be understood unless one looked into their historical origins, their development, and the environment in which they came to have meaning for believers. With this approach, he contributed to the founding of the academic discipline of the history of religions, which was divorced from the old academic tradition of theology because of its insistence on "bracketing" questions about truth or falsehood and taking the outsider's perspective on all manifestations of religion, including Christianity.

What is so horrible about this approach in the eyes of fundamentalists? Scholars working from the assumptions of the historical-critical method typically assume that miracles should be understood as expressions of superstition, or simply as human interpretations of natural events. They also challenge the Bible's own views concerning the authorship of the books in the Old Testament, claiming that Moses could not possibly be the author of the Pentateuch. In several of the first five books of the Old Testament, the text tells us that Moses wrote down the words of the Lord. The critical scholar, however, insists that the different sections of the books of the Pentateuch, including the Mosaic laws, were written down much later than the time of Moses, if he ever lived, and were composed by a number of different authors. When the modern scholar rejects the authorship of Moses, he or she necessarily rejects the authority of the Bible itself. Christian fundamentalists of the early 1900s saw this academic rejection of the absolute authority of the Bible as a grave threat to the faith.

If we take a look at the articles found in *The Fundamentals*, one is struck by the great concern with the status of the Bible. Almost one-third of all the articles in this collection were concerned with Scripture, and the most popular subject was the status of the Pentateuch.[15] "The effects of historical-critical Bible research are very serious," wrote Sir Robert Anderson in 1910 in an article called "Christ and Criticism."[16] Higher criticism has dethroned the Bible in the home, Anderson wrote, and as a result the old practice of family worship is dying out. Christians now had to take a stand, the author asserted. There was a choice between Christ and criticism. The historical-critical approach to the Bible was undermining Christianity, and it was spreading through modern Christian culture. More and more Christians abandoned the fundamental truths of their religion and embraced a vague and relativistic worldview in which the certainties of dogma had to yield to the modern culture of critical science, liberalism, and humanism.

Higher criticism was the name normally given to historical-critical research about the Bible and the history of Christianity by fundamentalist Christians. In order to understand the origins of American fundamentalism, we need to look into the arguments that the fundamentalist Christians of the period 1900–1920 had with this tradition of research and its approach to the Bible. For an overview, I believe we can reduce the quarrel to two main points.

First, the rejection of the history and authorship of the Bible as described in the Bible itself is an obvious challenge to Scripture. If the Bible says that Moses wrote the laws, there is nothing to argue about from the fundamentalist point of view. If the Bible says that Jesus performed a miracle, it is a grave error to explain the event as something else. It is typical of the arguments of the defenders of Christian fundamentals when Sir Robert Anderson ends his article "Christ and Criticism" by saying that he himself

[15] Mark A. Noll, *Between Faith and Criticism: Evangelicals, Scholarship and the Bible in America,* 2nd edition (Vancouver: Regent College Publishing, 2004), pp. 39–40.

[16] Robert Anderson, "Christ and Criticism," in Dixon, Meyer, and Torrey, *The Fundamentals,* vol. 1, p. 126.

is in fact not a champion of rigid orthodoxy and welcomes a full and free criticism of Holy Scripture with only one limitation: that the words of Lord Jesus Christ "shall be deemed a bar to criticism and an 'end of controversy.'"[17] When the New Testament records Jesus as saying something about a subject, that must be the end of all discussion. The contradiction of scripture is obviously a problem for people who take the words of their holy book in a literal sense and insist that they are the words of God.

However, a second point is even more important, I believe, and a bit harder to understand. It is about conceptions of time and history. *Evolution* is one of the keywords for understanding culture in the second half of the nineteenth century. Most books about fundamentalism observe that fundamentalists have a problem with the theory of evolution by natural selection as an explanation of the origin of species in the natural world, including *Homo sapiens.* Evolution as a biological concept has been a main target for attacks from both Christian and Muslim fundamentalists. What is often overlooked is the very close link between conceptions of evolution in the natural world and in the world of religion and culture.

Most accounts of fundamentalism treat historical-critical research in the humanities and research on evolution in the natural world as two separate challenges to fundamentalist Christians. They may seem to constitute two separate attacks on the Christian worldview of the nineteenth and twentieth centuries because higher criticism arose earlier than Darwin and because the two research traditions developed in two very different academic communities. Higher criticism originated in Germany in the early 1800s, whereas biological evolution was the revolutionary idea of Charles Darwin first espoused publicly in 1859. However, fundamentalist attacks on higher criticism and its treatment of the Bible are in reality attacks on ideas of evolution applied to religion and culture. Many Christian

[17] Ibid., p. 126.

fundamentalists speaking and writing at the beginning of the twentieth century saw evolution as the theoretical foundation of modern biblical scholarship that questioned the truths of Scripture.

Evolution is the background to the entire picture that biblical scholars want people to believe, wrote Franklin Johnson, one of the lesser-known authors included in *The Fundamentals.* He asserted that an important fallacy of higher criticism was "its dependence on the theory of evolution as the explanation of the history of literature and of religion. [...] The Spencerian philosophy of evolution, aided and reinforced by Darwinism, has added greatly to the confidence of the higher critics."[18] There would be no higher criticism without the underpinnings of the theory of evolution, Johnson argues, but the theory of evolution is a fallacy when applied to the history of religion. It leaves us unable to account for Homer or Shakespeare, as well as Moses and Christ.

Franklin Johnson refers to *Spencerian evolution,* a theory of evolution proposed by Herbert Spencer (1820–1903). Spencer was among the most influential academic writers in the last decades of the nineteenth century, and he coined the notorious term *survival of the fittest* to describe the processes that drive progress in the natural and social worlds. Spencer believed that universal laws meant that everything developed from less complex to more complex forms. This was true, in his view, about plants and animals, as well as human societies and institutions. According to such general ideas about evolution, a world religion such as Christianity had to develop through history into more complex and differentiated stages, and the task of the scholar would be to uncover and understand this development. Spencer's ideas about evolution had little to do with Darwin's theory of evolution by natural selection, but in the general culture of Europe

[18] Franklin Johnson, "The Fallacies of the Higher Criticism," in Dixon, Meyer, and Torrey, *The Fundamentals,* vol. 1, p. 61.

and America from the 1860s onward the different concepts of evolution shaped much of the thinking about how to analyze religion.

The most famous exponent of a theory of evolution in the study of religion was Friedrich Max Müller (1823–1900), professor of comparative theology at the University of Oxford and editor of the popular series *Sacred Books of the East*, translations of important religious works from Oriental cultures. Müller stated: "I certainly am and mean to remain an evolutionist in the study of language, mythology and religion – that is to say, I shall always try to discover in them intelligible historical growth."[19] This was a very common approach to religion around the turn of the century and informed much of the academic debate both in the humanities and the social sciences.

Fundamentalists reacted strongly against this approach. An article by a learned evangelical Christian, Professor William Henry Griffith Thomas (1861–1924), attacking higher criticism, shows why evolution was perhaps more difficult to stomach in the realm of history and philology than in the study of the natural world. Griffith Thomas wrote: "The great law of the universe, including the physical, mental, and moral realms, is said to be evolution, and though this doubtless presupposes an original Creator, it does not, on the theory before us, permit any subsequent direct intervention of God during the process of development."[20] Thus, Griffith Thomas pointed out, a theory of evolution applied to the study of a historical subject, like the affairs of the people of Israel, "tends to minimize divine intervention."[21] Griffith Thomas was a noted Evangelical writer and speaker and taught theology first in Oxford and later in Toronto. He was also a cofounder of the Evangelical Theological

[19] F. Max Müller, *Natural Religion: The Gifford Lectures* (London: Longmans, Green, & Co., 1892), p. 143.

[20] W. H. Griffith Thomas, "Old Testament Criticism and New Testament Christianity," in Dixon, Meyer, and Torrey, *The Fundamentals*, vol. 1, p. 136.

[21] Ibid., p. 137.

Seminary in 1924, which would become Dallas Theological Seminary and today teaches biblical inerrancy and dispensationalist and premillennialist theology.

There are important conservative Christian thinkers who try to bridge the gap between evolution and biblical inerrancy, but they all insist that any viable conception of evolution must leave room for divine intervention. B. B. Warfield made very important contributions to the modern Christian fundamentalist idea of biblical literalism, but at the same time he believed that evolution might be a useful key to understanding changes in the world after the initial act of divine creation. However, he was careful to note that even if one accepts evolution, there must be room for divine providence and the occasional supernatural interference.[22]

So, in the minds of Christian fundamentalists, the problem with evolution in the study of sacred Scripture and the history of Christianity is that it closes off these realms from the intervention of God. Evolutionary thinking applied to the history of religions and the history of Holy Scripture denies God a role in the affairs of humans. An evolutionary view of the history of sacred Scripture leads people toward a diffuse kind of religion with a distant God who lacks the will or power to intervene. The same problem arises with the theory of evolution applied to the origins of humans as a biological species. If humans have developed over long periods through natural mechanisms only, God is denied any role in the appearance of humans on the stage of history. In conclusion, evolution throws God out of the equation, whether we want to explain the origins of humans, of the Bible, or of Christian doctrine. This is why the concept of evolution was and still is a threat to conservative believers in the realms of both history and biology.

[22] David N. Livingstone and Mark A. Noll, "B.B. Warfield (1851–1921) – Biblical Inerrantist as Evolutionist," *Isis* 91, no. 2 (June 2000): 283–304; see especially p. 296.

ISLAM AND CREATIONISM

There is no one simple Muslim fundamentalist position on the question of the relationship of religion to science, but one recurring issue has been the search for ways to demonstrate how Islam encompasses modern scientific truths.

A main contention in Part I of this book, especially Chapter 3, was that fundamentalism is a movement mainly driven by laypeople under circumstances where traditional religious elites are seen to be impotent in the struggle to adjust religion to the modern world. Quite a few of the lay Muslims (I am still using this expression with the reservations mentioned in Chapter 3) who are concerned with the relationship between Islam and modern science are scientists themselves. A common assertion is that modern science is positive in the sense that it offers effective ways to meet practical problems but that science also carries with it a worldview that is deeply problematic. This worldview is fragmented because science insists on analyzing all problems in their smallest units. (Indeed, the Greek word "analysis" means breaking something into smaller units.) A basic concept in Islamic theology is *tawhid*, which means *oneness* and is a description of the nature of God. Taking this oneness as their point of departure, many fundamentalists would assert that Muslim scientists should feel a responsibility to work against the fragmentation of the modern worldview by contributing to an Islamization of science.

Darwin's theory of evolution was part of a rapid development in the sciences in the mid-nineteenth century, and it is part of that general movement that I called "modernism" in Chapter 1. This movement was introduced in many parts of the world through the channels and networks of globalization created by colonialism. We need to keep in mind the context created by colonialism if we want to understand reactions to European and American science in the leading nations of Africa and Asia. This was a main argument in Chapter 2, where I argued that we should see fundamentalism as parallel reactions in all the world religions against global forces of differentiation. British officials and military men expanding and consolidating the British Empire in the nineteenth and early twentieth centuries were accompanied by scientists, and science was an integrated part of the colonizing and modernizing project of empire. Nations that were not colonized – such as Turkey, Thailand, or Japan – rapidly understood the importance of adopting Western scientific methods in order to strengthen national self-determination through economic and military progress. Therefore, many of the reactions for or against aspects of science in Asia and Africa must be understood not as neutral responses to purely academic ideas but at least partly as attempts to reassert cultural self-confidence and pride.

How did Muslims react to the theory of evolution? Just as we need to understand reactions against evolution in rural Tennessee in the context of the struggle between a modernizing state and traditional culture, we need to understand reactions for or against evolutionary theory in the Muslim world against its broader political background. A fundamental aspect of this background was the expansion of European colonialism and rapid modernization, which included the novel application of science in many spheres.

Sayyid Ahmad Khan was perhaps the most prominent representative of modernist South Asian Islam in Darwin's time. Khan was typical of the progressive Muslim leaders because he believed that Muslims needed to work hard to integrate their own cultures with modern values and practices brought by the British. Khan was concerned first of all with education and thought that educational reforms were the key to socially uplifting the Muslim population in British India (which also comprised today's Pakistan and Bangladesh). In order to promote education among Muslims, he founded Aligarh College, one of the most important Islamic centers of learning in South Asia.

Sayyid Ahmad Khan took a very positive stance toward modern science, to the extent that he advocated allegorical reading of the Qur'an in cases where the sacred text could not be aligned with science.[23] In several tracts and articles appearing in the last decade of the nineteenth century, Khan wanted to demonstrate how the Qur'an, if interpreted correctly, could be reconciled with modern biological and geological theories. Using Qur'anic verses as the point of departure, he discussed the development of species from common ancestors, the concept of the survival of the fittest, and the geological theories of the age of the earth. Science had to be reconciled with Islam, and the best way to do this was to show Muslims how modern science was really implied in the holy book from the start.

A number of other modernist Muslims of the South Asian continent took similar approaches to the reconciliation between science and religion, reason and belief. I cannot discuss all of them in detail, but mention should be made of one key figure in the shaping of modern Islam during the nineteenth century: Jamal ad-din al-Afghani. In a text called *The Truth about the Neicheri Sect and an Explanation of the Neicheris*, published in 1880–81, al-Afghani attacked the philosophical position of what he calls the *neicheris*. The term *neicheri* referred to naturalism and materialism. The reason for writing a book criticizing naturalist views was that the word *neicheri* and the naturalist perspective on the world were spreading rapidly to every corner of British India at this time, according to al-Afghani. Naturalism was a position in philosophy that had been around a long time, al-Afghani explained, and he traced it back to Greek philosophy and in particular to Democritus.

In modern times, it was mainly Charles Darwin that had caused the new fashion, al-Afghani asserted: "He wrote a book stating that man descends from the monkey, and that in the

[23] Martin Riexinger, "Reactions of South Asian Muslims to the Theory of Evolution," unpublished manuscript.

course of successive centuries as a result of external impulses he changed until he reached the stage of the orangutan."[24] Al-Afghani continued his exposition of Darwin's theory in long passages stating how the followers of Darwin saw Caucasian man as the highest stage of development. His treatment of Darwin's work was a caricature and no more balanced than that of the most ardent Christian critic. The imperfect resemblance of man and monkey had cast the unfortunate Darwin into the desert of fantasy, al-Afghani insisted.[25]

Most of al-Afghani's pamphlet about the *neicheris,* however, is not concerned with the details of Darwinian naturalism but is rather a discussion of the social consequences of the materialist view of the world. Al-Afghani asserted that religion in different forms had served a vital function in all human societies by upholding social virtues such as honor, shame, trustworthiness, and truthfulness. Such virtues are vital for societies and cultures to survive, he wrote, and the materialists destroy the foundations for healthy societies by undermining religious beliefs. These virtues are linked to religious beliefs about man holding a special position in the cosmos and to the assumption that humans have the capacity for attaining the perfection that will transfer him to a better world, to heaven. The *neicheris* have destroyed several great civilizations before, al-Afghani explained, and now they are about to destroy both the West and Islam. In modern times, the *neicheris* have often called themselves by other names, such as socialists, communists, or nihilists, but the godless philosophy leads to destruction all the same.

Sayyid Ahmad Khan and al-Afghani were both modern Muslim thinkers, although they parted ways on certain questions. They worked hard to find strategies to reconcile Islam with science, and sometimes they ended up asserting that science was quite all

[24] Al-Afghani quoted in Nikki R. Keddie, *An Islamic Response to Imperialism: Political and Religious Writings of Sayyid Jamal ad-Din "al-Afghani"* (Berkeley: University of California Press, 1983), p. 135.

[25] Quoted in ibid., p. 136.

right because it was in fact contained or implied in the Qur'an. This was a strategy of cultural self-assertion in the face of imperialism. On the other hand, there were large sections of the older Muslim elites that were very hostile to science and tended to reject all ideas that were not obviously in line with a traditional understanding of Islam. The *ulama*, the traditionally educated "priestly" class, had little patience with modern science, and this was one reason for their gradually decreasing relevance in Islamic societies in modern times.

But what about the fundamentalists? In the 1940s, Maulana Maududi wrote that the theory of evolution was in conflict with Islam's belief in a creator God. He dismissed suggestions by modernist Muslims that the Qur'anic story of the creation of Adam from clay could be read allegorically as evolution from simpler forms of matter to complex life forms. This was in line with his modern position on how to read Holy Scripture. He made it clear in the introduction to his own translation and commentary on the Qur'an that he did not intend to offer a new, literal translation for people well versed in classical Arabic but rather that his aim was "an explanatory or interpretative exposition, rather than a literal translation."[26] In his commentary on Sura 3:7 about the distinction between the clear and the ambiguous verses of the Qur'an, Maududi expressed his wish to keep things simple for the lay Muslim and explained why it is important that Muslims should refrain from trying to understand the ambiguous verses. The clear and simple sections of the Qur'an are those that deal with how the good Muslim should live his or her life, Maududi explained, and these are really the only verses that the believer needs. The difficult verses deal with deeper things that cannot be expressed clearly in words. The person who seeks truth will be satisfied with the obvious meaning of the unambiguous verses, and wherever he finds complications and

[26] Sayyid Abul A'la Maududi, *Towards Understanding the Quran*, Volume 1: *Surahs 1–3*, trans. and ed. Z. I. Ansari (London: Islamic Foundation, 1988), p. 4.

ambiguities he abstains from pursuing their solution and avoids wasting time splitting hairs, Maududi asserts.[27]

From such a literalist approach to the story of creation in the Qur'an, it was clear that evolutionary theory had to be discarded, but to the fundamentalist Maududi there were more arguments against Darwinism, in particular the argument from design. When one observes living organisms, one cannot avoid the conclusion that their characteristics are the result of conscious design, he said. In order to demonstrate this, Maududi used a parable. He asked his readers to think of a professor from Mars visiting the earth with his students. The only problem with the Martians is that they cannot see human beings. Thus, they observe vehicles moving about and they see new and more advanced vehicles being produced in factories. Should they assume some conscious designer behind the origin of the vehicles, or should they start speculating about a hidden force of nature driving the development?[28]

Maududi's rejection of evolution as fundamentally opposed to Islamic views has been crucial to Muslim fundamentalists' attitudes. However, for Maududi, the greatest problem with the theory of evolution was not its conflict with theology but rather its social and political consequences. Evolutionary thought equaled materialism, he asserted, and materialism caused humans to see themselves as unfettered by religious and moral constraints and to treat each other in terrible ways. Darwinism and materialism placed humanity in the center of the universe and resulted in moral decay and political catastrophe, Maududi wrote. The same view is championed by organized Islamic antievolutionism today.

Although the theory of evolution was debated among Muslim intellectuals almost from the time Darwin published *Origin of Species* in 1859, it was much later that antievolutionism became

[27] Ibid., p. 238.

[28] Riexinger, "Reactions of South Asian Muslims to the Theory of Evolution."

an organized movement in the Muslim world. This process started in Turkey in the 1980s, when several works by American Protestant creationists were translated into Turkish.[29] Soon, anti-evolutionism got a foothold in the educational system in Turkey, and the theory of evolution was in certain periods banned as a subject in primary and secondary schools. The reason was that the theory of evolution was seen by some to be closely linked to other materialist systems of thought, such as communism and secularism. There is a certain irony here, as Turkey has been a strongly secularist state since its founding in the 1920s, although much of Turkish society is still Muslim. In the eyes of Turkish creationists, however, the materialism they find in evolutionary theory is deeply problematic because it contradicts the vaguely religious and ethical basis for Turkish nationalism. Materialism can be seen as an ally of anti-Turkish forces, such as the Marxist Kurdish separatist movement, the PKK.

The most important thinker among these Turkish Muslim antievolutionists is Adnan Oktar, who writes under the pseudonym Harun Yahya. Yahya has published a very large number of books in Turkish, and many of these have been translated into English and other languages. His main idea is to refute evolutionary theory and prove that the world and all life forms must have been created by God. In one book, called *Design in Nature*, he goes through a number of phenomena, such as the flight of insects and birds, to demonstrate how the natural world is full of what he calls "irreducible complexity," complex organs that cannot possibly come into existence step by step because the different parts of the organ are of no benefit to the organism carrying it.[30] Such biological systems "demolish Darwin's theory," he insists. The harshest attacks on evolutionary theory are launched in books with titles such as *The Evolution Deceit* and *The Disasters*

[29] Martin Riexinger, "The Islamic Creationism of Harun Yahya," *International Institute for the Study of Islam in the Modern World Newsletter* (December 2002): pp. 5–6.

[30] Harun Yahya, *Design in Nature* (London: Ta-Ha Publishers, 2002).

Darwinism Brought to Humanity. Here the main argument is not only that evolutionary theory is wrong but that the theory has been the foundation for all the violent ideologies of modernity. According to Yahya, the totalitarian ideologies and practices of Nazism, fascism, racism, imperialism, and communism were all really Darwin's ideas put into practice. Apologists who insist on separating the theory of evolution from the ideology of social Darwinism are simply naive, Yahya insists.

Yahya is also founder of an organization called the Science Research Endowment, which is active in antievolution campaigns targeted at key institutions and persons in Turkish society. One of Yahya's goals is to demonstrate that modern evolutionary theory is incorrect and builds on forged evidence. Like Christian antievolutionists, he uses a number of archaeological and paleontological arguments to show where modern biology got it all wrong. Yahya and his movement are clearly inspired by Protestant creationism, and the contacts between the Christian and Muslim creationists seem to grow. In the late 1990s, the Science Research Endowment began holding large conferences in Turkey where they invited important creationists from Christian fundamentalist milieus in the United States.[31] On certain points, however, there are notable differences. Yahya and Muslim creationism seem to tolerate the idea of deep time that has troubled many Christian creationists, and young earth creationism has not caught on among Turkish antievolutionists. This is because the story of creation in the Qur'an is slightly different from the one found in the Old Testament and does not easily support ideas of a young earth.

At the beginning of the twenty-first century, the struggle between antievolutionists and science-friendly modernists seemed to harden in several Islamic societies, most notably Turkey. Harun Yahya is fighting what he perceives as a global conspiracy hatched by a mafia consisting of scientific communities

[31] Riexinger, "The Islamic Creationism of Harun Yahya."

in universities, scientific journals, and big scientific organizations promoting mainstream biology. The goal of such a materialist conspiracy is to weaken the nations of the world by undermining their moral and religious foundations. On this point, Yahya has something in common with both the modernist al-Afghani and the fundamentalist Maududi. It is difficult to say how important the issue of evolution will become to Muslim fundamentalists, but it is quite possible that it will become far more central to their rejection of modernism than it has been so far. One reason is that many Muslim societies only quite recently have been able to implement systems of mass education to expose ever-larger sections of the population to the worldview of modern science. If we look at some recent statistics from big Islamic countries, it is evident that evolution is not seen to be easily reconcilable with religion.[32] Perhaps we will see stronger claims to build science on Islamic foundations in countries such as Pakistan, Egypt, and Turkey in the coming years.

ANCIENT HINDUISM AND MODERN SCIENCE

One day in 1898, Swami Vivekananda visited the zoological gardens in his hometown of Calcutta together with a small group of friends and followers. They stopped in front of a cage containing a python snake. Somebody mentioned how the tortoise had developed from the snake, and the conversation shifted to the subject of biological evolution. The group sat down for some tea and cakes, and one of Vivekananda's admirers asked the Swami what he thought about Darwin's theory of evolution. Vivekananda thought for a second. Darwin was certainly correct, the Hindu leader replied, but that does not necessarily mean his answer offered a complete explanation for everything in the biological world. Vivekananda briefly reminded the group about

[32] Salman Hameed, "Bracing for Islamic Creationism," *Science* 322, no. 5908 (2008): 1637–38.

the fundamentals of Darwin's theory according to which change and development in nature arise from "the struggle for existence, survival of the fittest, natural selection, and so forth."[33] These principles explain how most individuals in a population of animals will die and only a few will survive, he continued, and they lead to the development of new animal species. However, Darwin's theory is not sufficient to explain development among humans, he said. Mankind develops not through physical competition and destruction but rather through conscious development of the spirit and the rational faculties, the Swami asserted. In these matters, the ancient Hindu philosophers had in fact given a better and more comprehensible explanation than Darwin. In fact, Vivekananda insisted, the Hindu seers who wrote down the Vedas in ancient times, and the later Hindu philosophers who followed them, had long ago given the most complete explanation for development and change both in nature and in human history.

Vivekananda belonged to that crucial period of rapid globalization in the late nineteenth century when the different nations became increasingly aware of each other. It was a period of dramatic changes in national consciousness and identity for many people. Leaders like Vivekananda laid the foundation for new ways of talking and writing about global concerns. Science, with its worldview, its practices, and its discoveries, was a field, a function system, that spread through the channels of globalization established by new modes of communication across the continents. Science shone in the eyes of late nineteenth-century Indians like a thousand bright suns, Vivekananda wrote. He was well read in popular science. Evolution and other recent theories and discoveries were the subject of several of his talks and essays. The Swami always discussed these matters as part of a

[33] The conversation is recorded in Swami Vivekananda, *The Complete Works of Swami Vivekananda* (Calcutta: Advaita Ashrama, 1992), vol. 7, p. 154. (All references to Vivekananda's work will be to the same edition.)

larger debate concerning the relationship between the "East and the West."

To Vivekananda, the East and the West were two fundamentally different cultures. The East had spirituality and religious insight, and the West had science and technology. Both cultures were necessary, and the problems facing mankind were often explained by too much emphasis on one and a lack of competence in the other. This rather simplistic idea about East and West and their essential traits arose in communication between Western and Asian leaders, and Vivekananda would not have been able to formulate his ideas if he were not part of a globalized debate about the nature of the world's cultures and religions. In this debate, science was never presented as a threat to the Hindu worldview because, as Vivekananda and many others insisted, Western science was encompassed by ancient Hindu philosophy. Modern scientific insights could be found in ancient Hindu texts, and the Western world was simply repeating many of the discoveries made in India two or three millennia earlier. It was a positive sign that the Christian world was finally able to allow scientists to think freely, according to Vivekananda. If Christianity still dominated Europe, Charles Darwin would have been burned by the Inquisition, he wrote.[34]

Swami Vivekananda's intellectual attempt to encompass modern science in his vision of Hinduism was a struggle to improve self-confidence among Hindus and create a new foundation for a modern Hindu identity. Later Hindu writers taking their cue from Vivekananda have produced large numbers of books that aim to prove how the ancient Indian scientific tradition contained and encompassed modern scientific knowledge. Many of these books also claim that the only way to realize personal and social harmony is to return to ancient truths and abandon the artificial boundaries between religion and science. These books have names such as *India's Glorious Scientific Tradition,*

[34] Ibid., vol. 5, p. 533.

Modern Science in the Vedas, *The Algebra of Vedic Science*, and *Human Devolution: A Vedic Alternative to Darwin's Theory*. Most of the books are in Hindi and are published for an Indian audience by local publishing houses.

For instance, one book, by Om Prakash Pande, a professor of Sanskrit in Allahabad, explains how different terms and concepts of Vedic literature refer to scientific facts that have been discovered only recently by modern science.[35] For instance, Pande explains how the goddess Durga, worshiped by Hindus as Shakti, which means "power" in Sanskrit, has nine forms that correspond to the nine forms of energy known to modern physics, and he explains how references in the great Hindu epic the Mahabharata are evidence of advanced cloning technology in ancient India. Similar claims are made about most areas of modern science; the ancient Hindu texts knew everything two or three millennia back, and the way toward resurgence and strength for the Hindus starts with the realization of this heritage.

This modern Hindu worldview would perhaps be seen as just eccentric were it not for the fact that it is shared by powerful politicians in India today. In Chapter 5, I related how it came about that a Hindu fundamentalist and nationalist organization called the Rashtriya Swayamsevak Sangh (RSS) managed to put their leaders and ideologues into government through the Bharatiya Janata Party (BJP) in the late 1990s and early 2000s. The RSS are fundamentalists in the sense that they want to create an organic Hindu culture where religion infuses all spheres of life from the life of the individual, through community activities in villages and towns, to the policies of the state of India. They are critical of secularist policies of the Congress Party and what they see as the state's preferential treatment of minorities.

When in power, the BJP embarked on a policy of de-differentiation of key sectors, and to the Hindu fundamentalists

[35] Om Prakash Pande, *Drashtavya jagat ka yathartha* (New Delhi: Prabhat Prakashan, 2005), vols. 1 and 2.

science was an important sphere for the infusion of Hindu religion and culture. The Hinduization of science in India under the BJP government started as soon as their coalition (the NDA) had occupied the government offices in Delhi. The man chosen for the task was Murli Manohar Joshi, a senior figure in the fundamentalist milieu of the RSS and the BJP. Joshi has strong Hindu fundamentalist credentials and has for a long time been the most important Hindu fundamentalist thinker in the sphere of science. He is a long-time member of the RSS and was one of the leaders who were arrested by Indira Gandhi during the period of emergency in 1975–77. Joshi, like many RSS ideologues, was deeply influenced by the writer and thinker Deendayal Upadhyay (1916–1968). As we saw in Chapter 5, Deendayal was one of the key figures in the Bharatiya Jana Sangh and argued for a completely new approach to science and education that would get rid of India's dependence on Western concepts and return to an integral view of the person and society. However, on top of all this, Joshi had a scientific background, with a PhD in physics from a recognized Indian university and a career as a university teacher. Through his ministership at the Ministry of Human Resource Development (HRD), Joshi had great power to change the course of Indian policy concerning science. The HRD is divided into the Department of School Education and Literacy and the Department of Higher Education. The Department of Higher Education oversees the country's universities and scientific councils and controls much of the funding, and under Joshi there was a marked change of policy, with the aim of making scientific departments and higher education more Hindu.

THE SCIENTIFIC RELIGION OF THE BUDDHA

Buddhism in its various local manifestations in Asia in premodern times was no more or less scientific than other religious traditions. Throughout its long history, Buddhism has incorporated numerous magical practices, superstitions about gods, spirits, and demons, and nonscientific assumptions about the workings of the universe, but in modern times Western and Asian intellectuals and leaders have created a conception of Buddhism as a scientific religion. This development started in the late nineteenth century and was part of the processes of modernization and globalization that I discussed in Part I.

In 1893, at the important World Parliament of Religions in Chicago, Anagarika Dharmapala presented Buddhism as the scientific alternative to Christianity. This was a period when there was considerable concern in the United States about how to reconcile Christian doctrines with new scientific perspectives on the natural world and history, and it was an opportune time to launch a "scientific religion." To bring home the message of Buddhism's scientific nature, Dharmapala picked a few central concepts from Buddhist philosophy and from modern science and discussed how they were interrelated. The American audience was told how the fashionable scientific concept of evolution and the concept of cause and effect had almost exact equivalents in Buddhist thought and how this convergence of modern science with Buddhism confirmed the scientific nature of the religion represented by Dharmapala.

Evolution was simply another word for the Buddhist concept of *pratityasamutpada*, Dharmapala insisted. *Pratityasamutpada*, often translated as "dependent origination," is an important idea in Buddhist philosophy. It describes how the psychological and physical elements that make up a living being give rise to each other as cause and effect in a neverending chain. *Pratityasamutpada* shows how existence, which according to Buddhism is suffering, is a process that keeps perpetuating itself unless one actively works to stop it. In the same way, the scientific concept of law and effect was contained in the ancient Buddhist doctrine of *karma*, according to which any action, including thoughts, has necessary consequences either in this life or the next. Dharmapala would typically address his Western audiences by saying: "The Buddha taught [...] a scientific religion containing the highest individualistic, altruistic ethics [...] and a cosmology which is in harmony with geology, astronomy, radio-activity and reality."[36]

By showing how Charles Darwin's ideas, and other ideas of modern science, were part of ancient Buddhist teachings, Dharmapala implied that Buddhism both preceded and surpassed Western intellectual traditions, especially Christianity, which was generally seen as a dated collection of superstitious beliefs both by Buddhists and by many modernist Westerners. This attack on the foundations of Christian doctrine was part of those currents of thought that gave rise to the formidable defensive reaction by American fundamentalists beginning at the turn of the twentieth century. Dharmapala was not alone in the attack on Christianity and the defense of Buddhism's scientific status. A number of Buddhist leaders participated eagerly in the assault on Christian culture mounted by secularist Americans and Europeans. Several important Japanese Buddhist leaders entered a new global discourse about religion and science.

This global discourse about the status of science relative to the world religions of Christianity and Buddhism became possible during the decades leading up to the turn of the twentieth century because of accelerating globalization and increased communication. All continents were being connected by telegraph lines, there was a rapid expansion of newspapers and other popular publications, and English was becoming a global language used by intellectual elites across the world. This was one of the most intense periods of globalization in the history of the world, and the new networks and new global debates profoundly shaped people's conception of the religious traditions of the world. In Part I, I used terms such as *the objectification of religion* to hint at some of the conceptual transformations.

[36] Dharmapala in a lecture in New York in 1893, quoted in David L. McMahan, "Modernity and the Early Discourse on Scientific Buddhism," *Journal of the American Academy of Religion* 72, no. 4 (2004): 897–933 at p. 904.

Paul Carus was among the most important Western supporters of Buddhism at the time. He was a German immigrant to the United States and once a devout Christian, but he had experienced a personal religious crisis as a consequence of the incompatibility of contemporary science and Christian doctrine. As a result, he spent much of his life looking for a new and scientific religion, or a Religion of Science as he called it, and he thought he saw the core of such a system when he heard Dharmapala and other Buddhist leaders at the World Parliament in Chicago in 1893. He started learning about Buddhism from the orientalist scholarship that was being published at the time, and he wrote an enormous amount of articles and books in which he tried to place Buddhism firmly in the context of the modern world. Carus's books were widely circulated in Asia, and he was a key contributor to the formation of a global discourse about scientific Buddhism.

Carus may be said to have represented a crisis in the religious worldviews of quite a few Americans and Europeans produced by the exceptional self-confidence enjoyed by science starting in the last decades of the nineteenth century. Dharmapala clearly represented a crisis in the worldview and culture of a great number of Asian Buddhists produced by colonial subjugation or self-imposed modernization. In the last decade of the nineteenth century, these groups started a global dialogue about the relationship of Christianity and Buddhism to science and modernity. The dialogue has continued up to today and still follows at least some of the original questions, although many new issues have been brought up. For instance, there are scholars and research programs devoted to the study of Buddhist meditation practices and their effects on the human brain and body that apply recent medical technologies. A different expression of the same impulses may be seen in several of the modern Asian Buddhist sects started by laypeople claiming that their version of Buddhism is not only scientific but more scientific than science itself. Leaders of the Japanese Buddhist sect Soka Gakkai make claims to this effect.

It is obvious, then, that the motivation of people espousing scientific Buddhism from the late nineteenth century to today are different from those of Christian fundamentalists who attack elements of science. Christian fundamentalists reject the theory of evolution because it collides with religious doctrine, whereas the aim of scientific Buddhism is partly adaptation to modernity and partly defense of Buddhist culture. Modern critical scholarship applied to sacred scripture is far less of a problem for conservative Buddhists than for Christians. When one reads the papers of an early Buddhist fundamentalist such as Anagarika Dharmapala, one is struck by his concern with formulating the fundamentals of Buddhism, but this idea does not result in a serious discussion about the principles of interpretation for the canonical texts of Buddhism.

This does not mean that modern Buddhism has been completely free from negative reactions to applications of historical research. Some Buddhists, too, have had problems with some of the modern textual scholarship applied to their Holy Scriptures. For instance, in a 1932 issue of the journal *Mahabodhi* (which was established by the fundamentalist Dharmapala), there was a fierce attack on the scholarship of an important contemporary British scholar of Buddhism, Rhys Davids. The article was entitled "Mrs. Rhys Davids and the 'Higher criticism'" and written by Arya Dhamma. In the article, the Buddhist critic claimed that Rhys Davids's latest writings on Buddhism "may be euphemistically termed 'higher criticism' but more appropriately called pedantic hypocriticism."[37] The Buddhist critic asserted that the higher criticism that Rhys Davids brought to the Pali texts she worked on was not only full of errors. She had only "cheap contempt" for the canonical texts and the great tradition of Buddhist scholarship, the critic claimed. Since the late nineteenth century, there have been several lay Buddhist

[37] Arya Dhamma, "Mrs. Rhys Davids and the 'Higher Criticism,'" *The Mahabodhi* 40, nos. 4–5 (1932): 160.

organizations in Asia that sought new ways to integrate traditional Buddhist science with the modern science they encountered in Western institutions. Modern science and its power could be seen in a number of areas, such as communications technology, military technology, or architecture. However, it was in the area of medicine that many of the early Buddhist revivalists and fundamentalists would search for a place for what they felt were their own traditional values and techniques related to the body and health. In 1913, the Mahabodhi Society, established by Anagarika Dharmapala, had developed plans for the establishment of a hospital devoted to the revival of local Buddhist medical practices called Ayurveda. Ayurveda is a traditional Indian system of medicine mostly associated with Hinduism, but varieties of this system have developed in many of the Buddhist cultures in Asia, too. In Sri Lanka, there was a long tradition of Ayurvedic practices, and this was associated with the Buddhist past that was under threat from aggressive proselytization by Christian missionaries. In 1914, the Mahabodhi Society set up the Foster-Robinson Memorial Hospital in Colombo in order to revive the ancient Sinhalese medical knowledge.

8

The Struggle over Education

In premodern society, schools were almost always religious institutions. The development of modern education is closely connected to the development of fundamentalism in all the world religions. The differentiation of education and the development of a broad-ranging secular educational system are key components of modernity.[1] Modern public education is generally organized according to an ideology of secularism, which means that the methods of teaching and the curricula assume that religion can be clearly separated from other secular subjects, such as science, history, and languages. It does not mean that the teaching of religion is banned from schools, but it does mean that religion is taught as a delimited subject with no implication for the teaching of other subjects. So differentiation in society at large is replicated in the modern educational systems of most modern states.

For this reason, fundamentalists see schools as an important arena for a struggle against a hostile worldview comprising humanism, secularism, and modernism. They believe that it is a grave problem that religion has this delimited status and

[1] Parsons, *The System of Modern Societies*, p. 94ff.

position in public schools, and there are several ways to approach this problem. On the one hand, fundamentalists often struggle to change teaching and curricula. Some of the most important Supreme Court cases about the status of religion in American society are about the place of religion in schools, and there are similar battles for the minds of children in other societies. On the other hand, fundamentalists may try to take the education of their children out of the hands of the state. They may argue that education of children is a private matter and that the public authorities should have nothing, or very little, to say about what parents teach their children. This is the strategy chosen by the homeschool movement in the United States, and it is the ideology behind some of the religious schools that we find in Muslim or Hindu societies.

In other words, the struggle for control over education is also a struggle about the boundaries between the public and the private. Religious beliefs and symbols that have been forced into the private sphere by the modern state may be put back into the public sphere, or, alternatively, education may be reclaimed from the public sphere and brought back into the private sphere. The private sphere was where education of children belonged before education was taken out of the hands of the family through the processes of modernization. So the educational system – the primary and secondary schools as well as the institutions of higher education – is a place where important negotiations are going on about where to draw the lines between the public and the private and about the place of religion in society.

RELIGION IN THE AMERICAN CLASSROOM

From the 1920s up to today, Protestant fundamentalists in the United States have seen the educational system as an important arena for the struggle to defend their religion, culture, and identity against secularization. In the eighteenth and nineteenth centuries, educational opportunities were limited and expensive, and work toward free public education was a key component of the modernization of society in the latter half of the nineteenth century. At the beginning of the twentieth century, public education was established as the default option for most American children. The development of a public education system was an important element in the general process of differentiation: education became a separate societal sphere. Secularization has taken place inside the public schools, too, in their teaching and textbooks. Through a large number of cases, especially from the 1960s, U.S. courts have decided that public schools are secular institutions. This means that all teaching, texts, and curricula used in classes must have a secular purpose. They must neither advance nor inhibit religion, and they must not foster excessive government entanglement with religion. If teaching in public schools breaks these principles, it is unconstitutional, according to the U.S. Supreme Court.[2]

Some fundamentalists meet the challenge from secularism by taking the education of their children out of the hands of public authorities. The homeschool movement has grown in popularity among fundamentalists since the 1980s. In 2003, about 1.1 million children were homeschooled in the United States. This meant that 2.2 percent of the school-age population was being homeschooled, which was a significant increase from 1999, when about 850,000 children, or 1.7 percent of the school-age population, were taught at home. The parents of 30 percent of the children who were homeschooled in 2003 said that the primary reason for their choice was that they wanted to provide religious or moral instruction for their children.[3]

A less radical option is to organize private religious schools that enjoy greater freedom from interference from the authorities. The Christian school movement became an important

[2] The principles of secularism were set out by the Supreme Court in the *Lemon v. Kurtzman* decision of 1971.

[3] National Center for Education Statistics (http://nces.ed.gov/nhes/homeschool/), retrieved on December 5, 2010.

part of the U.S. educational landscape in the 1980s and has continued to grow, as many conservative believers feel that to pass responsibility for the education of their children to a secular public school would mean rejection of a God-given responsibility to raise children in their faith.[4] Protestant fundamentalist schools in the United States have their organization and curricula designed to protect children from the evils of the outside world and to impart a religious education that will make them good Christians. The school is often seen by parents to be part of an organic community that also includes family and church. They want to set up strict boundaries between their own local communities and the contaminated and corrupted secular world outside.[5]

However, most fundamentalists are more concerned with changing the content of the *public* schools. They want to roll back secularism inside public school classrooms, where about 90 percent of American pupils get their basic education. Two sensitive issues may illustrate how fundamentalists have worked to challenge the secularism of public schools espoused by federal laws. The first is the teaching of evolution and creationism. The second is the place of prayer. I will take a look at both of these issues.

In the chapter about science, I looked at how the new biology arising out of Charles Darwin's theory of evolution created strong reactions from conservative circles in the Christian churches in many countries, but it was not until the theory of evolution entered the classrooms of high school students that the controversy developed into a real battle for the hearts and minds of Christian America. If we look at the history of the anti-evolution movement in U.S. high schools, it is clear that this struggle was and is about much more than a clash between

4 See, for instance, Steven L. Jones, *Religious Schooling in America* (Westport, Conn.: Praeger, 2008), chap. 2.

5 Susan D. Rose, *Keeping Them Out of the Hands of Satan: Evangelical Schooling in America* (New York: Routledge, 1988).

science and religion. It was also a struggle of rural communities against the imposition of modern urban culture in American public education. The struggle focused on the issue of biology teaching partly because this subject was designed in a way that conflicted with a religious and traditional worldview. But the struggle over the subject of biology was also a result of several larger historical developments in U.S. high school education between 1910 and 1920.

In this period, big American publishers, such as the American Book Company, produced a new generation of biology textbooks for the high school market. Naturally, these new textbooks used modern insights in the life sciences. There was nothing very surprising in the fact that the new generation of textbooks taught evolutionary theory and integrated the teaching of human biology with other branches of the life sciences, such as zoology. The evolutionary view of biology had been accepted in the American science communities and had been the foundation of university education in biology for decades. However, the new textbooks for the high school market had greater ambitions than teaching biology according to modern scientific principles. They aimed at promoting modern culture and civic values through biology courses. The new textbooks were explicitly written for urban pupils and often presented urbanization and industrialization as key elements of human progress. The authors of these books believed that the new generation of urban Americans needed a new way of understanding the role of biology in everyday life.

The most important and famous example of the new biology textbooks was called *Civic Biology*. It appeared in 1914 and was written by George W. Hunter. This book consistently developed all major biological subjects into practical problems of modern life in order to equip young people to become good citizens. Cell theory was the foundation for teaching about microbes, public sanitation, and hygiene, the book's treatment of metabolism led to a discussion of healthy diets and a detailed treatment of the dangers of alcohol, heredity was the natural groundwork for a discussion of human reproduction and sexual health, and evolutionary principles led to issues of eugenics and the improvement of animals and plants for human use.[6] In other words, there was a lot of politics in the book, and both author and publisher saw clearly that they touched on controversial issues that would counter reactions from sections of the American public.

In the same period, a rapid expansion of compulsory high school education took place in the rural south of the United States. In Tennessee, which would soon become the focus of the war over the teaching of evolution in schools, a generation of rural young people were exposed to modern education, with all its explicit and implicit values and ideologies. In 1924–25, about 4,000 Tennessee high school students, comprising over 90 percent of the students taking biology classes, used the book *Civic Biology*. For the publisher, the book was a great success, and without it there probably would not have been a Butler Act in 1925 prohibiting the teaching of evolution.[7]

In the conflict over biology textbooks in the United States in the 1910s and 1920s, one easily recognizes some of the big issues in the conflict between modernity and tradition. Authors and publishers based in big northern cities, such as New York and Chicago, wrote textbooks promoting modern civic values. In their textbooks, the understanding of human biology was a precondition for social progress along with industrialization and modern economic principles. From the point of view of people living in the rural south, the values and worldview found in books like *Civic Biology* and promoted by an expanding system of public education were threats to traditional culture.

Civic Biology was the textbook used by John T. Scopes, a local teacher in the small town of Dayton, Tennessee, when he violated the Butler Act and was tried in the famous Scopes trial in 1925.

[6] Adam R. Shapiro, "Civic Biology and the Origins of the School Antievolution Movement," *Journal of the History of Biology* 41, no. 3 (2008): 409–33. My treatment of *Civic Biology* is based on Shapiro's article.

[7] Ibid., p. 5.

This case has become the symbol of the clash between defenders and opponents of teaching evolutionary theory in American schools. The Butler Act was a law passed in the state of Tennessee in 1925 prohibiting the teaching of evolution in public schools. The American Civil Liberties Union (ACLU) challenged the law with the help of John T. Scopes, who agreed to stand trial on charges of teaching evolution to his students. When the case came up in Dayton, it made the headlines throughout the country, mostly because of the prominence of the lawyers arguing the case.

William Jennings Bryan was the most famous member of the prosecution team representing the state of Tennessee. He had been presidential candidate for the Democratic Party three times and had been secretary of state in the administration of Woodrow Wilson. Defending Scopes was a team headed by Clarence Darrow, a famous lawyer and member of the ACLU. The case ended with the conviction of Scopes, who was fined 100 dollars. The decision was appealed to the Supreme Court of Tennessee and was reversed because of a technical fault with the legal procedures in Dayton, but the court left the Butler Act standing and did not discuss its relation to the Constitution.[8]

Many fundamentalists saw the Scopes trial as a victory for Bible-believing Christians over modernist and immoral scientists. The Christian fundamentalists in the United States retreated at least partly from the public scene around 1930 to reemerge with new intensity in the wake of the cultural transformations of American society in the 1960s and 1970s. In spite of the symbolic victory in the Scopes trial, conservative Christians in the United States realized, at least starting in the 1960s, that the educational system was an arena for the rapid secularization

[8] For a full treatment of the case, see Edward J. Larson, *Summer for the Gods: The Scopes Trial and America's Continuing Debate over Science and Religion* (New York: Basic Books, 1997).

of American society and the relegation of traditional Protestant religion to a far more limited position than it had enjoyed to that point in American history. The status of prayer and Bible reading in public schools became showcases for the process of secularization.

Some decades after the Scopes trial, a less famous, but more important, legal case about religion and schools reached the courts. In 1951, the New York State Board of Regents had crafted a short prayer and decided that this should be read aloud by pupils and teachers in the schools of the state of New York. The Board of Regents was a committee chosen by the state legislature and had the power to make decisions concerning the public schools in the state. The prayer was carefully worded, and very short, in order to make it as nonsectarian as possible and acceptable to all pupils and their families. However, several parents, especially among people who had recently moved into the state, were unhappy with the fact that their children had to pray in class.

During the 1950s, people were moving from the city of New York to the suburbs, and among some of the newcomers resistance to school prayer grew into organized legal action. Lawrence Roth, who had moved to the county of Nassau on Long Island and enrolled his children in the Herricks School District, was the man who took the first steps. Roth was of Jewish background, as were all the plaintiffs in the case. They saw this as an unconstitutional lack of separation of church and state and an infringement on their private lives. Many would also see school prayer as an imposition of a Protestant Christian culture in spite of the loose wording of the prayer. Being members of a religious minority, they were worried that the public authorities would decide when and how their children should pray. Roth contacted the New York branch of the ACLU, which hired a New York lawyer, William Butler, to take the case to court. In the New York Court of Appeals, the school board argued that the prayer was acceptable because pupils were not forced to pray and had the option of remaining silent if they so wished. The trial judge supported the school board.

Through several appeals, the case finally ended up with the U.S. Supreme Court. The school board argued again that the prayer was voluntary and that the wording of the prayer was so general that it was simply part of a civil religion shared by almost all Americans regardless of religious background. These facts made the practice constitutional, they claimed. The plaintiffs and Butler insisted that prayer in public school was in violation of the separation of church and state laid down in the First Amendment to the Constitution. The Supreme Court agreed with the plaintiffs who had brought the case to court. The decision was issued on June 25, 1962, and the U.S. Supreme Court decided in the *Engel v. Vitale* case that it was unconstitutional for a public school to ask pupils to pray in school even when the prayer was worded in very general terms and did not promote one particular religion. The *Engel v. Vitale* case (the *Engel case* for short) changed the course of the history of American religion in the public sphere.[9] The Supreme Court's opinion regarding the role of religion in the educational system was elaborated in several subsequent cases. In 1963, the Supreme Court made a decision in two similar cases: *Abington School District v. Schempp* and *Murray v. Curlett.* Now the court decided that it was unconstitutional for states to have laws requiring children to hear or read the Bible in public schools.

There were strong reactions to the *Engel* decision. Many conservative Protestants felt that their national culture was being undermined by the Supreme Court, and large sections of the political elite in the country called for a constitutional amendment to overturn it. The families who took the case to court experienced threats and violence because of their role as

[9] I rely on the account of the case in Bruce J. Dierenfield, *The Battle over School Prayer: How Engel v. Vitale Changed America* (Lawrence: Kansas University Press, 2007).

plaintiffs.[10] This became a struggle about much more than the actual prayers. It became a struggle for the defense of the status and power once enjoyed by Protestant Christianity in America, and it became a struggle for the right to define American identity. Protestant fundamentalists have organized themselves to reintroduce their version of Christianity into public school curricula. The Bible Creation Association was founded in 1964 in order to promote the teaching of creationism in public schools, whereas religious liberals have founded organizations that struggle to keep creationism out of public schools. The struggle continues: the National Council on Bible Curriculum in Public Schools (NCBCPS) was founded in 1993 to promote the place of Christianity in the public school system.[11]

With the differentiation of a public school system in the United States starting in the late nineteenth century, the education of children and adolescents has gradually been taken out of the hands of parents and families. This has given unprecedented opportunities for learning to the majority of the population and has transferred some of the burden for raising and training new generations to the state. However, this process also entails a loss of control and power of parents and families over what kinds of persons their children grow up to be. For quite a few religious people, this is a serious problem. From the 1960s, it became abundantly clear to all Americans that the modern public school system is built on secular values. Religion must have no place in American public schools except as a neutral subject of historical and sociological inquiry and understanding. Prayer and devotional Bible reading are prohibited by federal law, and the teaching of creationism never became the challenge to evolutionary theory in schools that the fundamentalists had hoped. Secularization has come very far in the public

[10] Ibid., p. 142.

[11] Mark A. Chancey, "A Textbook Example of the Christian Right: The National Council on Bible Curriculum in Public Schools," *Journal of the American Academy of Religion* 75, no. 3 (September 2007): 554–81.

classrooms of America. This has led to a large movement of religious schooling where families, local communities, and several organizations have joined in the struggle to change the place of Protestant religion in the sphere of education. The struggle takes several forms. Some want to desecularize public schools by pushing Protestant religion back into the classrooms. The only way to achieve this would be to challenge the many legal decisions about religion and schools made by the Supreme Court and lower courts. Others choose to organize private religious schools instead or simply retreat from the secular public sphere to educate their young at home.

SAFFRON-COLORED EDUCATION IN INDIA

In Chapter 5, I explained how Hindu fundamentalists succeeded in launching a political party, the BJP, as part of their family of organizations intent on infusing Hinduism into all societal spheres. The result was that between 1999 and 2004 India was governed by a coalition called the National Democratic Alliance (NDA), with the BJP as the coalition leader and holder of key government posts. On questions regarding education, the BJP was very keen to follow the fundamentalist line of the mother organization, the RSS, by carrying out a large-scale restructuring of the education system. It is a testimony to the importance of education in the vision of Hindu fundamentalists that they filled the posts at the head of government ministries and organizations responsible for education with some of the most profiled Hindu fundamentalist leaders.

In the presentation of the Hinduization or saffronization of science in the last chapter, I discussed the key role played by M. M. Joshi, the senior RSS member, and BJP politicians. (Saffron is the color associated with Hinduism, especially with today's revivalist Hinduism, and "saffronization" refers to the infusion of Hindu values and ideas.) During the rule of the NDA coalition headed by the BJP, Joshi headed the Ministry of Human

Resources Development. This ministry is in charge of primary, secondary, and higher education through its Department of School Education and Literacy and Department of Higher Education. Another key institution in the struggle over education was the National Council of Educational Research and Training (NCERT), which is a government agency assisting the Indian authorities in planning education and by producing schoolbooks. During the NDA government, the director of the NCERT was J. S. Rajput, a Hindu fundamentalist hardliner appointed to the directorship by Joshi.

Joshi headed the BJP's policies to Hinduize education in India. As part of the plan to change the education of Indian children, the Hindu fundamentalists of the NDA government published a National Curriculum Framework for School Education in 2000, a year after they gained power. In this and other documents, the ideology of Hinduizing education is very clear. The ideology guiding the educational reforms brought by the NDA government in the early 2000s revolved around certain assumptions and attitudes that are comparable to those found in fundamentalist movements in other world religions. First of all, the BJP politicians who dominated the NDA alliance believed that the vast majority of Indians had forgotten the fundamental values of India. In the worldview of Hindu fundamentalists, there is a timeless Hindu religious and philosophical ethos that is natural to Indians. Closely linked to this ethos is a conception of Hindu society as an organic whole built on economic and political principles different from those found in modern societies.

In modern times, the middle classes and most educated Indians have distanced themselves from this heritage, and this is India's great tragedy in the eyes of politicians like Joshi and Rajput. In the policy statements, speeches, and semiacademic articles about education produced by the Hindu fundamentalists, this historical development is discussed extensively. Globalization and Westernization are often identified as the main causes of India's problems, and the educators of the BJP are eager to raise new generations of Hindus that are conscious and critical of the fragmentation and differentiation resulting from these processes. The problem has deep roots, they feel. With the introduction of Western educational and scientific standards in the nineteenth century, the indigenous schools suffered. Traditional Hindu education lost its status, and Indians became increasingly alienated from their own values and culture.

Joshi and like-minded Hindu fundamentalist educators often insist that the ancient Indian ideal of education and science was in fact superior to the Western model. Indian civilization, they assert, pursued knowledge in fields such as mathematics, linguistics, astronomy, and economics long before most other cultures knew how to till the soil. In fact, it is part of any Indian's genes and psyche to be inclined to pursue knowledge, according to Joshi. The big difference between ancient Indian science and modern Western science was that the Indians did not put up false barriers between religion and science. Here is the key to understanding the problem of modernity, according to Hindu fundamentalists. The ancient Indians understood that one could not separate religion and ethics from the study of natural or social sciences. Modernity, starting with the European scientific revolution during the Enlightenment era, insisted on separating what could in fact not be separated. The result is societies that are fragmented and alienated.

In order to reverse the trend of fragmentation and differentiation, the education policies of the NDA government from 1999 to 2004 had the aim of reintroducing ancient Hindu subjects into the national curriculum. These subjects included Vedic science, Vedic mathematics, Vedic astronomy, and the study of the Hindu language Sanskrit. ("Vedic" refers to the oldest Hindu texts, the Vedas.) Children in public schools should be taught a holistic approach to the world and the universe, and they should understand that there is a deep interconnectedness between the individual, society, and the laws of the cosmos. The Hindu ethos must be brought into all other subjects, according to the fundamentalists, as this would reconnect Indians with their real identity and the culture found in the ancient Hindu texts.

Such a Hinduized education would also match the latest truths in Western science, according to the Hindu fundamentalist politicians. M. M. Joshi said on several occasions that modern science really proved that the ancient Hindus had been right all along, as when modern physics reached conclusions about the dissolution of strict distinctions between cause and effect and between an observer and the external world. Modern physics approached the truth about oneness expressed in the Hindu concept of Brahman and described in the Upanishads, texts composed several centuries before Christ.

The education policies of the Hindu fundamentalists in charge of the NDA coalition government of India between 1999 and 2004 aimed to set in motion a de-differentiation of public education by introducing an essentialized version of ancient Hindu knowledge into all branches of national school curricula. Key persons and organizations saw this as a way to reconnect with the fundamental truths of Hinduism and to re-create a social order that had been partly lost since the period of colonization and from self-imposed Westernization after independence in 1947. In addition, the reintroduction of what they often called "value-education," in order to avoid the constitutional prohibition of mixing religion and politics, was also a project of national pride. By showing that ancient Hindu science was better than Western science, they wished to raise the self-esteem of the coming generation of Hindus.

In spring 2004, the NDA government was voted out of office in parliamentary elections, and shortly after leaving his post as the head of the HRD, M. M. Joshi was interviewed by the magazine *Organiser*, which is published by the RSS. The *Organiser* asked Joshi what he thought of the plans announced by the new government headed by the Congress Party for reversing the changes he had made to Indian education. Joshi explained that policies aimed at the Hinduization or saffronization of education were in line with the constitution and the demands of the people and the parliament of the country. Joshi, countering the criticism from the secular politicians, said: "Some people certainly said education has been saffronised but they do not know the meaning of saffronisation. In fact, saffron is the color that represents the very ethos and psyche of this country. Saffronisation means to go back to the holy traditions of this country. If they want to remove it, people will judge it."[12]

ISLAMIC SCHOOLS: GOVERNMENT PAWNS OR NESTS OF TERRORISM?

The basic problem for Muslim fundamentalists with regard to education is similar to that faced by fundamentalists in other world religions: when modern states developed in Asia and Africa in the nineteenth century, the independence and status of the Islamic tradition of learning, and the class of clerics embodying this tradition, was undermined by centralizing states that saw Islamic charitable endowments as nice sources of income for the state and the clerics as potential allies in the process of modernization. By narrowing down the field of religious subjects and introducing a host of new, completely secular subjects, governments from Egypt to Indonesia followed the logic of modernity by introducing a differentiated, and therefore secularized, worldview in education. They also narrowed the authority of the religious elites, and they set clear boundaries for the influence of religion over subjects that were deemed nonreligious.

The modern states of the Muslim world have wanted to reform the Islamic schools (*madrasas*) at different points in history and in different ways. However, underlying the reform of the system of Islamic education in most or all Islamic societies was the

[12] M. M. Joshi, interview in *Organiser*, June 6, 2004 (retrieved at http://www.organiser.org/dynamic/modules.php?name=Content&pa=showpage&pid=26&page=3).

modern idea that the traditional subjects could be divided into strictly religious and nonreligious subjects and many of them could be taught more efficiently by new, secular schools. Most of the modern governments would impose new restrictions on teaching in the *madrasas*, and by narrowly defining Islamic subjects as those dealing with the Qur'an, the Hadith, and religious law, the modern states restricted the autonomy and power of the teacher-scholars.

This trend is obvious in the modern development of Islamic education in Egypt. Under Muhammad Ali's reign (1805–48), a massive project of centralization was started in all spheres of society in order to make Egypt into a modern state. As ruler of Egypt on behalf of the Ottoman sultan, and as witness to the recent effective military technology and tactics of Napoleon's Egyptian campaign, Muhammad Ali realized that any attempt to make Egypt into a powerful state would start by adopting the inventions of Europe.[13] Ali created a centralized government and army, reformed taxation, developed local industry to make products for export, introduced reforms in agriculture, and created new and modern policies on education. Egypt needed officers, engineers, printers, doctors, and nurses to make modernity penetrate society and create economic growth, and during the first half of the nineteenth century schools and colleges were established that taught modern subjects according to European methods.[14]

The status of Islamic education and of the scholars and teachers of this tradition, the *ulama*, was partly destroyed as a result of Muhammad Ali's centralization and bureaucratization. In the second decade of the nineteenth century, he decided to tax the charitable endowments (*waqf*) from which the Islamic schools and mosques got their funds. As a consequence, a large

[13] John Dunn, "Egypt's Nineteenth-Century Armaments Industry," *Journal of Military History* 61 (April 1997): 231–54.

[14] Afaf Lutfi al-Sayyid Marsot, *Egypt in the Reign of Muhammad Ali* (Cambridge: Cambridge University Press, 1984).

number of smaller and middle-sized Islamic schools in the country simply had to close their doors, and their teachers became redundant. The undermining of the economic independence and livelihood of Islamic schools and scholars also had an effect on the Islamic University al-Azhar in Cairo. Al-Azhar was established around 970 CE and has for long periods been the most famous and respected institution of learning in the Sunni Muslim world, but at the accession of Muhammad Ali the university was in a state of physical decline and its academic reputation was questioned both by Muslims and Europeans. Beginning in the early nineteenth century, the status of al-Azhar deteriorated steadily as a new elite was formed by the introduction of Western-style education in new schools and colleges. Graduates from al-Azhar could not compete in the job market of a modernizing state: their knowledge was useless in the civil service or the army.[15]

The undermining of the status of Islamic education and scholars continued in the twentieth century. During the Nasser administration (1956–70), al-Azhar was reformed by the government in order to modernize the *ulama* and teaching at the university. In the 1960s, the Nasser government nationalized the charitable endowments, and the university was placed under the administration of the Ministry of Endowments. In effect, al-Azhar lost most of the independence it had retained since the reforms of the nineteenth century. Nasser created a state-controlled religious monopoly in Egypt, and the religious scholars were brought into complete submission to the modern state. Egyptian presidents Nasser, Sadat (1971–81), and Mubarak (1981–2011) have all exercised control over al-Azhar through their power over leadership appointments and economic matters, and they have used the Islamic university to give legitimacy to state policies.

[15] Indira Falk Gesink, *Islamic Reform and Conservatism: Al-Azhar and the Evolution of Modern Sunni Islam* (London: I. B. Tauris, 2010).

Egyptian fundamentalists never liked the close ties between traditional scholars and the state. Islamists have often loudly criticized al-Azhar's role as a government tool in destroying Islam and deceiving the public into believing that the infidel government is ruling according to Islam and acting on behalf of the population. The Muslim Brotherhood has often criticized the traditionally educated *ulama* of the al-Azhar because it sees them as irrelevant to the problems facing Egypt, and the more radical groups carrying out terrorist attacks in Egypt in the 1990s were at least partly motivated by what they perceived as the co-optation by the state of religious institutions and the inability of *ulama* to defend true Islam.[16] This development in the relations between state authorities, established religion, and religious/political protest groups in Egypt is part of the picture presented in Part I about the global shift in religious authority.

In Pakistan, the status of Islamic education has suffered, too. Maulana Maududi realized that the Pakistan that was born in 1947 did not possess the kind of people needed to institute a true Islamic state and did not possess the educational institutions to give a new generation the right worldview and skills for such a task. Both the old Islamic educational system and the modern secular schools introduced after the Western model were inimical, or at best irrelevant, to shaping the minds of good Muslims running an Islamic state. In a 1948 speech addressing the question of Islamic law in Pakistan, he said that Pakistanis needed a thorough reorientation of the educational system. At present, he said, Pakistan has two kinds of educational systems running simultaneously: the old religious *madrasas* and the modern secular universities and colleges. In Maududi's words: "The old-fashioned schools are steeped in conservatism to such an extent that they have lost all touch with the modern world. [...]

[16] Tamir Moustafa, "Conflict and Cooperation between the State and Religious Institutions in Contemporary Egypt," *International Journal of Middle East Studies* 32, no. 1 (February 2000): 3–22.

As for our modern, secular institutions, they produce people who are ignorant of even a rudimentary knowledge of Islam and its laws."[17]

Under the dictatorship of General Zia, Pakistan underwent a number of political reforms that were meant to strengthen Islam in Pakistani society. In 1979, Zia commissioned a report on how to reform the *madrasas* to make them more relevant to modern conditions. In the report, it was suggested that those *madrasas* and their leadership that accept reforms should be awarded financial aid, scholarships, and government recognition of the degrees they offered. Zia and his regime wanted to lift the *madrasas* into the modern age and entrench Islam in the culture of the country, and through the introduction of new secular subjects and the differentiation of religious subjects, the Pakistani government has continued to change the *madrasas* into institutions that are very different from the Islamic schools that existed in the past.

Thus, the Pakistani governments, to different degrees but particularly under Zia in the late 1970s and 1980s, continued reforms of the *madrasas* that were started during British rule. In British India, the colonial government saw that reform of the *madrasas* clearly undermined the status and authority of the Muslim scholarly elites in society. This was also obvious to the Muslim elites themselves, who often saw government initiatives to reform the *madrasas* as a conspiracy to destroy Islam. Government support from the British came with demands for teaching subjects useful to the state. In the eyes of several conservative Muslim scholars, the reforms carried out in Pakistan after it became an independent state in 1947 have had the same effect: they create loyal government servants while undermining the authority of the religious scholars and destroying the

[17] The speech "Islamic Law: Its Introduction in Pakistan" was given at Lahore Law College in February 1948 and is included in Maududi, *Islamic Law and Constitution*, pp. 51–52.

tradition of real Islamic learning by restricting the religious to a few narrow subjects and introducing a host of new secular subjects.[18]

Muslim fundamentalists are not among the defenders of the traditional *madrasa* system, simply because they realize that they are powerless, as Maududi pointed out, and here we see the distinction between conservative and fundamentalist reactions to the differentiation of religion from other spheres of society. The people who lose out from the decline of the traditional Islamic system of education are the religious scholars with traditional educations, who cling to the religious authority they think they rightfully possess. Fundamentalists are mainly found among the much larger group of people with educations in the secular mainstream educational institutions. Fundamentalists may be engineers or medical doctors, sometimes with an extra degree in a religious subject, but they seldom belong to the class of religious scholars. They are concerned about religion and its place in society, but often they see the *ulama* as useless and outdated.

What, then, about the dangerous *madrasas*? One of the recurrent themes in Western media in recent years has been the fear of Islamic schools and their supposed role in creating fundamentalist cultures associated with terrorism. Numerous newspaper articles and media reports have asserted that the system of Islamic schools (*madrasas*) is expanding in countries such as Pakistan and that this leads to a veritable Islamization of society that sets it on a collision course with the Western world and with liberal and democratic sections of local communities. A large number of reports and articles by newspapers and think tanks have claimed that anywhere from 10 percent to 33 percent of Pakistani students and children are enrolled in *madrasas* and that these schools often teach intolerance and even espouse

[18] Muhammad Qasim Zaman, "Religious Education and the Rhetoric of Reform: The Madrasa in British India and Pakistan," *Comparative Studies in Society and History* 14, no. 2 (1999): 294–323 at pp. 315–16.

violence against non-Muslims, but such articles are often based on very dubious sources. A critical look at *madrasa* enrollment in Pakistan shows that *madrasas* account for less than 1 percent of overall school enrollment in the country. Among the families who send a child to a *madrasa*, 75 percent send other children in the same household to other schools, public and private, which means that religiosity or poverty cannot explain why some families send a child to a *madrasa*, as is often assumed in Western media.[19]

So the important conditioning factor in the sphere of education for Muslim fundamentalism is probably not the *madrasa* system as such but rather the spread of higher education of a modern type, as it is in other religions. Mass education started to have a real impact on the religious culture of Middle Eastern societies in the 1960s, and in some countries the options for getting a higher education appeared even later. The spread of higher education in the Muslim world has changed the way that Muslims view their own tradition and how they approach the foundational texts of this tradition, including the Qur'an.[20] Mass education is an important factor in the formulation and spread of an objectified and deculturalized concept of religion, as I discussed in Chapter 2, and it fosters a new and direct relationship to religion that we discussed earlier as an element in the global shift in religious authority.

The struggle of traditional religious elites against the differentiation of society is a difficult, even impossible, struggle in most places. The modern state is simply far too strong. The religious scholars themselves have resisted and criticized government reforms of the *madrasa* system, but in most countries

[19] Tahrir Andrabi, Jishnu Das, Asim Ijaz Khwaja, and Tristan Zajong, "Religious School Enrollment in Pakistan: A Look at the Data," in *Islam and Education: Myths and Truths*, ed. Wadad Kadi and Victor Billeh (Chicago: University of Chicago Press, 2007).

[20] Eickelman, "Mass Higher Education and the Religious Imagination in Contemporary Arab Societies," p. 646.

they have no power to reverse the trend by which *madrasas* are brought under the control of the state and religious subjects are restricted and downgraded relative to the secular subjects of public education.

BUDDHISM AND EDUCATION

During the past 150 years, the education offered to laypeople in Sri Lanka has gradually been differentiated from Buddhism. Both in Sri Lanka and in other Theravada Buddhist societies, there has been a long historical trend of differentiation of education from religion, which started in the nineteenth century, and we can find reactions against this process that resemble the reactions found in Muslim and Christian communities in other parts of the world.

In both Sri Lanka and Thailand, traditional education was organized and controlled by the Buddhist monkhood. Monks ran schools for laypeople and also the education for monks and for the novices who aspired to become monks. These temple schools were organized in a very different fashion from Western types of schools. Normally, in a temple school for laypeople, a monk would gather around him a handful of young pupils who would be part of his household; they would do household work in exchange for some instruction and perhaps a meal a day. These schools were part of the village community and constituted an element in the organic relationship between monkhood and laypeople, where monks rely on the laity for their material well-being and laypeople rely on monks for some religious services. In temple schools, pupils would learn certain Buddhist texts by heart and would often learn some basic astrology and other "religious" subjects.[21] The education would be informal, and pupils would not normally attend to a high age because they would enter the economic activity of the village community.

[21] Michael Ames, "The Impact of Western Education on Religion and Society in Ceylon," *Pacific Affairs* 40, nos. 1–2 (Spring/Summer 1967): 19–42.

In Sri Lanka, the British colonial government believed these temple schools and the whole system of traditional Buddhist education were absolutely useless, and from the British occupation in 1815 officials and missionaries worked to expand a system of Western-style education on the island. Between the early nineteenth century and Sri Lankan independence in 1948, several thousand schools were created by British missionaries and by the colonial government. As early as 1828, just a decade after the British gained military and political control in Sri Lanka, there were 236 Protestant mission schools, enrolling more than 9,000 pupils. These numbers would grow rapidly over the following decades, as the missionaries saw education as the foremost means of spreading Christianity.[22]

Until 1865, only Protestant mission schools received government aid, and there was never any doubt that education was part of a massive project of changing society from the bottom up. Other schools, including some traditional ones, started receiving government funding toward the end of the nineteenth century, but a precondition for receiving such funds was that a school organize itself along British lines, with a Western curriculum emphasizing subjects such as science, English, and math. The number of Buddhist schools that would receive funding was very limited, and those that wanted such assistance had to change their approach to education in fundamental ways.

From the end of the nineteenth century, the influence of traditional temple education on laypeople in Sri Lanka had been largely destroyed through these transformations. This was part of a revolution in the relationship between monkhood and laypeople that took place in all Theravada Buddhist societies whereby the religious authority of the monkhood was gradually undermined and a new class of cultural agents came forth: Western-educated middle-class Buddhists who would redefine their own religion and create modern religious movements,

[22] Ibid., pp. 26–27.

mindsets, and organizations, among them Buddhist fundamentalism. Educational changes were part of a basic transformation of the societies of Theravada Buddhist countries associated with modernization, and the transformations were not the circular, recurrent changes happening within the framework of a relatively stable social structure but rather linear changes that transformed social structures in fundamental and irreversible ways, as I discussed earlier when pointing out the nature of the changes caused by modernity.

There were wide reactions against the transformations, as in many colonized societies. The Buddhist middle class that emerged in Sri Lanka toward the end of the nineteenth century generally believed that a fundamental change in the education of children was necessary to save the religion and culture of the country from the Christian missionaries, and the establishment of new Buddhist schools was seen as an emergency measure to save a generation of young Buddhists. At the same time, the Buddhist men and women of Sri Lanka who worked to establish schools with Buddhist values were more often than not inspired and encouraged by both men and women arriving in Sri Lanka from Western countries, first of all members of the Theosophical Society. These Westerners were deeply critical of the hegemonic ambitions of Christian missionaries in Asia and provided important support for Buddhist initiatives to counter the missionary influence.

The revival of Buddhist education from the late nineteenth century was perhaps the most important work undertaken by Buddhist monks and laypeople in Sri Lanka who wished to stop the influence exerted by the British on their society. Many middle-class lay Buddhists saw the organizational superiority and economic advantage of Christian schools as a threat to the survival of their culture, and many of the most resourceful among them got engaged in work to promote and revive Buddhist education. Two of the most important organizations devoted to this revival were the Mahabodhi Society and the Young Men's Buddhist Association (YMBA) of Colombo.

The Mahabodhi Society was started in 1891 by Anagarika Dharmapala, the fundamentalist Buddhist leader we discussed earlier, and the YMBA was an organization established by a group of enthusiastic Buddhists in Colombo, the capital of Sri Lanka, in 1898 in order to defend Buddhism against the onslaught of Christian missionaries and to promote Buddhist education.[23] The obvious Christian model for the YMBA is one more testimony to the necessity of struggling against Western and Christian influence in the language and through the institutional models provided by the British. The globalization of religious, cultural, and organizational forms in the nineteenth century meant that local reactions against modernization mimicked the forms of the Christian world: Buddhist revival was conceptualized as Christian-style revival with different contents.

Buddhist schools for boys started being organized in the mid-nineteenth century, but among Buddhist activists of this period there was also a growing awareness that the girls, too, were being Christianized, and from the 1880s sound Buddhist education for girls was seen as the top priority.[24] Girls and women would have to play a key role in stopping the destruction of Buddhism, activists believed, and in 1889 the Women's Education Society of Ceylon (WES) opened in the capital city of Colombo, with the aim of establishing schools for Buddhist girls. Anagarika Dharmapala's mother was among the first members of the WES and the movement to create such girls' schools, and when Dharmapala embarked on his own religious and political career in the mid-1890s, he would continue the focus on girls and women in the revival of Buddhism in Sri Lanka. The position of women in fundamentalist movements is the subject of the next chapter.

[23] Donald Swearer, "Lay Buddhism and the Buddhist Revival in Ceylon," *Journal of the American Academy of Religion* 38, no. 3 (September 1970): 255–75.

[24] Bartholomeusz, *Women under the Bo Tree*, pp. 49–53.

9

The Struggle over Women

In Chapter 1, I briefly divided the concept of secularization into three components: differentiation, privatization, and decline in religious authority. Over the last few chapters, I have looked at how fundamentalists in the world religions have struggled to de-differentiate religion in important spheres such as politics, law, science, and education. In the chapter on education, however, I mentioned that the work of fundamentalists is also a challenge against the ever-increasing power and authority of the modern state and about the redrawing of boundaries between public and private spheres. The struggle about the role of women in society is also a conflict over who has the authority to draw the boundaries between the public and the private.

Secular and modern states insist on defining public space and limiting or proscribing those uses of public space that may seem to question the basic ideology of the state. If a state is founded on a strong secular ideology, such as the *läicite* of France, bringing religious symbols into public space is easily perceived as a challenge to the core values of society. If a state in addition has developed an explicit ideology of gender equality, as is the case in most Western countries, using symbols that may signify inequality between men and women meets with strong reactions. And when symbols are perceived as signaling both religious identity and gender inequality at the same time, the reactions become very strong indeed. That is why the veil, or the headscarves of Muslim women, created such intense debates in many European countries in the 1990s.

Aggressively secular governments see religion as conservative backwardness obstructing the participation of women in public life. The modernizing regime of Josef Stalin's Soviet Union was very concerned with rooting out what was seen as backwardness in the societies of Central Asia in order to pave the way for a new reality. In the 1920s, several traditions and customs were outlawed as "crimes of custom." In Central Asian regions such as Uzbekistan and Turkmenistan, traditional Islamic family patterns had a strong hold on societies, and the Soviet authorities decided early on that Islam was holding women back from becoming good socialists. From the 1920s, the most important symbol of the socialist emancipation of Muslim women inside the Soviet Union was a great campaign of unveiling. The Soviet authorities staged large meetings in which veils were taken off and burned in public.[1] In some Soviet districts, these aggressive campaigns to root out the veil resulted in increased attachment to the veil as a cultural symbol among Muslim women, just as they have done more recently in Western Europe.

AUTHORITY AND OBEDIENCE IN THE CHRISTIAN FUNDAMENTALIST FAMILY

Values among fundamentalist Christians are anchored in beliefs about human nature that are different from those found among liberals and less committed Christians. Fundamentalist Christians generally take the creation story of the Old Testament in a literal sense, and although this story is lacking in detail about the

[1] Adrienne Lynne Edgar, "Emancipation of the Unveiled: Turkmen Women under Soviet Rule, 1924–29," *The Russian Review* 62 (January 2003): 132–49.

actual social roles of men, women, and children, it does contain some very general principles that are the point of departure for fundamentalist reasoning about issues of gender and family. In addition to Genesis, Christian fundamentalists often refer to a number of key passages in the New Testament to explain and legitimate what they believe are correct principles on which to build gender roles in everyday life. The two most prominent principles are *difference* and *complementarity*.

Man and woman were created *differently* according to Genesis. There is a long and fascinating history of interpretation of the biblical creation story in all three Abrahamic religions. The story has been used to defend divergent stands on issues about male and female status and roles. However, to Christian fundamentalists, the difference between Adam and Eve is crucial. The insistence on difference does not mean that fundamentalists generally believe that men are more valuable than women.

To Aristotle, the founding father of moral philosophy, the concept of justice was formal and simple. Like cases must be treated alike, and different cases must be treated differently. Most people can agree on such a general statement, but our problems start when we begin to reason about what *like* and *different* really mean. Are men and women different cases? Both feminists and fundamentalists (and everybody else) can easily observe that men and women have different bodies, but they would disagree if we asked them about the *relevance* of the biological differences. Feminists would claim that the differences are not relevant to our reasoning about the roles and status of men and women. Fundamentalists would say that the differences are in fact highly relevant to the place of men and women in the family and in society, and they will often refer to the creation story or New Testament passages about men and women to defend this view.

The differences between men and women are important and relevant to their social and public roles according to a Christian fundamentalist worldview. Men and women are different, and they complement each other when they work together and do their different things. Many fundamentalists are of the opinion that motherhood is an important part of being a woman, and the responsibility for creating a warm and comforting home is often seen to flow naturally from the role of motherhood. Men have other responsibilities. First of all, they should be strong leaders and provide for the family by earning money and dealing with the outside world.

The differences and complementarities between men and women are apparent in a wide range of Evangelical Christian sex manuals for guiding married couples. These manuals typically present the sexuality of men and women as fundamentally different. Men are generally thought to be less in control of their impulses, and wives are responsible for satisfying their husband's biological needs. Such realizations of basic needs, coupled with a positive will to respond to them, are presented as a key to marital happiness in manuals and guides for marriage and sex that have an Evangelical or fundamentalist Christian viewpoint.

So from what they see as biblical principles of gender difference and complementarity, Christian fundamentalists tend to deduce ideals about family life where women are associated with motherhood, caring, and nurturing and men are associated with leadership, strength, and responsibility. Leadership is also an important aspect of being a father. In fundamentalist literature and media statements, many of the evils of modern society – such as crime, drug abuse, and divorce – are consequences of the inability or unwillingness of fathers to exert authority and teach children obedience. Disobedience in the home may translate into disobedience on matters of law and social norms according to this view.

Authority is a key word in understanding Christian fundamentalists' ideas about what is wrong and right in family matters. In the beginning, God established authority in the world and ordered people to obey authority. In a literalist Christian worldview, the troubled history of mankind began with a revolt against

God's authority when Adam and Eve broke the rules in the Garden of Eden and were thrown out. The struggle for authority goes further back in time: Satan himself fell from heaven as a result of his revolt against divine authority. From the conservative Christian perspective, then, the essence of evil is in a sense the will to reject God-ordained authority, and this inclination is a part of our human nature that it is our duty to fight and overcome.

These ideas are widespread in fundamentalist ideology and can be found in the writings of leading figures such as Jerry Falwell, Tim LaHaye, Pat Robertson, and James Dobson. Let me give just one example to illustrate the reasoning. In an article in the magazine *FrontLine* (the magazine of the Fundamental Baptist Fellowship International), one retired Baptist pastor from Florida discusses the parallels between the authority in the universe and the authority within the family: "When God established authority, He included that of the home. God made man and woman for specific functions. The Biblical home has God's order, which is discussed quite fully in Ephesians 5:21–6:4. We see that God made the husband the head of the home."[2]

This does not mean that the husband should be tyrannical against his wife. On the contrary, the fundamentalist pastor asserts, the husband should love his wife dearly and the wife should revere her husband. There is a subtle difference between the love of the husband and the reverence of the wife, which implies a sense of submission to the authority of the husband. The authority established by God in the family must be obeyed, and many Christian fundamentalists would agree that the most important source of social problems in the modern world is the lack of Christian virtues and attitudes that are the corollaries of divine authority in the family as in society in general. The retired Florida Baptist pastor sums up important fundamentalist ideas

[2] Reynold Lemp, "Authority: Right or Wrong?" *Frontline* (September/October 2007): 17ff. at p. 17.

about family life when he continues, "'Obedience' and 'honor' are two important words that apply not only to family but to every area of life!"[3] These key concepts, and this way of reasoning, are typical of fundamentalist writing and preaching about the relations between men and women.

A key person shaping the Christian fundamentalist debates about family and gender relations is Dr. James Dobson. Dobson is a child psychologist and best-selling author of books about Christian family life. He is one of the most influential fundamentalist Christians in the United States today and has shaped American political debate about issues such as abortion and same-sex marriage through his many books and his widely broadcast radio programs. Dobson is in charge of an important and influential organization called Focus on the Family, which produces a range of materials about family matters with a Christian fundamentalist perspective, such as the magazine *Citizen*, with ten issues per year defending conservative Christian family values.

Most of James Dobson's books take as their point of departure that the modern world has gone wrong on a number of important issues. According to Dobson, modern American families are under threat by selfishness, divorce, infidelity, and a general lack of a Christian understanding of marriage. The problems are clear also in the lives of children and adolescents, according to Dobson, and many of his books are about how to raise children as good and God-fearing Christians in the modern world. The books about children carry titles such as *Dare to Discipline*, *Bringing Up Boys*, *Bringing Up Girls*, and *The Strong-Willed Child*, and they are all written in a very personal style that emphasizes examples from the real world and practical strategies for handling the problems and challenges of raising children. These books focus on the necessity of disciplining children (Dobson is careful to note that this does not mean being violent) and

[3] Ibid., p. 18.

providing solid role models. Understanding the issues of authority – in the universe, in society, and in the family – is the heart of the matter for Dobson and several other Christian fundamentalists engaged in family policy in America. In one of his bestselling books, Dobson explains that respect for authority in the family is important because young children "identify their parents, and especially their fathers, with God," which means that if mom and dad are not respected, neither are their country and their faith.[4]

SITA OR DURGA? HINDU FUNDAMENTALIST WOMEN AND THEIR DIVINE MODELS

There is ambivalence in Hindu fundamentalist circles about the public and private roles of women. On the one hand, Hindu fundamentalists believe that women are assigned very specific positions and roles in society and in the family. The basis for the assignment of these positions and roles is dharma, the important Hindu concept I have discussed earlier that refers to the natural order of things and the rights and obligations of all beings in the cosmos. On the other hand, some fundamentalists, including a number of prominent women, believe that it is important that women take on new roles that do not conform to the ideas associated with the dharma of traditional Hinduism.

The female roles that conform to the standards of Hindu dharma, according to fundamentalists, are those of the wife and the mother. In the fundamentalist vision of society, the ideal Hindu wife stays at home, does not engage in economic activity outside the household, is very devoted to her husband, and sacrifices her own needs and desires in order to support him. In modern Hindu fundamentalist imagination, the epic Ramayana gives the best illustration of the ideal wife. This is the story of

[4] James Dobson, *The New Dare to Discipline*, Carol Streams, Ill.: Tyndale House, 1992), p. 19.

King Rama and his wife, Sita, who is kidnapped by a terrible demon but waits patiently to be rescued by the hero. At the end of the story, Rama is worried that Sita may have been unfaithful to him during her years in captivity, and the only response she can think of is to plan for her own ritual suicide by fire. As she is pure and innocent, the gods rescue her before she kills herself. In the discourse of fundamentalist women in India, Sita gives a blueprint for the chastity and patience of the perfect wife.

The role of the mother is perhaps even more important both to Hindu nationalists and fundamentalists (the two categories overlap to a large degree). Motherhood is given a high status, and the perfect mother sacrifices her own needs for her children, especially for her sons. In many parts of South Asia, including India, sons are more highly valued than daughters, and this results in statistically poorer living conditions for girls than for boys. Motherhood is also associated with the motherland, and India is often referred to as "mother India" or "Bharatmata."

The tension between, on the one hand, the image of the idealized Hindu woman, with an emphasis on wifely and motherly virtues and self-sacrifice, and, on the other hand, the image of a modern woman with equal rights can be traced back to the nineteenth century, when India came into close contact with the West through processes of globalization in general and the channels of the British Empire in particular. The intellectual and reformer Rammohan Roy (1772–1833) was very critical of the way women were treated in the Hindu tradition, and he worked zealously to change the situation. He was committed to ending the practice of *sati*, the ritual in which a widow let herself be burned on the funeral pyre of her husband after the model of the perfect wife in Hindu mythology.

In a treatise called *A Second Conference between an Advocate and Opponent of the Practice of Burning Widows Alive*, Roy opposes a Brahmin defender of the traditional position of women in Hindu society: "By ascribing to them all sorts of improper conduct, you have indeed successfully persuaded the Hindoo community to look down upon them as contemptible and mischievous creatures, whence they have been subjected to constant miseries."[5] He discusses the natural properties of women and points out that women are equal or even better than men in understanding, in resolution, in trustworthiness, in the subjection of passions, and in virtuous knowledge.[6] The quarrel between Rammohan Roy and orthodox Hindu Brahmins can be seen as an early precursor to later debates between modernists and fundamentalists. Roy was inspired by Western liberal ideas, although he was keenly aware of the paradoxes of the illiberal colonial regime. His conservative Hindu opponents held the traditionalist view that the ultimate source of all authority must be the ancient Hindu texts, and they lamented Roy's modernism.

The famous Hindu leader Swami Vivekananda, working at the very end of the nineteenth century, was also intent on changing the position of women in Hindu society, and his reasons were both religious and political. On his travels in America and England, Vivekananda encountered societies where he felt that the uplift of women had come a very long way in comparison with India. Indeed, one of the things that made him admire America was the position of its women. The average American woman is far more cultivated than the average American man, he said.[7] He observed that "…nowhere in the world is woman so free, so educated, so cultured. They are everything in society."[8]

At the same time, Vivekananda saw the West's lament over women's fate in India as an aspect of a general attack on Indian culture, and he refused to condemn the treatment of women in his own society in the way Rammohan Roy did. Instead, he talked in romantic terms of the Indian woman as the ideal Mother as

[5] Rammohan Roy, *Translation of Several Principal Books, Passages, and Texts of the Vedas and of Some Controversial Works on Brahmunical Theology* (London: Parbury, Allen, & Co., 1832), p. 251.

[6] Ibid., p. 252.

[7] Vivekananda, *The Complete Works of Swami Vivekananda*, vol. 5, p. 22.

[8] Ibid., vol. 8, p. 325.

opposed to the American woman as the Wife.[9] For Vivekananda, the Indian woman was the epitome of purity. This did not mean that he was happy about the contemporary position of women in India. Women in India had "many and grave problems," according to the Swami.[10] But, at the same time, the solution to the problems was to be found at home, in the Hindu tradition, and he looked to ancient India to find the ideal relation between men and women, quoting classical literature in Sanskrit, which he knew well, in order to demonstrate that there was a strong tradition in Indian history for gender equality: "Again, could anything be more complete than the equality of boys and girls in our old forest universities?"[11]

In the twentieth century, Mahatma Gandhi would continue the debate about the status of women in Hindu culture, but he would introduce several new elements into it. Whereas some Hindu reformers of the late nineteenth and early twentieth centuries saw Hindu women as helpless creatures who had to be protected, Gandhi saw women as potentially independent actors both in the private and public spheres. He did not deny that women had a natural role in the home, but at the same time he insisted that women had the ability and obligation to change their relative status in society through their own efforts. They needed to be fearless, he asserted, and emulate the great female models of Hindu mythology.

Gandhi's female role models were not different from those of Hindu fundamentalists. He would often point to Sita, Rama's wife, as an ideal for contemporary women, but he would emphasize different aspects of Sita's character and behavior. In Gandhi's rhetoric, Sita was independent and strong-willed; she was pure and chaste, but she was not submissive and dependent.[12]

[9] Ibid., vol. 8, p. 53ff.

[10] Ibid., vol. 5, p. 231.

[11] Ibid.

[12] Madhu Kishwar, "Gandhi on Women," *Economic and Political Weekly* 20, no. 40 (October 5, 1985): 1691–1702.

Gandhi did not favor equality in the sense that men and women should do the same types of work, but his emphasis on female fearlessness and independent engagement was important in channeling women into his movement of protest against British policies.

The idealized roles of Hindu women that we find in the thought of leaders such as Vivekananda and Gandhi, such as the wife, the sister, and the mother, are often discussed or depicted in symbolic form in Hindu fundamentalist propaganda. It is common to print images of important Hindu goddesses, especially Lakshmi, the perfect wife of the god Shiva, on the pages of propaganda issued by organizations such as the RSS and the VHP and their female branches. Lakshmi, with her chastity, patience, and devotion to her husband, is the embodiment of wifely values for Hindu fundamentalists. However, there is another current of female ideals running through the history of Hindu fundamentalism according to which women, too, need to come out of the home, leave the domestic chores and rituals behind, and take on public roles in the defense of Hindu culture. The political and militant roles of fundamentalist women are pointed to in propaganda through pictures and stories about fierce, unmarried goddesses who carry weapons and slay demons. Durga is the most famous of them. There is a tension, then, between the ideals concerning women in Hindu fundamentalism that is also found in many nationalist movements.

This tension is clear if we look at the political activities of female Hindu fundamentalists in modern Indian politics. The Rashtriya Swayamsevika Samiti (which I will refer to as the Samiti) is the women's branch of the RSS, the most important organization of Hindu fundamentalism. The Samiti was established by a woman called Lakshmibai Kelkar in the mid-1930s. Kelkar approached K. B. Hedgewar, the founder and leader of the RSS, with a wish to join the RSS, and through their discussions they agreed that she should organize the women's wing of the movement.[13] At the time, Kelkar was a widow with eight children, and according to the Samiti's own narration, its founding mother had to struggle for a long time to gain acceptance of her political activity from her extended family. Her motivation arose largely from a realization that many Hindu women were weak and needed strength to resist physical exploitation by men.

On a more ideological level, the Samiti was started because Kelkar, Hedgewar, and other early ideologues of Hindu fundamentalism saw a grave threat to the Hindu family, the basic unit of Hindu culture and society, in the feminine ideals espoused by liberal, Westernized women and from communists and socialists. Hindu fundamentalist women generally believe that the Western and modernist focus on equal rights for women is a threat to Hindu culture. They feel that the focus on equal rights championed by modern women's groups in India is the result of Western influence and has resulted in broken families, unhappy children, and other kinds of misery. A good, pure Hindu woman will find the happiness she needs in being a mother and sacrificing herself for the happiness of the family, leading fundamentalist women point out.[14] Proper Hindu culture, in their view, teaches Hindu girls and young women to behave and dress modestly and accept a subordinate position as servants for the male members of the household. The ideal is "worship of the husband" (*pativrata* in Hindi) as if he were a god.

To some Hindus, both women and men, the most powerful symbol of such devotion and worship is the act of *sati*. I mentioned that the great reformer Rammohan Roy engaged in a campaign to stop this practice in which Hindu wives mount the funeral pyres of their deceased husbands and kill themselves in an act of religious piety. This is an act that has strong

[13] For the early histoty of the Samiti, I rely on Paola Bacchetta, *Gender in the Hindu Nation: RSS Women as Ideologues* (New Delhi: Women Unlimited, 2004).

[14] Tanika Sarkar, "Pragmatics of the Hindu Right: Politics of Women's Organisations," *Economic and Political Weekly* 34, no. 31 (July 31– August 6, 1999): 2159–67. For quotations, see p. 2165.

resonances in parts of Hindu mythology, and to some modern fundamentalists it is a sign of anti-Hindu policies and degenerate Westernization that *sati* is outlawed in India. *Sati* is certainly rare today, but when a young Hindu woman was burned to death with her deceased husband in the town of Deoras in the state of Rajasthan in 1987, it created significant enthusiasm in fundamentalist circles, and a conflict ensued between authorities that wanted to ban the communal glorification of wife-burning and fundamentalist organizations that defended this practice as an integral part of Hindu culture.[15]

The women of the Samiti are organized along the same lines as the male organization: it consists of *shakhas*, small groups of people who come together regularly to discuss aspects of Hindu culture and history and to receive physical exercise. From the 1930s to the 1980s, the Samiti was not a terribly important part of the Sangh Parivar, or the wider family of Hindu fundamentalists associated with the RSS, although it always did engage in some public activity. However, the role of the Samiti, as with some other fundamentalist women's organizations in India, started to change in the 1980s. This was the decade when the Hindu fundamentalists saw their opportunity to work more realistically toward their goal of gaining political power, both on a national level and in the important state assemblies that work as parliaments in the states that make up the federation of India.

Since the late 1980s, some of the most vocal supporters of violence against Indian Muslims (and sometimes against Christians) were women. In the propaganda produced by the Samiti through the decades, Muslims have consistently been presented as a dangerous threat to Hindu women and to the Hindu nation. The following is a typical quotation from a fundamentalist woman talking about Muslims: "They deserve to die. They should all be killed. They spill our blood. They rape

[15] John Stratton Hawley, *Fundamentalism and Gender* (New York: Oxford University Press, 1994), pp. 79–111.

our women. Let their blood be spilled, the bloody bastards."[16] Two prominent militant woman leaders are Uma Bharati and Ritambhara. Uma Bharati is a very prominent BJP politician and former member of Parliament, and Ritambhara is a self-styled Hindu female ascetic who has become famous for her aggressive preaching. Both have contributed significantly to the violent politics of Hindu fundamentalism over the past twenty years. During the most violent period of the Hindu fundamentalist agitation in the early 1990s, thousands of women took part in the violent attacks on Muslim persons and buildings in India.

It is difficult to say anything exact about the number of women who take part in Hindu fundamentalist politics because the Samiti and several other organizations do not have reliable statistics. It is clear, however, that the religious image of women – the mother, the wife, the sister – is at the core of Hindu fundamentalist ideology and that hundreds of thousands of Hindu women have played key roles in Hindu fundamentalism for some decades and will probably continue to do so in the future.

WOMEN, MODERNITY, AND FUNDAMENTALISM IN EGYPT

The landing of Napoleon Bonaparte outside Alexandria in 1798 marked the beginning of the Middle East's step into an age of rapid modernization and globalization. The French invasion of Egypt was part of a larger strategy in the global war against Britain, and Napoleon's plan was to use Egypt as a first stop on the way to India, where he planned a campaign against the British Indian empire, which was being expanded and consolidated at this time. Although Napoleon gave up on Egypt in 1801 and traveled back to Europe, eventually to be defeated at Waterloo, his arrival in Egypt ushered in great changes.

[16] This is a quotation from one scholar's interviews with a young Hindu fundamentalist woman. See Bacchetta, *Gender in the Hindu Nation*, p. 85.

The imbalances brought by the invasion created the opportunity for a new leader to emerge, Muhammad Ali, who acted as virtually independent governor of the Ottoman sultan in Istanbul. Muhammad Ali's vision for a modern Egypt included all members of society, and the period was the starting point for great changes in the public roles of Muslim women.[17] During the nineteenth century, the modernizing processes affected the lives of all Egyptians. Businessmen and traders were hit by reforms in the economy, peasants were hit by sweeping changes in agriculture, and the lower sections of society were hit by the use of forced recruitment to the army or to the work of digging canals. The *ulama*, the religious elite, were hit hard by a rapid erosion of their authority in society, a process that took place globally from the nineteenth century onward, as we saw in Part I.

The position of women in Egyptian society changed dramatically through the nineteenth century, and debates about these changes were carried out in a wide range of magazines and books. Paradoxically from a modern point of view, most of the authors and readers of the articles on what was called "the woman question" were men until the later decades of the nineteenth century.[18] However, from the early 1900s, quite a few Egyptian women did take part in the debates and founded feminist organizations and publications.[19]

The great reformist Muhammad Abdu discussed the role of women in Muslim society extensively in the magazines he published during the 1880s and 1890s. In his view, the position of women in Egypt needed to be changed, but this certainly did not entail a wholesale rejection of Islam or Egyptian culture. In order to develop Egyptian society, one should adopt new

[17] Leila Ahmed, *Women and Gender in Islam* (New Haven, Conn.: Yale University Press, 1992). See in particular chaps. 7–11.

[18] Marilyn Booth, "Woman in Islam: Men and the 'Women's Press' in Turn-of-the-20th-Century Egypt," *International Journal of Middle East Studies* 33 (2001): 171–201.

[19] Ahmed, *Women and Gender in Islam*, chap. 9.

organizational forms and traditions. Customs that were clearly in the way of progress, such as the seclusion and subjection of women, must be changed, Abdu asserted, but he insisted that this realization had not been brought to the Muslim world by contacts with the West. On the contrary, it was Islam that first recognized the equal humanity of women, he said. In Islam, women and men are equal before God, Abdu argued, so changing the position of women in contemporary Egypt was really a way of going back to real Islamic principles of gender equality.[20]

This position was rejected in a controversial book that appeared in Egypt in 1899. It was written by a man called Qassim Amin and was entitled *The Liberation of Woman*. Amin argued that Muslim civilization in general, and Egyptian civilization in particular, was a failure. Egyptians of both sexes were lazy, dirty, and stupid. The only way to change this sad state of affairs would be to embrace superior Western culture, he argued. Thus, British occupation was a good thing, Amin wrote, and Egyptians should be thankful for the justice, freedom, security, and knowledge that the occupants brought. The veil was the most obvious symbol of the inferior status of women in Egyptian society, according to Amin. In his opinion, Egypt should be unveiled as quickly as possible. He believed that boys and girls, and men and women, needed to mix freely with one another to develop a culture of learning, and he argued that veiling and seclusion made this impossible. Many other writers held the same views on education and public participation of women but rejected the claim that veiling made education and progress impossible. The heated debate over these issues was the starting point for the modern controversies on the issues of veiling and the public role of women in Egypt.

The debate expanded rapidly to include a number of women and men with different opinions on the proper public role of women. Huda Sharawi (1879–1947) was among the most

[20] Ibid., pp. 139–40.

important of the early Egyptian feminists. Sharawi was an upper-class Egyptian woman educated at the prestigious Sorbonne in Paris. She founded the Egyptian Feminist Union in 1923 in order to fight for women's suffrage and stayed in close touch with feminists in the Western world. Sharawi was the typical modernist. She wanted rapid change and saw traditional Egyptian Islam as an obstacle to equal rights. There were a number of devoted activist women working to strengthen the public role and the human rights of women through the early twentieth century in Egypt. Some embraced modern Western values and rejected Islam. Others argued, in line with Abdu, that change was necessary but that did not mean rejection of tradition. It meant going back to real Muslim values and practices.

What is the fundamentalist position? First of all, Muslim fundamentalists see Islam as the right answer, and they believe that a correct approach to the Islamic sources will yield a clear answer to the question of women's roles. The Muslim Brotherhood has espoused values and conceptions about women's role in society that show the complexities of fundamentalist worldviews on matters of public and private spheres and on the relationship between men and women. On the one hand, the Muslim Brotherhood sees the participation of women as crucial for success, and the debate on the potential social and political roles of women has been important to the political transformation that has taken place in the organization since the 1980s. The Muslim Brotherhood as a modern political party in Egypt has tried to field female candidates, and it believes that women should be allowed to hold offices of high political authority.

On the other hand, they have always had a religious worldview according to which men and women were created differently and assigned different roles in the world by God. This worldview comes with a set of values about the proper place of women in society, and the Muslim Brotherhood has generally been of the opinion that women should primarily fulfill their God-given duties of being mothers and wives and that their full participation in public and political life is wrong if it entails abandoning these duties.

The fundamentalist ideology that Islam is a total solution to questions of gender roles and the proper relationship between the public and the private was espoused by a famous twentieth-century Islamist woman close to the Muslim Brotherhood, Zaynab al-Ghazali (1918–). As a very young woman, al-Ghazali worked for the Egyptian feminist Huda Sharawi, but she realized at the age of eighteen that she disagreed with her mentor on many issues and decided to start her own organization, the Muslim Women's Association.[21] Al-Ghazali believed Sharawi was mistaken in the view that the Western model of feminism had anything to offer a Muslim society. On the contrary, Islam was the only guide, and the religion, as properly understood, provided women with all the freedom and rights they needed. Al-Ghazali had a close relationship with Hasan al-Banna, the founder of the Muslim Brotherhood. They met early in al-Ghazali's career as a political activist, and al-Banna tried to convince her to merge her organization with the Muslim Brotherhood. She refused to merge with al-Banna's group but continued to work closely with it to make the Egyptian nation live more in accordance with true Islam. In her opinion, it was absolutely necessary for women to take part in this political work.

What types of sources are used by fundamentalists to understand the proper roles of women? As an example of how the debates are shaped, we can take a look at how modern Muslims use a particular verse of the Qur'an – Sura 4:34 – in arguments about the position of women in the family and in society. This verse has become the focus of controversy because various translations of the verse imply different relationships between husbands and wives. The controversies have often revolved around the interpretation and translation of particular words, such as *qawwam.* This is variously translated as "guardian," "maintainer,"

[21] Ibid., p. 197.

or "caretaker," and, as is often the case with key terms in ancient texts, people with different interests insist on different interpretations. Those who advocate modernist values insist on a reading of the verse that implies gender equality, whereas conservative readers tend to see the verse as expressing a relationship of male authority and female submission.

Debates regarding the correct interpretation of this particular Qur'anic verse and other key verses have raged in many Muslim societies. In 1994, the Muslim Brotherhood explained their view on the term *qawwam*, or the "directing role," as they translated it into English. They say that the directing role of men does not apply to all men and all women in all things. The directing role is confined to the family, where the male should be the leader. The husband has the responsibility to provide all that is needed for the household, and he has no right to force the woman to pay anything, even if she is wealthy. The directing role of the husband must be based not on repression or hegemony but on kindness, love, and consultation between husband and wife, according to the Muslim Brotherhood:

> The general rule, therefore, is equality between men and women. The exceptions are from Allah, the All-Knowing and All-Aware because it is He who knows His creation best and the exceptions are in those specific characteristics that distinguish the female from the male. These differences are due to the separate functions that have been accorded to the male and female.[22]

To the Muslim Brotherhood, as to fundamentalists in general, these God-given differences between men and women refer mainly to women's obligations as mothers and keepers of the family household. Their public roles are necessarily secondary.

The word *qawwam* is just one of the relevant words for gender roles in the Qur'an, and the second half of Sura 4:34 is just as

[22] "The Role of Muslim Women in Islamic Society According to the Muslim Brotherhood," translation of a statement issued by the Muslim Brotherhood in Egypt, March 1994 (Cairo: International Islamic Forum), pp. 14–15.

contested because it refers to a husband's right to beat a wife if she displays disobedience or rebellion. Again, there have been numerous debates between defenders of different interpretations of the Qur'an, and again the sacred text itself offers several possible translations and interpretations, as ancient religious texts often do.[23]

PURDAH IN PAKISTAN

In Pakistan's history since independence in 1947, we see similar tensions between modernists calling for a new public role for women to strengthen the nation and civil society and a fundamentalist reaction that has insisted on the creation of roles for women that are truly Muslim, from their point of view, and do not mimic the gender roles of the West. Maulana Maududi insisted that Muslim women should wear the veil and spend their energies in the home. He argued for *purdah*.

Purdah is a word that has entered the South Asian languages from Persian and literally means "curtain" or "screen" but generally refers to the custom of keeping women strictly separated from society. This is a tradition with old roots in parts of South Asia and is not restricted to certain Muslim communities but is also practiced by some members of other religions. *Purdah* is a very clear expression of the ideology that women belong to the private sphere of the home, whereas men are responsible for all dealings with the public world outside. Maududi's concept of *purdah* entailed a clear separation of gender roles, based on what he believed to be God-given differences between men and women. In his fundamentalist vision of Islamic society, the good Muslim wife or daughter would not need to be forced to wear the veil and stay at home because a true Muslim woman would

[23] For a discussion, see for instance Shannon Dunn and Rosemary B. Kellison, "At the Intersection of Scripture and Law: Quran 4:34 and Violence against Women," *Journal of Feminist Studies in Religion* 26, no. 2 (2006): 11–36.

understand the importance of willingly accepting religiously sanctioned gender roles.[24]

Maududi's ideas about the natural God-given differences between men and women also had implications for the relationship between husbands and wives, and his exposition of their roles and relative status took as its point of departure Sura 4:34 of the Qur'an. In a book about the position of wives and husbands, Maududi chose a translation rendering the beginning of the verse as "Men are the maintainers of women…," pointing out that "*qawwam* also means guardian, protector, manager, supervisor."[25] Among South Asian Muslims today, debates over the position of women in the family and society are often based on divergent opinions about the correct translations of key terms in the Qur'an relating to men and women.[26]

Maududi asserted that Islam has clearly demarcated the sphere of work for the wife and the husband. A woman's duty is to stay at home and take care of household chores, and the husband must go out and work and make a living for the family. The role of the husband as the breadwinner is implied in the term *qawwam*, Maududi asserted: "Qawwam is a person who looks after and takes care of a thing and by virtue thereof has an authority over it."[27] This division of labor is a factor that elevates the husband's status above that of the wife, he continues, but it also gives the man great responsibilities. If he is not able to provide a livelihood and give his wife living expenses as well as dower, the marriage may be legally dissolved.

[24] Syed Abul A'la Maududi, *Purdah and the Status of Women* (Delhi: Markaza Maktabi Islami, 1996).

[25] Sayyid Abul A'la Maududi, *The Rights and Duties of Spouses* (Delhi: Human Welfare Trust, 2000), p. 23.

[26] See, for instance, how an important Indian Muslim scholar discusses the meaning of terms such as *qawwam* to support gender equality in Yoginder Sikand, "Maulana Wahiduddin Khan Responds to Contentious Points on Views about Women in Islam." http://www.islamopediaonline.org/fatwa/maulana-wahiduddin-khan-responds-contentious-points-views-about-women-islam (retrieved March 1, 2011).

[27] Maududi, *The Rights and Duties of Spouses*, p. 26.

The fundamentalists of the Jamaat-e-Islami, Maududi's religious and political movement, strengthened their position during the reign of General Zia ul-Haq in the years 1977–88. The Pakistani fundamentalists were successful in getting government support for a broad range of measures aimed at the Islamization of state and society, but on matters related to the status of women, the Pakistani fundamentalists were not very successful. They were not able to get political support for their goal of preventing women from working outside the home, and they failed to obtain legislation to repeal the Muslim Family Law Ordinance of 1961, which improved the rights of women in the family. The fundamentalists saw this law as contradictory to the *sharia*.[28] The lack of success in imposing fundamentalist values in legislation dealing with women resulted from the fact that the political elites were generally quite modern in their outlook. The political elites of Pakistan, people from the armed forces and high-ranking civil servants, had often been exposed to modern ideas and values through their education and their contacts with the larger world.

Maududi's view on women and *purdah* certainly had great significance for the Jamaat-e-Islami in particular and for South Asian Sunni Muslim fundamentalism in general. However, there was necessarily an ambiguity in the position of women, as in many fundamentalist ideologies and movements, because relegating half the population to the confines of the home deprives a movement of valuable resources. Some three decades after the founding of the Jamaat, important transformations started appearing in the thinking about the roles of women. Beginning in the 1970s, there appeared substantial criticism of Maududi's position, and several members of the Jamaat claimed that Islam in fact allowed women to take on important political

[28] Ann Elizabeth Mayer, "The Fundamentalist Impact on Law, Politics, and Constitutions in Iran, Pakistan and Sudan," in Marty and Appleby, *Fundamentalisms and the State*, pp. 110–52, especially pp. 128–29.

and economic roles in society and did not demand veiling and seclusion.[29]

Today, the Jamaat's branches in India and Bangladesh have edged closer to mainstream democratic and egalitarian views about the position of women in society, and even in the Pakistani Jamaat women are taking part in politics in new ways. The women's wing of Jamaat-e-Islami Pakistan describes itself as "the largest and most progressive women's organization in the world"[30] and organizes a number of activities for women outside the home, in the public sphere, and even has a separate department for dealing with issues of working women.

Muslim fundamentalists, like their Christian counterparts, are very aware that their movements need the active participation of women, and this often results in an ambiguous position on the status and role of women. The ambiguity is visible in the ideology and practice concerning gender in the Islamist terrorist organization Lashkar-e-Taiba (LeT). The LeT has been supported by the Pakistani authorities as allies in the war against India in the disputed region of Kashmir and is feared in India and Pakistan for its violent campaigns against civilians in the whole of South Asia, such as the large-scale attack on several sites in Mumbai in November 2008. The LeT owes part of its success to a conscious campaign to involve women in its world of militarism by playing on the emotions of mothers and sisters of the young men who enter the movement as terrorists or, in their eyes, as "freedom fighters" dying for the liberation of Muslims from suppression at the hands of Hindus and their Christian and Jewish allies. Getting parents to accept the choice of their sons to become martyrs is usually difficult, but in the ideology of the LeT, the greatest sacrifice a woman can perform is the giving away of one or more sons in LeT's war, and the women's mixed

29 Irfan Ahmad, "Cracks in the 'Mightiest Fortress': Jamaat-e-Islami's Changing Discourse on Women," *Modern Asian Studies* 42 (2008): 549–75.

30 http://jamaatwomen.org/site/page/4 (accessed February 8, 2011).

feelings of sorrow and pride are part of the warrior culture of the group. Through a women's wing, and through schools and publications targeting women, the LeT has been far better at creating a sustainable militant culture than competing terrorist groups in Pakistan.[31]

The women of the LeT are expected to take part in the fight for Islam. Their struggle does not entail active militant or terrorist operations but rather campaigns in the private sphere. They work to create a clean and conscious fundamentalist space inside the private realm by purging the household of all corrupting influences, such as TVs, pictures, magazines other than those published by the fundamentalists themselves, and all products associated with enemy societies, such as food or household goods produced in India or the West. By wearing black *burqas* and covering their bodies completely, they signal that they embrace the fundamentalist ideal of *purdah* – the strict separation of women from public life. Such complete covering has no roots in Muslim traditions of the regions where the LeT women live but is the invention of Muslim fundamentalists.

WOMEN BETWEEN FUNDAMENTALISM AND MODERNISM

We may return once again to the point I made earlier about modernity developing a set of reference points, a set of concepts, a language, that everybody needs to use in order to be listened to in debates about what matters. In the treatment of questions concerning families, and the role of women in particular, it is obvious that both fundamentalists and modernists (feminists included) must employ concepts such as justice and equality to make their points. Is it simply confusion about the concepts of equality and justice that causes fundamentalists and modernists to be at loggerheads over matters of women?

[31] Farhat Haq, "Militarism and Motherhood: The Women of the Lashkar-i-Tayyibiya in Pakistan," *Signs* 32, no. 4 (Summer 2007): 1023–46.

If we turn to the field of political philosophy to straighten our thoughts, we must admit that both *equality* and *justice* are extremely general terms that can refer to many things. The fact is that nobody who wants to be taken seriously in political debate would say that he or she is against equality or justice. I mentioned earlier that Protestant fundamentalists and feminists in the United States disagree about what differences between men and women are relevant. Fundamentalists believe that men and women are created different and therefore they must accept different roles and responsibilities in the world, although it is often hard to live up to those ideals. In the book *Islam and Gender*, feminist anthropologist Ziba Mir-Husseini gives a revealing account of her discussion with a traditionalist cleric, Ayatollah Madani: "We agreed on the principles of equality and justice, we both believed that men and women are entitled to them, yet we kept talking across each other."[32] The ayatollah and the academic agreed that equality and justice were very important. But they both realized that they were not talking about the same things.

In practical terms, justice and equality are often about hard material realities, and the ideologies of both fundamentalists and modernists regarding the roles of men and women are sometimes challenged by the economic constraints of everyday life. The extent to which women are willing and able to be part of the public realm is partly conditioned by the economy of the society in question. Women make up half of the potential workforce, and in many societies that are moving from a traditional to a modern economy there will be pressure on women to come out of their homes and enter offices and factories as wage earners. Capitalist economies rely on the mobilization and organization of labor, and keeping a large part of society out of the economy makes little sense from an economic point of view.

[32] Ziba Mir-Husseini, *Islam and Gender: The Religious Debate in Contemporary Iran* (Princeton, N.J.: Princeton University Press, 1999), p. 29.

In many capitalist economies, society is organized around the assumption that both men and women work.

As with many social movements, the fundamentalist organizations that work to change modern American family life often display a number of disparities between ideology and practice, and some of these disparities may be explained by the constraints put on families by a modern economy. The ideology of fundamental differences in gender and in the roles of men and women in the family is not always the only force shaping the everyday lives of fundamentalist Christians in America. On the contrary, many fundamentalist families experience that the ideals about the husband as leader and breadwinner and the wife as mother and housewife are difficult to put into practice because they need the extra income that the wife can provide by entering the labor market. Held up against the constraints of everyday life, it may seem like the fundamentalist Christian family values we find in books, magazines, and radio and TV programs are really the values and norms of a Christian elite.[33]

To believing Muslim women, too, economic incentives may pull in different directions. On the one hand, it is an advantage in many Muslim societies to display modern values if you want a job in the private sector and especially in the businesses that are part of the globalized economy, such as telecommunications, airlines, or the tourist industry. In other words, if a woman wants to join a multinational company in a country like Egypt, she might have a better chance if she does not wear a veil and dresses like a Westerner. In such a case, aligning with modern values and dress codes is the economically rational thing to do. On the other hand, if a woman stands no chance of getting a job with decent pay, for instance if she lacks higher education, the only option to secure a livelihood is often to enter into a marriage with a man who can provide for the family. However, in

[33] John Bartkowski, *Remaking the Godly Marriage: Gender Negotiation in Evangelical Families* (New Brunswick, N.J.: Rutgers University Press, 2001).

many Muslim societies, and particularly in conservative communities, a woman will stand a better chance of attracting suitors if she carries signs of piety and purity. In such a case, wearing a veil and adopting more traditional values might well be a highly rational choice.[34]

[34] Lisa Blaydes and Drew A. Linzer, "The Politicial Economy of Women's Support for Fundamentalist Islam," *World Politics* 60 (July 2008): 576–609.

Conclusion

The main argument in this book is that fundamentalism is a reaction to modernity and globalization found in all world religions. Fundamentalism includes movements, organizations, and people in many different religious cultures, and I have taken examples that I believe are important from Protestant Christianity in the United States, Islam in South Asia and the Middle East, Buddhism in South and Southeast Asia, and Hinduism in India. Fundamentalist movements in these religious cultures share several traits, as has been observed by many others, but I have argued that there is a much more important reason why we may use the word "fundamentalism" to describe all the movements I have looked at here and surely many others. The reason is that they are the results of the same global historical processes, and my goal in the first part of this book was to outline some of the main elements in these processes.

To outline the early global history of fundamentalism in world religions, I looked at the great political and cultural transformations that took place in almost every part of the world starting in the mid-nineteenth century as the result of the global spread of Western modernity. In many parts of Africa and Asia, the transformations came as the result of colonization, whereas in other societies – I have pointed to Turkey, Thailand, and Japan as important examples – modernity was hurriedly self-imposed in order to face a new and competitive international environment.

One important aspect of modernization, whether introduced by colonial governments or self-imposed by Western-inspired heads of state, was that element of secularization that is often called *differentiation*. This is the process whereby the spheres of society – law, politics, science, education, religion – become independent of each other and develop clear boundaries from other societal spheres. This is a necessary part of any modernizing process if that process is to include the setting up of bureaucracies, the framing of modern legal codes, the establishment of nation-building educational systems, and so forth. I discussed the thinking of sociologist Talcott Parsons to explain the process of differentiation in some detail because a grasp of this process is crucial if we want to understand what fundamentalists react against. Fundamentalists everywhere struggle to make religion regain some of its lost authority in other societal spheres, such as politics, law, science, and education, and it was the goal of the second part of this book to give some examples of how such struggles are fought.

The process of differentiation was closely linked to other important processes of change for religion in the modern world. Beginning in the nineteenth century, we can see the start of a process in which traditional religious authority was being challenged and undermined in many societies. The undermining of religious authority started in Western Christianity with the Reformation in the sixteenth century. Protestant ideas about individual religious authority and the universalization of priesthood surely had some effect in several Asian and African societies as a result of the global spread of Protestant Christianity, starting with the explosion of modern missionary activity in the early nineteenth century and continuing today with the charismatic movements across the globe.

However, there were several other very important reasons why a global challenge against traditional religious authority has taken place. The great political changes starting in the nineteenth century severed old ties between political power and established religious elites. The changes left the religious elites without the status and support they had enjoyed in premodern times, or the new and powerful states nationalized the religious establishment and forced it into complete submission. There was a global shift in the relationship between political and religious institutions that can be observed in Muslim, Buddhist, Hindu, and Sikh, as well as Christian, societies. In most places, the modern states severely curtailed the privileges of the religious elites, and states implemented regulations and state control over religious institutions and their activities.

Everywhere the religious elites lost their position in society, and they lost their roles as theological, moral, legal, educational, medical, and scientific authorities taking part in a complex division of labor with political elites. The process of differentiation was a fundamental cause of the loss of status and authority because it boxed religious elites into their limited societal sphere and denied them any say over the affairs of other areas of society. The undermining of traditional religious authority was exacerbated by the diffusion of new technologies, such as printing, which contributed to breaking the old monopoly of the priesthood over religious and other texts. Throughout the twentieth century, more and more people gained access to the sacred scriptures and other treasures of the world religions, and with growing access to the Internet the process is probably accelerating.

Most importantly, religious elites have lost much of their status in the eyes of laypeople. The details vary enormously, of course: in a country such as Thailand, the Buddhist monkhood still commands respect, whereas in many Christian countries of Western Europe the priesthood finds itself in a crisis, with declining prestige and falling recruitment. The fact is, however, that the position of the priesthood in all the world religions has taken a very severe beating, and there is no sign in today's world that this trend will be stopped or reversed. Of course, American pastors, Muslim mullahs, or Thai monks can still enjoy some prestige and authority, but that prestige has foundations different from the status enjoyed three centuries ago. Both the religious specialist and the lay follower today know that the authority of the priest or monk is not backed by special links to real political power, nor is it grounded in a monopoly on religious truths, and if the lay follower wants, he or she may simply withdraw support or even establish a new sect and claim the status of a pastor, monk, or nun. The recognition of such a claim comes down to how the environment perceives it: it comes down to charisma.

In the late nineteenth century, a new type of religious actor appeared on the scene. These are the middle-class people with some modern education who feel that their societies and their religious traditions are under threat from modernization and differentiation and who engage in political and religious activity to counter the threat. These new actors all share the modern concept of religion as an object that the believer should relate to in a conscious and active way. The process that we may call the *objectification* of religion took place in elite circles of educated people beginning in the late nineteenth century and can easily be observed if one reads the opinions of intellectuals in Egypt, India, Thailand, and many other places. After the Second World War, the process spread to more or less anybody with a minimum of access to education and some exposure to media debates about religion. A religion today is something that one belongs to exclusively, consciously, and unambiguously. Religion in premodern times could not be extracted from the cultures in which it was embedded, and its borders with law or science were fuzzy or nonexistent. Even borders *between* religions could be fuzzy, although saying so might be an offense to many modern believers. Today, most people take it for granted that Islam or Hinduism or Buddhism exist as timeless and universal things and that the mixture of these universal religions with local cultures entails pollution, or at least a muddling of the fundamentals.

The new middle-class people who took the responsibility to save their religious cultures from the destruction of modernity perceived clearly that their traditional religious elites had been sidelined and lost their authority. This led to the construction of new social and religious roles, and one of these new roles is that of the fundamentalist. The fundamentalist is somebody who realizes the impotence of traditional priesthood and steps into the vacuum with a new message of religious regeneration.

The prophet is the blueprint for the new roles created by lay religious leaders from the nineteenth century onward. In the thinking of Max Weber, the role of the prophet is a religious one that is opposed to the role of the priest. The priest is the caretaker of the traditional authority of an established church, whereas the prophet brings a new moral message from God to humanity and attacks established authority. The Old Testament is a main source for sociological reflections on prophethood, and we find the important ethical prophet in the Abrahamic religions: Judaism, Christianity, and Islam.

However, one important aspect of the global spread of Protestant Christianity and its institutions was a particular style of doing religion. This style emphasized the urgent message communicated by preaching. Many fundamentalist leaders in all world religions engage in preaching in ways that mimic the styles of Christian missionaries. We saw examples of the early beginnings of this new religious style in the late nineteenth and early twentieth centuries in the innovations of Buddhist monks in Sri Lanka as well as in itinerant Muslim preachers in India. In southern Africa, too, the transformations brought by colonialism produced a large number of new preachers and preaching movements. Preaching is also a hallmark of modern Buddhist movements in Japan, and the mimicry of Protestant preaching styles is evident today in global televangelists, whether Muslim, Buddhist, or Hindu.

Fundamentalist leaders are often lay religious leaders taking on the role of ethical prophet, preaching against impotent priesthoods, lukewarm co-religionists, and state power, in a struggle to halt or reverse modernism and its values and especially the process of differentiation, which has stripped religion of its influence over other societal spheres. Fundamentalism is the result of global processes that started in the Western world and spread, at different speeds and with different local adaptations, to all societies starting in the nineteenth century.

Today, many of the key processes seem to continue. Indicators of secularization as religious belief may be contradictory and complex, but differentiation is hard to reverse. The objectification of religion is continuing with increasing speed, and more and more people hold a concept of religion according to which it is an object detached from culture. Traditional priesthoods may try to reassert their position and authority now and then, but such traditionalist projects seem exceedingly difficult in a world where state regulation of religion is as strong as ever and where the development of communication technologies and the ideology of individual experience favor continued crumbling of traditional religious authority. New public spheres are created by groups that are deterritorialized, that is, by diasporas, which have considerable influence on the shaping of global discourses on how the world religions should be lived out by believers. All these trends and forces leave open a large territory and provide excellent conceptual tools for religious activism of different kinds, among them fundamentalism.

Bibliography

Primary Sources, Including Interviews

Anderson, Robert. "Christ and Criticism," in *The Fundamentals, a Testimony to Truth*, Volume 1, edited by A. C. Dixon, L. Meyer, and R. A. Torrey, 111–26. Chicago: Bible Institute of Los Angeles, 1917, reprinted by Baker Books in 2003.

Anonymous. "Evolutionism in the Pulpit," in *The Fundamentals, a Testimony to Truth*, Volume 4, edited by A. C. Dixon, L. Meyer, and R. A. Torrey, 88–96. Chicago: Bible Institute of Los Angeles, 1917, reprinted by Baker Books in 2003.

"Review of *Dominion Theology: Blessing or Curse?* by H. Wayne House and Thomas Ice." *Presbyterian: Covenant Seminary Review*, Spring 1989, p. 62ff.

Working Group Report. Presented to National Executive Bhopal, July 20, 1985. New Delhi: Bharatiya Janata Party Central Office, 1985.

Bahnsen, Greg L. *Theonomy in Christian Ethics*, 3rd edition. Nacogdoches, Tex.: Covenant Media Press, 2002.

Beach, Henry H. "Decadence of Darwinism," in *The Fundamentals, a Testimony to Truth*, Volume 4, edited by A. C. Dixon, L. Meyer, and R. A. Torrey, 59–71. Chicago: Bible Institute of Los Angeles, 1917, reprinted by Baker Books in 2003.

Carey, William. *An Enquiry into the Obligation of Christians to Use Means for the Conversion of the Heathen.* London: The Carey Kingsgate Press, 1792.

Carey, William to Andrew Fuller, 30 January 1795, IN/13. Angus Library, Regent's College, Oxford.

Carey, William to John Sutcliffe, 27 November 1800, IN/ 13 1 of 2. Angus Library, Regent's College, Oxford.

Cereghin, John. "From the Classroom." *Maranatha Baptist Watchman* (April 1992), p. 4.

Darwin, Charles. *On the Origin of Species by Means of Natural Selection, or The Preservation of Favoured Races in the Struggle for Life.* London: John Murray, 1859.

The Descent of Man and Selection in Relation to Sex. London: John Murray, 1871.

Dhamma, Arya. "Mrs. Rhys Davids and the 'Higher Criticism,'" *The Mahabodhi* 40, nos. 4–5 (1932): 160–65.

Dharmapala, Anagarika. *Return to Righteousness – a Collection of Speeches, Essays and Letters by the Anagarika Dharmapala,* edited by Ananda Guruge. Colombo: The Ministry of Education and Cultural Affairs, 1938.

Dobson, James C. *Straight Talk to Men and Their Wives.* Eastbourne: Kingsway, 1981.

Love Must Be Tough. Eastbourne: Kingsway, 1984.

The New Dare to Discipline. Carol Streams, Ill.: Tyndale House, 1992 (first published in 1970).

The Strong-Willed Child: Discipline While You Can. Eastbourne: Kingsway, 1993.

Bringing Up Boys: Practical Advice and Encouragement for Those Shaping the Next Generation of Men. Carol Streams, Ill.: Tyndale House, 2005.

Bringing Up Girls: Practical Advice and Encouragement for Those Shaping the Next Generation of Women. Carol Streams, Ill.: Tyndale House, 2010.

Einwechter, William O. "Paul Tillich and Biblical Theonomy." *Christian Statesman* 150, no. 2 (March–April 2007): 11ff.

Golwalkar, M. S. *Why Hindu Rashtra?* Bangalore: Kesari Press, 1962.

Bunch of Thoughts, 3rd edition. Bangalore: Sahitya Sindu Prakashana, 1996.

Griffith Thomas, W. H. "Old Testament Criticism and New Testament Christianity," in *The Fundamentals, a Testimony to Truth,* Volume 1, edited by A. C. Dixon, L. Meyer, and R. A. Torrey, 127–48. Chicago: Bible Institute of Los Angeles, 1917, reprinted by Baker Books in 2003.

Hunter, Sidney W. "Dominion Theology – Tried and Found Wanting." *Biblical Fundamentalist* (March 1, 1995), p. 1ff.

Ice, Thomas. "Hal Lindsey, Dominion Theology and Anti-Semitism." *Biblical Perspectives* (January–February 1992), p. 1ff.

Johnson, Franklin. "The Fallacies of the Higher Criticism," in *The Fundamentals, a Testimony to Truth,* Volume 1, edited by A. C. Dixon,

L. Meyer, and R. A. Torrey, 55–75. Chicago: Bible Institute of Los Angeles, 1917, reprinted by Baker Books in 2003.

Joshi, M. M. Interview. *Organiser*, June 6, 2004 (retrieved at http://www.organiser.org/dynamic/modules.php?name=Content&pa=showpage&pid=26&page=3).

Krekar, Mullah. *Med Egne Ord.* Oslo: Ashcehoug, 2004.

Interview. September 30, 2004.

Interview. November 27, 2004.

Lemp, Reynold. "Authority: Right or Wrong?" *Frontline*, September/October 2007, p. 17ff.

Maududi, Maulana. *Political Theory of Islam*, edited and translated by Khurshid Ahmad. Lahore: Islamic Publications, 1960.

Selected Speeches and Writings of Maulana Maududi, translated by S. Zakir Aijaz. Karachi: International Islamic Publishers, 1988.

Maududi, Syed Abul Ala. *Political Theory of Islam.* Lahore: Markazi Maktaba Jamaat-e-Islami, 1939.

Islamic Law and Constitution, edited by Khurshid Ahmad. Karachi: Jamaat-e-islami, 1955.

Towards Understanding the Quran. Volume 1: *Surahs 1–3*, translated and edited by Z. I. Ansari. London: Islamic Foundation, 1988.

Purdah and the Status of Women. Delhi: Markaza Maktabi Islami, 1996.

The Rights and Duties of Spouses. Delhi: Human Welfare Trust, 2000.

McCune, Roland. "Theonomy." *Frontline* (May–June 2007), p. 12ff.

Müller, F. Max. *Natural Religion: The Gifford Lectures.* London: Longmans, Green, & Co., 1892.

Muslim Brotherhood in Egypt. *The Role of Muslim Women in Islamic Society According to the Muslim Brotherhood.* Translation of a statement issued by the Muslim Brotherhood in Egypt, March 1994, pp. 14–15. Cairo: International Islamic Forum, 1994.

Pande, Om Prakash. *Drashtavya jagat ka yathartha*, Volumes 1 and 2. New Delhi: Prabhat Prakashan, 2005.

Prime Minister's High Level Committee, Government of India. *Social, Economic and Educational Status of the Muslim Community of India – a Report*, November 2006. Retrieved from Indian Ministry of Minority Affairs at http://minorityaffairs.gov.in/newsite/sachar/sachar.asp.

Roy, Rammohan. *Translation of Several Principal Books, Passages, and Texts of the Vedas and of Some Controversial Works on Brahmunical Theology.* London: Parbury, Allen, & Co., 1832.

Selbrede, Martin G. "The Blessing of Dominion Theology." *Faith for All Life* (March–April 2008), p. 13ff.

Shower, Renald E. "Christian Reconstructionism." *Israel My Glory* (December 1990–January 1991), p. 17ff.

Singleton, James E. "Fundamentalism – Past, Present and Future, Part 24," *Tri-City Builder* (September–October 1993), p. 2ff.

Turk, Ralph G. "The Mosaic Law and National Reconstruction." *Faith Pulpit* (January–February 1990), p. 1ff.

Unknown. "Cultural Mandate or Christian Missions." *Fundamentalist Digest* (September–October 1993), p. 3ff.

Upadhyay, Deendayal. *Integral Humanism.* Delhi: Bharatiya Janata Party Publication, 1965.

Vivekananda, Swami. *The Complete Works of Swami Vivekananda,* Volumes 1–8. Calcutta: Advaita Ashrama, 1992.

Waggoner, Jarl K. "The Lure of Reconstruction Theology." *Voice* (July–August 2000), p. 18ff.

Wright, George Frederick. "The Passing of Evolution," in *The Fundamentals, a Testimony to Truth,* Volume 4, edited by A. C. Dixon, L. Meyer, and R. A. Torrey, 72–87. Chicago Bible Institute of Los Angeles, 1917, reprinted by Baker Books in 2003.

Yahya, Harun. *Design in Nature.* London: Ta-Ha Publishers, 2002.

Secondary Sources

Adas, Michael. *Machines as the Measure of Men: Science, Technology, and Ideologies of Western Dominance.* Ithaca, N.Y.: Cornell University Press, 1990.

Ahmad, Irfan. "Cracks in the 'Mightiest Fortress': Jamaat-e-Islami's Changing Discourse on Women." *Modern Asian Studies* 42 (2008): 549–75.

Ahmed, Leila. *Women and Gender in Islam.* New Haven, Conn.: Yale University Press, 1992.

Ahmed, Rafiuddin. *The Bengal Muslims.* Delhi: Oxford University Press, 1996.

Almond, Gabriel A., R. Scott Appleby, and Emmanuel Sivan. *Strong Religion: The Rise of Fundamentalisms Around the World.* Chicago: University of Chicago Press, 2003.

Ames, Michael. "The Impact of Western Education on Religion and Society in Ceylon." *Pacific Affairs* 40, nos. 1–2 (Spring/Summer 1967): 19–42.

Ammerman, Nancy T. *Bible Believers: Fundamentalists in the Modern World.* New Brunswick, N.J.: Rutgers University Press, 1999.

Andrabi, Tahrir, Jishnu Das, Asim Ijaz Khwaja, and Tristan Zajong. "Religious School Enrollment in Pakistan: A Look at the Data," in *Islam and Education, Myths and Truths,* edited by Wadad Kadi and Victor Billeh. Chicago: University of Chicago Press, 2007.

Antoun, Richard T. *Muslim Preacher in the Modern World: A Jordanian Case Study in Comparative Perspective.* Princeton, N.J.: Princeton University Press, 1989.

Understanding Fundamentalism: Christian, Islamic, and Jewish Movements. Oxford: AltaMira Press, 2001.

Arjomand, Said Amir. "Iran's Islamic Revolution in Comparative Perspective." *World Politics* 38, no. 3 (April 1986): 384–414.

"The Crisis of the Imamate and the Institution of Occultation in Twelver Shiism; A Sociohistorical Perspective." *International Journal of Middle Eastern Studies* 28, no. 4 (November 1996): 491–515.

"Unity and Diversity in Islamic Fundamentalism," in *Fundamentalisms Comprehended,* edited by Martin E. Marty and R. Scott Appleby, 179–98. Chicago: University of Chicago Press, 2004.

After Khomeini: Iran under His Successors. New York: Oxford University Press, 2009.

Bacchetta, Paola. *Gender in the Hindu Nation: RSS Women as Ideologues.* New Delhi: Women Unlimited, 2004.

Bainton, Roland. *Here I Stand: A Life of Martin Luther.* London: Penguin Books, 2002.

Barkun, Michael. *Religion and the Racist Right: The Origins of the Christian Identity Movement.* Chapel Hill: University of North Carolina Press, 1995.

Bartholomeusz, Tessa. *Women under the Bo Tree.* Cambridge: Cambridge University Press, 1994.

and Chandra R. de Silva. *Buddhist Fundamentalism and Minority Identities in Sri Lanka.* New York: State University of New York Press, 1998.

Bartkowski, John. *Remaking the Godly Marriage: Gender Negotiation in Evangelical Families.* New Brunswick, N.J.: Rutgers University Press, 2001.

Bechert, Heinz. *Buddhismus, Staat und Geschellschaft in den Ländern der Theravada-Buddhismus. Erster Band: Allgemeines und Ceylon.* Frankfurt am Main: Alfred Metzner Verlag, 1966.

Bellah, Robert. "Religious Evolution." *American Sociological Review* 29 (1964): 358–74. Reprinted in *Sociology of Religion,* edited by Roland Robertson, 262–93. Harmondsworth: Penguin, 1969.

Beyond Belief: Essays on Religion in a Post-Traditional World. New York: Harper & Row, 1970.

Bentley, Jerry H. "Cross-Cultural Interaction and Periodization in World History." *The American Historical Review* 101, no. 3 (June 1996): 749–70.

Berger, Peter L. "Charisma and Religious Innovation: The Social Location of Israelite Prophecy." *American Sociological Review* 28, no. 6 (December 1963): 940–50.

Beyer, Peter. "The Religious System of Global Society: A Sociological Look at Contemporary Religion and Religions." *Numen* 45, no. 1 (1998): 1–29.

Religion in Global Society. London: Routledge, 2006.

Blaut, J. M. *Eight Eurocentric Historians*. London: The Guilford Press, 2000.

Blaydes, Lisa and Drew A. Linzer. "The Politicial Economy of Women's Support for Fundamentalist Islam." *World Politics* 60 (July 2008): 576–609.

Booth, Marilyn. "Woman in Islam: Men and the 'Women's Press' in Turn-of-the-20th-Century Egypt." *International Journal of Middle East Studies* 33 (2001): 171–201.

Brekke, Torkel. *Makers of Modern Indian Religion*. Oxford: Oxford University Press, 2002.

"Sinister Nexus: USA, Norge og Krekar-saken." *Internasjonal Politikk* 63, no. 2 (2005): 279–96.

"Mission Impossible? Baptism and the Politics of Bible Translation in the Early Baptist Mission in Bengal." *History of Religions* 45, no. 3 (February 2006): 213–33.

"The Concept of Religion and the Debate on the Rights of Women in the Constitutional Debates of India." *Nordic Journal of Religion and Society* 22, no. 1 (2009): 71–85.

Brock, Peggy. "New Christians as Evangelists," in *Missionaries and Empire*, edited by Norman Etherington, 132–53. Oxford: Oxford University Press, 2009.

Brown, Nathan J. "Sharia and State in the Modern Muslim Middle East." *International Journal of Middle East Studies* 29, no. 3 (August 1997): 359–76.

Bruce, Steve. *God Is Dead: Secularization in the West*. Oxford: Blackwell, 2003.

Casanova, Jose. *Public Religions in the Modern World*. Chicago: University of Chicago Press, 1995.

Cassirer, Ernst. *The Philosophy of the Enlightenment*, translated by Fritz A. Koelln and James P. Pettegrove. Princeton, N.J.: Princeton University Press, 1951. (First published in German in 1932.)

Chancey, Mark A. "A Textbook Example of the Christian Right: The National Council on Bible Curriculum in Public Schools." *Journal of the American Academy of Religion* 75, no. 3 (September 2007): 554–81.

Chavez, Mark. "Secularization as Declining Religious Authority." *Social Forces* 72, no. 3 (March 1994): 749–74.

Cicero. *De natura deorum. Academica*, with an English translation by H. Rackham. Cambridge, Mass.: Harvard University Press, 1994.

Comaroff, Jean. "Missionaries and Mechanical Clocks: An Essay on Religion and History in South Africa." *The Journal of Religion* 71, no. 1 (January 1991): 1–17.

Cox, Harvey. *Fire from Heaven: The Rise of Pentecostal Spirituality and the Reshaping of Religion in the Twenty-First Century*. Cambridge, Mass.: Da Capo Press, 2001.

Davie, Grace. *Religion in Modern Europe: A Memory Mutates*. Oxford: Oxford University Press, 2000.

Deegalle, Mahinda. "Buddhist Preaching and Sinhala Religious Rhetoric: Medieval Buddhist Methods to Popularize Theravada." *Numen* 44, no. 2 (May 1997): 180–210.

"Politics of the Jathika Hela Urumaya Monks: Buddhism and Ethnicity in Contemporary Sri Lanka." *Contemporary Buddhism* 5, no. 2 (2004): 83–103.

"JHU Politics for Peace and a Righteous State," in *Buddhism, Conflict and Violence in Modern Sri Lanka*, edited by Mahinda Deegalle, 233–55. London: Routledge, 2006.

"Contested Religious Conversions of Buddhists in Sri Lanka and India." Forthcoming.

Devji, Faisal. *Landscapes of the Jihad: Militancy, Morality, Modernity*. Ithaca, N.Y.: Cornell University Press, 2005.

The Terrorist in Search of Humanity: Militant Islam and Global Politics. New York: Columbia University Press, 2008.

DeVotta, Neil. "Sri Lanka in 2004: Enduring Political Decay and a Failing Peace Process." *Asian Survey* 45, no. 1 (January–February 2005): 98–104.

Dierenfield, Bruce J. *The Battle over School Prayer: How Engel v. Vitale Changed America*. Lawrence: Kansas University Press, 2007.

Dunn, John. "Egypt's Nineteenth-Century Armaments Industry." *Journal of Military History* 61 (April 1997): 231–54.

Dunn, Shannon and Rosemary B. Kellison. "At the Intersection of Scripture and Law: Quran 4:34 and Violence against Women." *Journal of Feminist Studies in Religion*, 26, no. 2 (2006): 11–36.

Edgar, Adrienne Lynne. "Emancipation of the Unveiled: Turkmen Women under Soviet Rule, 1924–29." *The Russian Review* 62 (January 2003): 132–49.

Eickelman, Dale F. "Mass Higher Education and Religious Imagination in Contemporary Arab Societies." *American Ethnologist* 19, no. 4 (November 1992): 643–55.

and James Piscatori. *Muslim Politics*. Princeton, N.J.: Princeton University Press, 1996.

El-Ghobashy, Mona. "The Metamorphosis of the Egyptian Muslim Brothers." *International Journal of Middle East Studies* 37, no. 3 (August 2005): 373–95.

Falk, Monica Lindberg. *Making Fields of Merit: Buddhist Female Ascetics and Gendered Orders in Thailand.* Copenhagen: NIAS Press, 2007.

Febvre, Lucien. *The Problem of Unbelief in the Sixteenth Century: The Religion of Rabelais,* translated by Beatrice Gottlieb. Cambridge, Mass.: Harvard University Press, 1982.

Ferguson, Niall. *Empire – How Britain Made the Modern World.* London: Penguin, 2004.

Fox, Jonathan and Ephraim Tabory. "Contemporary Evidence Regarding the Impact of State Regulation of Religion on Religious Participation and Belief." *Sociology of Religion* 69, no. 3 (2008): 245–71.

Frost, Mark. "'Wider Opportunities': Religious Revival, Nationalist Awakening and the Global Dimension in Colombo, 1870–1920." *Modern Asian Studies* 36, no. 4 (October 2002): 937–67.

Garvey, John H. "Fundamentalism and American Law," in *Fundamentalisms and the State: Remaking Polities, Economies, and Militance,* edited by Martin E. Marty and R. Scott Appleby, 28–49. Chicago: University of Chicago Press, 1993.

Gaustad, Edwin S., ed. *A Documentary History of Religion in America,* with revisions by Mark A. Noll. Grand Rapids, Mich.: Eerdmans, 2003.

Geertz, Clifford. *Local Knowledge: Further Essays in Interpretive Anthropology.* New York: Basic Books, 1983.

Gesink, Indira Falk. *Islamic Reform and Conservatism: Al-Azhar and the Evolution of Modern Sunni Islam.* London: I. B. Tauris, 2010.

Goering, Joseph W. "An Introduction to Medieval Christian Biblical Interpretation," in *With Reverence for the Word – Medieval Scriptural Exegesis in Judaism, Christianity and Islam,* edited by Jane Dammen MacAuliffe, Barry D. Walfish, and Joseph W. Goering, 197–203. Oxford: Oxford University Press, 2003.

Gombrich, Richard. "Is the Sri Lanka War a Buddhist Fundamentalism?" in *Buddhism, Conflict and Violence in Modern Sri Lanka,* edited by Mahinda Deegalle, 22–37. London: Routledge, 2006.

and Gananath Obeyesekere. *Buddhism Transformed: Religious Change in Sri Lanka.* Princeton, N.J.: Princeton University Press, 1988.

Gul, Aldikacti Marshall. "Ideology, Progress and Dialogue: A Comparison of Feminist and Islamist Women's Approaches to the Issues of Head Covering and Work in Turkey." *Gender and Society* 19, no. 1 (February 2005): 104–20.

Haas, J. W. "John Wesley's Views on Science and Christianity: An Examination of the Charge of Antiscience." *Church History* 63, no. 3 (September 1994): 378–92.

Hadden, Jeffrey K. and Anson Shupe, eds. *Prophetic Religions and Politics: Religion and the Political Order.* New York: Paragon House, 1986.

Hallaq, Wael B. "Can the Shari'a Be Restored?" in *Islamic Law and the Challenges of Modernity*, edited by Yvonne Y. Haddad and Barbara F. Stowasser, 21–53. Walnut Creek, Calif.: AltaMira Press, 2004.

The Origins and Evolution of Islamic Law. Cambridge: Cambridge University Press, 2005.

Hameed, Salman. "Bracing for Islamic Creationism." *Science* 322, no. 5908 (2008): 1637–38.

Haq, Farhat. "Militarism and Motherhood: The Women of the Lashkar-i-Tayyibiya in Pakistan." *Signs* 32, no. 4 (Summer 2007): 1023–46.

Harris, Harriet A. *Fundamentalism and Evangelicals.* Oxford: Clarendon, 1998.

Hawley, John Stratton. *Fundamentalism and Gender.* New York: Oxford University Press, 1994.

Horowitz, Donald. "The Qu'ran and the Common Law: Islamic Law Reform and the Theory of Legal Change." *The American Journal of Comparative Law* 42, no. 2 (Spring 1994): 233–93.

Hudson, Anne. *The Premature Reformation: Wycliffite Texts and Lollard History.* Oxford: Clarendon Press, 1982.

Israel, Benjamin. *Radical Enlightenment: Philosophy and the Making of Modernity, 1650–1750.* Oxford: Oxford University Press, 2001.

Jackson, Roy. *Mawlana Mawdudi & Political Islam: Authority and the Islamic State.* New York: Routledge, 2011.

Jaffrelot, Christophe. *The Hindu Nationalist Movement and Indian Politics, 1925 to the 1990s.* London: Hurst & Co., 1996. (English translation.)

"A Nationalist but Mimetic Attempt at Federating the Hindu Sects," in *Charisma and Canon – Essays on the Religious History of the Indian Subcontinent,* edited by Vasudha Dalmia, Angelika Malinar, and Martni Christof, 388–410. Delhi: Oxford University Press, 2001.

Jansen, Johannes. *The Neglected Duty: The Creed of Sadat's Assassins and Islamic Resurgence in the Middle East.* New York: Macmillan, 1986.

Johnson, Paul. *Modern Times: The World from the Twenties to the Nineties.* New York: Perennial Classics, 2001.

Jones, Steven L. *Religious Schooling in America.* Westport, Conn.: Praeger, 2008.

Juergensmeyer, Mark. *Global Rebellion: Religious Challenges to the Secular State, from Christian Militias to al Qaeda.* Berkeley: University of California Press, 2008.

Keddie, Nikki R. *An Islamic Response to Imperialism: Political and Religious Writings of Sayyid Jamal ad-Din "al-Afghani."* Berkeley: University of Calfiornia Press, 1983.

Kemper, Steven. "The Buddhist Monkhood, the Law and the State in Colonial Sri Lanka." *Comparative Studies in Society and History* 26, no. 3 (July 1984): 401–27.

Kepel, Gilles. *The Revenge of God: The Resurgence of Islam, Christianity and Judaism in the Modern World.* Cambridge: Polity Press, 1994.

Muslim Extremism in Egypt: The Prophet and Pharaoh. Berkeley: University of California Press, 2003.

Keyes, Charles F. "Buddhist Politics and Their Revolutionary Origins in Thailand." *International Political Science Review* 10, no. 2 (1990): 121–42.

Kippenberg, Hans G. "'Consider That It Is a Raid in the Path of God': The Spiritual Manual of the Attackers of 9/11." *Numen* 52, no. 1 (2005): 29–58.

Kishwar, Madhu. "Gandhi on Women." *Economic and Political Weekly* 20, no. 40 (October 5, 1985): 1691–1702.

Kors, Alan Charles. *Atheism in France, 1650–1729.* Volume 1: *The Orthodox Sources of Disbelief.* Princeton, N.J.: Princeton University Press, 1990.

Larson, Edward J. *Summer for the Gods: The Scopes Trial and America's Continuing Debate over Science and Religion.* New York: Basic Books, 1997.

Lawrence, Bruce. *Defenders of God: The Fundamentalist Revolt against the Modern Age.* Columbia: University of South Carolina Press, 1989.

Lia, Brynjar. *The Society of the Muslim Brothers in Egypt – The Rise of an Islamic Mass Movement.* Reading, Mass.: Ithaca Press, 1998.

Irak og terrortrusselen: Eit oversyn over terrorgrupper med tilknyting til det irakiske regimet. FFI/Rapport/2003/00940. Kjeller: Forsvarets forskningsinstitutt, 2003.

Livingstone, David N. and Mark A. Noll. "B.B. Warfield (1851–1921) – Biblical Inerrantist as Evolutionist." *Isis* 91, no. 2 (June 2000): 283–304.

Lombardi, Clark B. *State Law as Islamic Law in Modern Egypt: The Incorporation of the sharia into Egyptian Constitutional Law.* Leiden: Brill, 2006.

Long, Kathryn. "The Power of Interpretation: The Revival of 1857–58 and the Historiography of Revivalism in America." *Religion and American Culture* 4, no. 1 (Winter 1994): 77–105.

Low, Morris. *Building a Modern Japan: Science, Technology and Medicine in the Meiji Era and Beyond.* New York: Palgrave Macmillan, 2005.

MacCulloch, Diarmaid. *Reformation – Europe's House Divided.* London: Penguin Books, 2004.

Marsot, Afaf Lutfi al-Sayyid. *Egypt in the Reign of Muhammad Ali.* Cambridge: Cambridge University Press, 1984.

Martin, David. *Pentecostalism: The World Their Parish.* Oxford: Blackwell, 2002.

Martin, Vanessa. *Creating an Islamic State: Khomeini and the Making of a New Iran.* London: I. B. Tauris, 2000.

Marty, Martin E. *Modern American Religion.* Volume 2: *The Noise of Conflict, 1919–1941.* Chicago: University of Chicago Press, 1991.

and R. Scott Appleby. *Fundamentalisms and Society: Reclaiming the Sciences, the Family and Education.* Chicago: University of Chicago Press, 1993.

and R. Scott Appleby, eds. *Fundamentalisms and the State: Remaking Polities, Economies, and Militance.* Chicago: University of Chicago Press, 1993.

and R. Scott Appleby, eds. *Accounting for Fundamentalisms: The Dynamic Character of Movements.* Chicago: University of Chicago Press, 1994.

and R. Scott Appleby, eds. *Fundamentalisms Observed.* Chicago: University of Chicago Press, 1994.

and R. Scott Appleby, eds. *Fundamentalisms Comprehended.* Chicago: University of Chicago Press, 1995.

Mayer, Ann Elizabeth. "The Fundamentalist Impact on Law, Politics, and Constitutions in Iran, Pakistan and Sudan," in *Fundamentalisms and the State,* edited by Martin E. Marty and R. Scott Appleby, 110–52. Chicago: University of Chicago Press, 1993.

McMahan, David L. "Modernity and the Early Discourse on Scientific Buddhism." *Journal of the American Academy of Religion* 72, no. 4 (2004): 897–933.

Menski, Werner. *Hindu Law – Beyond Tradition and Modernity.* New Delhi: Oxford University Press, 2003.

Minnis, A. J. "Material Swords and Literal Lights – The Status of Allegory in William of Ockham's Breviloquium on Papal Power," in *With Reverence for the Word – Medieval Scriptural Exegesis in Judaism, Christianity and Islam,* edited by Jane Dammen MacAuliffe, Barry D. Walfish, and Joseph W. Goering, 292–308. Oxford: Oxford University Press, 2003.

Mir-Husseini, Ziba. *Islam and Gender: The Religious Debate in Contemporary Iran.* Princeton, N.J.: Princeton University Press, 1999.

Moustafa, Tamir. "Conflict and Cooperation between the State and Religious Institutions in Contemporary Egypt." *International Journal of Middle East Studies* 32, no. 1 (February 2000): 3–22.

Nasr, Seyyed Vali Reza. *Maududi and the Making of Islamic Revivalism.* Oxford: Oxford University Press, 1996.

Noll, Mark A. *Between Faith and Criticism: Evangelicals, Scholarship and the Bible in America,* 2nd edition. Vancouver: Regent College Publishing, 2004.

Oberoi, Harjot. "Sikh Fundamentalism: Translating History into Theory," in *Fundamentalisms and the State: Remaking Polities, Economies, and Militance,* edited by Martin E. Marty and R. Scott Appleby, 256–85. Chicago: University of Chicago Press, 1993.

Parsons, Talcott. *Societies – Evolutionary and Comparative Perspectives.* Englewood Cliffs, N.J.: Prentice–Hall, 1966.

The System of Modern Societies. Englewood Cliffs, N.J.: Prentice-Hall, 1971.

Social Systems and the Evolution of Action Theory. New York: The Free Press, 1977.

Peshkin, Alan. *God's Choice: The Total World of a Fundamentalist Christian School.* Chicago: University of Chicago Press, 1986.

Peters, Rudolph. "Divine Law or Man-Made Law? Egypt and the Application of the sharia." *Arab Law Quarterly* 3, no. 3 (August 1988): 231–53.

Philo. *On the Creation. Allegorical Interpretation of Genesis II, III,* Volume 1, with an English translation by F. H. Colson and G. H. Whitaker. Cambridge, Mass.: Harvard University Press, 1929.

Rajagopal, Arvind. "Sangh's Role in the Emergency." *Economic and Political Weekly* 38 (July 5–11, 2003): 2797–98.

Ranger, Terence. "Christianity and the First Peoples: Some Second Thoughts," in *Indigenous Peoples and Religious Change,* edited by Peggy Brock, 15–33. Leiden: Brill, 2005.

Raychaudhuri, Tapan. "Shadows of the Swastika: Historical Perspectives on the History of Hindu Communalism." *Modern Asian Studies* 34, no. 2 (May 2000): 259–79.

Reynolds, Frank E. "Dhamma in Dispute: The Interactions of Religion and Law in Thailand." *Law & Society Review* 28, no. 3 (1994): 433–52.

Riesebrodt, Martin. *Pious Passion: The Emergence of Modern Fundamentalism in the United States and Iran,* translated by Don Reneau. Berkeley: University of Calfornia Press, 1993.

Riexinger, Martin. "The Islamic Creationism of Harun Yahya." *International Institute for the Study of Islam in the Modern World Newsletter* (December 2002): 5–6.

"Islamic Opposition to the Darwinian Theory of Evolution," in *Handbook of Religion and the Authority of Science,* edited by Hammer Olav and James R. Lewis, 484–509. Leiden: Brill, 2010.

"Reactions of South Asian Muslims to the Theory of Evolution." Unpublished manuscript.

Robertson, Roland and Bryan S. Turner, eds. *Talcott Parsons: Theorist of Modernity.* London: Sage Publications, 1991.

Robinson, Francis. "Technology and Religious Change: Islam and the Impact of Print." *Modern Asian Studies* 27, no. 1 (February 1993): 229–51.

Rose, Susan D. *Keeping Them Out of the Hands of Satan: Evangelical Schooling in America.* New York: Routledge, 1988.

Roy, Olivier. *Globalised Islam: The Search for a New Ummah.* London: Hurst & Co., 2006.

Secularism Confronts Islam, translated by George Holoch. New York: Columbia University Press, 2007.

Holy Ignorance: When Religion and Culture Part Ways, translated from French by Ros Schwartz. London: Hurst & Co., 2010.

Rutherford, Bruce K. "What Do Egypt's Islamists Want? Moderate Islam and the Rise of Islamic Constitutionalism." *Middle East Journal* 60, no. 4 (Autumn 2006): 707–31.

Ruthven, Malise. *Fundamentalism: A Very Short Introduction.* Oxford: Oxford University Press, 2007.

Saffari, Said. "The Legitimation of the Clergy's Right to Rule in the Iranian Constitution of 1979." *British Journal of Middle Eastern Studies* 20, no. 1 (1993): 63–82.

Sandeen, Ernst. "Toward a Historical Interpretation of the Origins of Fundamentalism." *Church History* 36, no. 1 (March 1967): 66–83.

Sarkar, Tanika. "Pragmatics of the Hindu Right: Politics of Women's Organisations." *Economic and Political Weekly* 34, no. 31 (July 31–August 6, 1999): 2159–67.

Sedgwick, Adam. "Objections to Mr. Darwin's Theory of the Origin of Species," in *Darwin*, edited by Philip Appleman, 265–67. New York: Norton, 1979. (Article originally published in 1860.)

Seneviratne, H. L. *The Work of Kings: The New Buddhism in Sri Lanka.* Chicago: University of Chicago Press, 1999.

Shapiro, Adam R. "Civic Biology and the Origins of the School Antievolution Movement." *Journal of the History of Biology* 41, no. 3 (2008): 409–33.

Sharkey, Heather J. "Christians among Muslims: The Church Missionary Society in the Northern Sudan." *The Journal of African History* 43, no. 1 (2002): 51–71.

Shupe, Anson. "Religious Fundamentalism," in *The Oxford Handbook in the Sociology of Religion*, edited by Peter B. Clarke. Oxford: Oxford University Press, 2011. Oxford Handbooks Online, March 8, 2011, http://dx.doi.org/10.1093/oxfordhb/9780199279791.001.0001.

Sikand, Yoginder. "Maulana Wahiduddin Khan Responds to Contentious Points on Views about Women in Islam." http://www.islamopediaonline.org/fatwa/maulana-wahiduddin-khan-responds-contentious-points-views-about-women-islam (retrieved March 1, 2011).

"Zakir Naik: 'Islamic Media' Mogul Faces New Foes." http://newageislam.com/NewAgeIslamArticleDetail.aspx?ArticleID=3922 (accessed January 30, 2010).

Sivan, Emmanuel. *Radical Islam: Medieval Theology and Modern Politics.* New Haven, Conn.: Yale University Press, 1985.

Smalley, Beryl. *The Study of the Bible in the Middle Ages.* Oxford: Blackwell, 1952.

Som, Reba. "Jawaharlal Nehru and the Hindu Code: A Victory of Symbol over Substance." *Modern Asian Studies* 28, no. 1 (1994): 165–94.

Southard, Barbara. "Colonial Politics and Women's Rights: Woman Suffrage Campaigns in Bengal, British India, in the 1920s." *Modern Asian Studies* 27, no. 2 (1993): 397–439.

Stout, Harry S. *The Divine Dramatist: George Whitefield and the Rise of Modern Evangelicalism.* Grand Rapids, Mich.: Eerdmans, 1991.

Subramanian, Narendra. "Legal Change and Gender Inequality: Changes in Muslim Family Law in India." *Law & Social Inquiry* 33, no. 3 (Summer 2008): 631–72.

"Making Family and Nation: Hindu Marriage Law in Early Postcolonial India." *The Journal of Asian Studies,* in press.

Sud, Nikita. "Secularism and the Gujarat State: 1960–2005." *Modern Asian Studies* 42, no. 6 (2008): 1251–81.

Swearer, Donald. "Lay Buddhism and the Buddhist Revival in Ceylon." *Journal of the American Academy of Religion* 38, no. 3 (September 1970): 255–75.

"Fundamentalistic Movements in Theravada Buddhism," in *Fundamentalisms Observed,* edited by Martin E. Marty and R. Scott Appleby, 628–91. Chicago: University of Chicago Press, 1994.

The Buddhist World of Southeast Asia. New York: State University of New York Press, 1995.

Talbot, Ian. *Pakistan – A Modern History.* New York: St. Martin's Press, 1998.

Tambiah, Stanley J. *World Conqueror and World Renouncer: A Study of Buddhism and Polity in Thailand against a Historical Background.* Cambridge: Cambridge University Press, 1976.

Taylor, J. L. "New Buddhist Movements in Thailand: An 'Individualistic Revolution,' Reform and Political Dissonance." *Journal of Southeast Asian Studies* 21, no. 1 (March 1990): 135–54.

Troll, Christian W. "Two Conceptions of Da'wa in India: Jama'at Islami and Tablighi Jama'at." *Archives de Sciences Sociales des religions* 39e, no. 87 (July–September 1994): 115–33.

Vatuk, Sylvia. "Islamic Feminism in India: Indian Muslim Women Activists and the Reform of Muslim Personal Law." *Modern Asian Studies* 42, nos. 2–3 (2008): 489–518.

Watson, Alan. *Legal Transplants – An Approach to Comparative Law.* Charlottesville: University of Virginia Press, 1974.

Weber, Max. *The Sociology of Religion*, translated from the German by Ephraim Fischoff. Boston: Beacon Press, 1993. (Originally published in 1922.)

The Protestant Ethic and the Spirit of Capitalism, translated from the German by Talcott Parsons, foreword by Anthony Giddens. London: Routledge, 2001.

Worthen, Molly. "The Chalcedon Problem: Rousas John Rushdoony and the Origins of Christian Reconstructionism." *Church History* 77, no. 2 (June 2008): 399–437.

Wuthnow, Robert. *The Restructuring of American Religion: Society and Faith Since World War II*. Princeton, N.J.: Princeton University Press, 1988.

Yilmaz, Ihsan. "Secular Law and the Emergence of Unofficial Turkish Islamic Law." *The Middle East Journal* 56, no. 1 (Winter 2002): 113–31.

Zaman, Muhammad Qasim. "Religious Education and the Rhetoric of Reform: The Madrasa in British India and Pakistan." *Comparative Studies in Society and History* 14, no. 2 (1999): 294–323.

Zehner, Edwin. "The Protestants and Local Supernaturalism: Changing Configurations." *Journal of Southeast Asian Studies* 27, no. 2 (September 1996): 293–319.

Zollner, Barbara. The Muslim *Brotherhood* – Hasan al-Hudaybi and Ideology. London: Routledge, 2009.

Index

Lightning Source UK Ltd.
Milton Keynes UK
UKHW010609060120
356397UK00001B/11/P

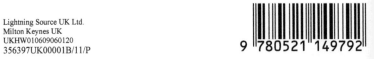